The Resilient Rural Leader

MELISSA A. SADORF

The Resilient Rural Leader

Rising to the Challenges of Rural Education

Arlington, Virginia USA

2800 Shirlington Road, Suite 1001 • Arlington, VA 22206 USA
Phone: 800-933-2723 or 703-578-9600
Website: www.ascd.org • Email: member@ascd.org
Author guidelines: www.ascd.org/write

Richard Culatta, *Chief Executive Officer;* Anthony Rebora, *Chief Content Officer;* Genny Ostertag, *Managing Director, Book Acquisitions & Editing;* Susan Hills, *Senior Acquisitions Editor;* Mary Beth Nielsen, *Director, Book Editing;* Jennifer L. Morgan, *Editor;* Thomas Lytle, *Creative Director;* Donald Ely, *Art Director;* Bailey Gregory/The Hatcher Group, *Graphic Designer;* Valerie Younkin, *Senior Production Designer;* Cynthia Stock, *Typesetter;* Kelly Marshall, *Production Manager;* Shajuan Martin, *E-Publishing Specialist;* Kathryn Oliver, *Creative Project Manager*

Copyright © 2024 ASCD. All rights reserved. It is illegal to reproduce copies of this work in print or electronic format (including reproductions displayed on a secure intranet or stored in a retrieval system or other electronic storage device from which copies can be made or displayed) without the prior written permission of the publisher. By purchasing only authorized electronic or print editions and not participating in or encouraging piracy of copyrighted materials, you support the rights of authors and publishers. Readers who wish to reproduce or republish excerpts of this work in print or electronic format may do so for a small fee by contacting the Copyright Clearance Center (CCC), 222 Rosewood Dr., Danvers, MA 01923, USA (phone: 978-750-8400; fax: 978-646-8600; web: www.copyright.com). To inquire about site licensing options or any other reuse, contact ASCD Permissions at www.ascd.org/permissions or permissions@ascd.org. For a list of vendors authorized to license ASCD ebooks to institutions, see www.ascd.org/epubs. Send translation inquiries to translations@ascd.org.

ASCD® is a registered trademark of Association for Supervision and Curriculum Development. All other trademarks contained in this book are the property of, and reserved by, their respective owners, and are used for editorial and informational purposes only. No such use should be construed to imply sponsorship or endorsement of the book by the respective owners.

All web links in this book are correct as of the publication date below but may have become inactive or otherwise modified since that time. If you notice a deactivated or changed link, please email books@ascd.org with the words "Link Update" in the subject line. In your message, please specify the web link, the book title, and the page number on which the link appears.

PAPERBACK ISBN: 978-1-4166-3286-3   ASCD product #123028   n4/24
PDF EBOOK ISBN: 978-1-4166-3287-0; see Books in Print for other formats.
Quantity discounts are available: email programteam@ascd.org or call 800-933-2723, ext. 5773, or 703-575-5773. For desk copies, go to www.ascd.org/deskcopy.

Library of Congress Cataloging-in-Publication Data

Names: Sadorf, Melissa A., author.
Title: The resilient rural leader : rising to the challenges of rural education / Melissa A. Sadorf.
Description: Arlington, Virginia USA : ASCD, 2024. | Includes bibliographical references and index.
Identifiers: LCCN 2023053360 (print) | LCCN 2023053361 (ebook) | ISBN 9781416632863 (paperback) | ISBN 9781416632870 (pdf)
Subjects: LCSH: Education, Rural—United States. | Educational leadership—United States. | Rural schools—United States. | Community and school—United States. | Education and state—United States.
Classification: LCC LC5146.5 .S28 2024 (print) | LCC LC5146.5 (ebook) | DDC 370.9173/4—dc23/eng/20231215
LC record available at https://lccn.loc.gov/2023053360
LC ebook record available at https://cn.loc.gov/2023053361

33 32 31 30 29 28 27 26 25 24   1 2 3 4 5 6 7 8 9 10 11 12

The Resilient Rural Leader

Rising to the Challenges of Rural Education

Introduction: The Unique Nature of Rural Education 1

Chapter 1: The Rural School Leader 12

Chapter 2: Rural Teacher Recruitment and Retention 31

Chapter 3: The Rural Principal 48

Chapter 4: The Effective and Efficient Rural School Leader 64

Chapter 5: Access in Rural Communities 84

Chapter 6: Rural Poverty 107

Chapter 7: Diversity in Rural Communities 128

Chapter 8: The Death of the Rural Community Center 140

Chapter 9: Leaning into Rural Strengths 164

References 185

Index 194

About the Author 199

Introduction: The Unique Nature of Rural Education

City people make the most fuss about the charms of country life.

Mason Cooley

When I tell people that I am the superintendent of a rural school district, they respond in various ways. They often remark how difficult it must be, given the lack of resources in rural areas. Sometimes they bring up difficulties with teacher recruitment and retention in rural schools. Increasingly, after the COVID-19 pandemic, they ask questions about access to technology and broadband for the students in my district. Some have asked when I plan to move to a larger urban district, now that I've "done my time" in rural education (spoiler alert: I have no plans or desire to!). And sometimes the "rural" part of my work in education is simply glossed over or not acknowledged at all. To be fair, colleagues who live and work in suburban or urban communities may not comprehend the concept of "rurality" and the many facets it entails. Part of what makes my job enjoyable, and part of the challenge of leading a rural district, is the opportunity to lay the foundation for understanding the barriers and innovations inherent in rural school districts.

Even I, when I was a new leader in a rural district, had misconceptions about what rural was and was not. Although I had been a rural student, and then a rural teacher and principal, I did not yet have a clear picture of the full scope of rural school district leadership. When I was hired by my governing board in 2012, no resources focusing specifically on rural places and people were available to use as a framework. This lack forced me to draw from urban-centric leadership resources, being creative with the tools at hand in my community, and drove me to create networks of support that I still tap into when I run into a new issue or concern.

For example, when massive school closures in response to the pandemic prompted a shift to online learning environments, many of us felt like we were new leaders all over again. Rural leaders in my area and state banded together to support each other and share ideas for addressing teaching and learning, community concerns, home-based trauma, and the fear of the unknown. These connections highlighted for me the importance of our communities of practice and the necessity for rural communities to apply others' successes to our own context. The pandemic-inspired innovation happening all over the country was not a new phenomenon in rural schools! Rural leaders typically have to think about problems and their solutions differently than other school leaders. The "duct tape and baling wire" approach is often the best solution to a rural education problem.

The word "rural" does not call to mind the same scenario for everyone. Rural places in the high desert of the Arizona borderlands, where I was both a student and a teacher, differ greatly from the woods of rural Maine, the Badlands of the Dakotas, or the wilds of Alaska. Not only are the locales varied, but the people who choose to live and work in a rural place and the assets that the rural community can provide are astoundingly diverse. The term "rural" is often used to refer to anything that is not urban, but rural is not a monolithic description. The context of a place has an impact on its people and its way of life—and, as this book explores in depth—context is vital to developing innovative solutions to rural challenges.

Yes, I Am a Rural Educator

My family moved from the suburbs of Chicago, Illinois, to Douglas, Arizona, on the border between the United States and Mexico, when I was a preteen. I experienced, firsthand and in living color, the differences between rural and nonrural places and people. The only non-Hispanic student in my class, I attended school in Douglas, where the lessons were six months or more behind those taught in my private school in Chicago. The classroom resources and even the buildings were older and in need of updating. When we subsequently moved an hour north to Sierra Vista, Arizona, I experienced a different rural environment and school setting. The traditions, the culture, and the issues of both locations had commonalities, but they were not identical. As they say, if you have seen one rural school, you have seen one rural school!

I have been an educator for more than 30 years at a variety of levels: in the classroom, as a site-level administrator, and as superintendent for the last 13 years. I served all of that time in rural schools and districts. The appeal of being part of a rural school community is difficult to quantify. For me, making connections with students and their families outside school is rewarding, though it sometimes impinges on privacy! The Rural Schools Collaborative and National Rural Education Association (n.d.) have developed an excellent promotional campaign celebrating rural teachers at https://iamaruralteacher.org. The platform, supported by the Bill & Melinda Gates Foundation, communicates why the unique rewards of rural teaching are truly a draw for many.

So why does it matter that some people understand rurality, and others do not? In the last 15 years, there has been an increase in conversation around rural issues, people, and places. The contributions of rural voters to the 2016 U.S. presidential election were heavily scrutinized, with the predominant media narrative characterizing rural voters as largely white, uneducated farmers. This is certainly not the case! While it is important that awareness of and consideration for rural issues are being raised, if the public's understanding of such issues is only surface-level and based in erroneous beliefs, policymakers and others with decision-making authority may effect unintentional harm to rural communities. It is vital that rural educators tell their stories about the challenges and barriers they face and share the innovations developed in response to that adversity. Not only might sharing spark ideas for educational solutions in all types of settings, but it can also ensure that rural concerns are a part of decision making at all levels. In an era of increasing political polarization, which often influences educational issues, a basic understanding of rural education can highlight how leaders in all locales can benefit from each other's insights and successes.

What Does Rural Mean?

Most people have a stereotypical concept of rural communities based on movies, books, social media, or what they have heard from friends. Friday night football game attended by the whole town? High school students making bad decisions down by the river after the game? Sitting on the porch with lemonade while Grandpa waxes poetic about the good ol' days? While my own experiences growing up in a rural community included two of the three, it's important to note that there is no template that applies to all such communities. Rurality is context-driven. Rural places exist in almost every state and are so varied and complex that it's difficult to create a single, inclusive definition for them. In fact, the U.S. Department of Agriculture (USDA) uses 15 different definitions of "rural" to determine which localities receive federal dollars (*The Washington Post,* 2013).

This lack of understanding makes sense in light of U.S. Census Bureau (America Counts Staff, 2017) reports that only one in five Americans live in a rural area, despite such areas making up almost 97 percent of the country's land mass (leaving the 80 percent of Americans who live in urban areas to reside on only 3 percent of the available land). To further complicate the issue, the U.S. Census Bureau does not define what rural *is,* but rather quantifies what it *is not.* It's no wonder that the definition of "rural" lacks consensus. Regional differences; local economic industries; racial, ethnic, and cultural variances; and proximity to urban resources all have an impact on rural spaces, preventing the generalization of attributes assigned to a community that calls itself rural.

Some interesting shifts in population are also affecting rural communities. While the total rural population percentage is down from almost 25 percent in 1990, research by The Aspen Institute (Community Strategies Group, 2019) points out that there are nuances to that statistic. They note that certain rural areas in the country have actually shown growth, while the migration of residents from suburban and urban areas to rural areas has caused many places formerly identified as rural to be reclassified.

To get further into the weeds, we should break down different types of rural. The National Center for Education Statistics (NCES, n.d.c) designates locale codes based on the proximity of an area to an urban cluster with a population of between 2,500 and 50,000. There are three locale codes used for rural education:

- **41: Fringe.** Census-defined rural territory that is less than or equal to 5 miles from an urbanized area, as well as rural territory that is less than or equal to 2.5 miles from an urban cluster.

- **42: Distant.** Census-defined rural territory that is more than 5 miles but less than or equal to 25 miles from an urbanized area, as well as rural territory that is more than 2.5 miles but less than or equal to 10 miles from an urban cluster.
- **43: Remote.** Census-defined rural territory that is more than 25 miles from an urbanized area and also more than 10 miles from an urban cluster. (NCES, n.d.c)

My rural district is classified as "distant," as we are within 20 miles of an urbanized area to both the east and west. The locale code of an area is an important distinction because it is attached to federal grant dollars that can be applied to innovations. Locale codes can also be integral to putting together a teacher recruitment and retention plan.

The American Rural Education System

The education system in America has deep rural roots. If you research the oldest operating school in your state or region, it's likely that it was a rural school, at least at the start! In truth, many one-room or small schoolhouses have historically served students in both large agricultural areas and small towns. According to NCES (2017), of the 88,835 schools across the United States, 25,188 serve rural students—and each of these schools taps into strengths that are unique to their location.

One of the things I tell policymakers about my district is that the school serves as the hub of the community. Given the distance to services, government buildings, and retail stores, it is the optimal place for the area's residents to congregate. (One could argue that the Cow Town Bar could also fill that role, but that's a different book!) Rural schools are typically one of the largest employers in their area as well, acting as an economic driver. And finally, our school is the recipient of the largest share of local taxes. Without our school, the community would be in danger of dying—and my district is not unique in these community connections.

Even though rural schools have long been important to their communities, in the mid-20th century, fewer rural students graduated high school than their urban counterparts. Because educational attainment is directly correlated to the economic prosperity of a community, this disparity leads to problematic circumstances. While the percentage of high school graduation from rural schools has shown growth, the gains have been variable. In 2000, the percentage of urban students who graduated high school and went on to some type of postsecondary education was 53.9; by 2019, it had grown to 63.2. In the same time frame, the proportion of rural high school graduates pursuing higher education grew from 40.2 percent to 51.4 percent (USDA, 2021).

In their report *Rural Education at a Glance, 2017 Edition,* the USDA Economic Research Service (USDA ERS, 2017) notes that rural Americans are more educated than ever and describes the following trends affecting rural communities and schools:

- **Educational attainment in rural areas is on the rise.** Research shows that while more than half of rural students graduated with a high school diploma or passed the GED in 1970, the graduation rate is now 85 percent. However, this rate varies according to student demographics.
- **The urban-rural gap in college degree attainment increased from 11 percent in 2000 to 14 percent in 2015.** This trend may be attributed to the rural "brain drain" that communities experience when rural students choose to reside in nonrural areas after completing their degree, often due to higher wages offered for skilled and educated workers.
- **Rural women are increasingly more educated than rural men,** with a gap of 2 percent more women completing college degrees than men from 2000 to 2015. The same time frame showed no gender difference in college completion in urban areas.
- **Educational attainment is lower for rural minority and ethnic students than for their white peers.** This disparity causes growing concern as rural America becomes increasingly diverse.

The innovations presented in this book address such trends while offering ways to overcome barriers for rural students and their school communities.

Rural Is Not a Monolith

Recently, my rural district revitalized our mission and vision by focusing our view of who we are as a school community and how we serve the community at large on three basic ideas:

- We are a family.
- We are academically focused.
- We are whole-child centered.

We are also a values-driven organization that is informed by data. These tenets, based on identified strengths of our district, were created by staff and community members invested in the school who value what the school provides for both local children and community residents. They are also a way for the school to showcase our contextual assets.

Rural schools are typically not imbued with the same levels of resources that schools in suburban and urban districts might be able to tap for support. Infrastructure issues, employee housing concerns, technology barriers, declining enrollment leading to fiscal impact, and aging buildings and facilities are just some of the difficult realities that rural leaders face. Despite such challenges, rural schools across the country generate outstanding examples of ingenuity and accomplishment.

I have explained that rural education is not monolithic. Rural educational offerings depend on the nature of the assets, resources, and professionals available to the schools. One community may have access to broadband, while another might not have any type of internet service available—and won't for years to come. Some rural schools employ educators who grew up attending the schools in which they now teach, while others have to think in new ways to attract teachers to their community. The assets that a rural education leader can tap into also vary from place to place. It is imperative that the leader be able to identify strengths of the rural areas they serve and leverage these resources, programs, or initiatives to promote positive outcomes for the school and its stakeholders. Understanding that innovations are driven out of necessity and crafted with the tools at hand is at the heart of rural education. Later, this book will go deeper into how the local community and what it offers play a part in the success of the rural school in myriad ways, including staff retention, place-based education, and closure decisions.

Rural Native or Rural Immigrant?

My experiences growing up in rural communities have benefited me in my different roles during my career. I know about pitfalls, such as neglecting to build relationships or talking to the wrong person about an issue, and I know how to negotiate with and enlist members of the local community to support school programming and initiatives. Research has shown that educators often end up teaching close to where they grew up (McArdle, 2019). It's important that educators from nonrural areas who are considering working in a rural school be aware of the challenges of transitioning to a rural way of life.

One common issue for educators newly arrived in a rural community is the diminished professional support that is a characteristic of small rural schools. With everyone wearing multiple hats, a mentoring program may not be available, and if it is, it may not be formally structured or led by trained personnel. Additionally, there may be a lack of academic or professional support both within grade levels and vertically from grade to grade. If the school district consists of a single site, there may not even be the opportunity to bring together staff from multiple campuses for collaboration. These limitations can lead to stagnation and a discouraging lack of drive to try new things.

Another circumstance that can take newly rural staff by surprise is the lack of resources available for instruction and initiatives. Whether due to a depressed tax base, the inability to secure grant funding, or dwindling local industry opportunities, resource scarcity is often a concern in rural communities. The structure of school funding in different states may also have an impact on the fiscal vitality of rural schools and what resources they are able to provide. It is vital for rural leaders to know and be able to advocate effectively on policy issues related to rural education.

The location of a rural area and the distance to amenities like shopping and entertainment often affect basic living conditions. Limitations on housing, whether in terms of affordability or available stock, are another potential barrier to recruiting nonrural staff. Many rural districts must provide employee housing or offer it as a benefit to attract candidates. Younger employees relocating to unfamiliar areas can feel isolated and lack social peers, especially in remote areas, which can lead to high employee turnover. Even restricted access to healthcare can be a hardship that can outweigh the benefits of living in rural places.

To counter these obstacles, I encourage those already in rural schools or considering working in them to explore the strengths of rural America. Spending time to expand one's understanding of rural places and people is worth the effort. Given the wide variety of rural localities that serve the nearly 9 million students, many candidates can find appealing positions outside of suburban and urban areas. The key is to recognize misconceptions about rurality and embrace the differences found in rural schools as the opportunities they are. It comes down to the fact that all communities want the same things for their children, no matter what type of locale they call home.

Looking Ahead

With so many students learning in rural areas of the country, it is hard to overlook the importance of investigating their educational journeys and exploring the lessons they can teach us. In response to barriers and challenges, rural educators are implementing a range of innovations to address the needs of their community. When shared between other leaders, these new ways of looking at issues can spark solutions that spread success beyond rural schools. This is not old wine in new bottles but rather new thinking to address problems both perennial and novel.

Rural school leadership has much in common with urban school leadership. However, in most rural schools, the filling of leadership roles depends on available personnel and their strengths. Often, the superintendent of a rural district is also a school principal. Because these varied responsibilities require diverse skill sets, mentoring, professional development, and collaboration with other rural leaders are key. Chapter 1 examines the many hats a rural leader must wear and how they have an impact on success filling those roles. It also explores laying the groundwork for an effective working relationship with a district's governing board and the importance of being a rural advocate. The chapter also identifies support networks that can assist with the varied duties and responsibilities of a rural leader.

Chapter 2 begins a deep dive into rural challenges and rural innovations, starting with teacher recruitment and retention. After examining this challenge and sharing some innovative solutions found across the country, the chapter offers practical strategies for creating recruitment plans, marketing effectively, using creative scheduling, and keeping teachers under contract.

We know that strong leaders create strong schools. However, there is an ever-growing problem keeping the pipeline to rural principalship flowing. Chapter 3 probes this problem, analyzing the current state of the pipeline and its gaps. It also dives into what rurality means for rural newcomers, the challenges related to finding professional development for leaders, and how stress is a factor in leader turnover. You will then be presented with strategies to secure the leadership pipeline in your community, including how to build "grow-your-own" programming and mentor and support rural leaders.

Chapter 4 focuses on enhancing the effectiveness of rural school leaders, who are called on to fill a multitude of roles. Strong organization and time management skills are a must for those tasked with both being an instructional leader and managing a school site. The chapter presents relevant strategies along with frameworks for decision making.

Chapter 5 addresses limitations of access to amenities in rural communities—disparities exacerbated by the COVID-19 pandemic and its societal effects. The chapter discusses these access pain points and offers innovative solutions for challenges such as broadband internet access, food insecurity, inadequate medical care, and lack of housing. You will learn about strategies such as telehealth and school-based clinics, grant funding opportunities, and examples of how rural leaders across the country have successfully filled access gaps.

Poverty afflicts students in all types of communities. However, the impact of poverty on rural students varies as a function of the availability of services and resources. Chapter 6 investigates rural poverty and suggests solutions that leaders may be able to implement, such as trauma-informed care and positive youth development programs. It also presents ways to determine how well a program fits the local context.

Chapter 7 takes a look at the increasingly rich diversity found in rural places across the country. It examines what diversity, equity, and inclusion look like in a rural setting and offers strategies to address barriers, such as innovations in providing underrepresented students with access to higher education and ways to meet the needs of Native American and multilingual and English language learners.

One of the most devastating things that can happen in a rural community is the closure or consolidation of its school. Chapter 8 explores the impact of the death of a local rural school and investigates possible ways to head off a restructuring. The chapter also outlines practical steps to ensure that the loss of the school does not destroy the community.

Rural flight—also called "brain drain"—is an issue for many rural communities. What can be done to mitigate the migration of young professionals out of these locations? How can a rural school and the surrounding community attract rural native adults back to the area? Chapter 9 describes the effects of the loss of this vital community asset and provides strategies rural leaders can use to grow the community at large, along with two powerful tools: rural needs assessments and rural asset mapping.

For Further Exploration

Throughout this book, you will find references to a variety of online materials you may use to further investigate the content of each chapter. These materials can serve as a starting point for conversations at the local level, a toolkit for a particular activity or effort within your rural school community, or a deeper dive into a concept or idea. To assist with ease of access, I have created a companion website at www.velaconsultants.com to collate these resources and offer additional ones to help you navigate your rural leadership journey. You can also contact me directly through the website to get specific support and information.

Now let's dive into the heart of the book and take a look at some insights and strategies that will help empower you in your role as the rural leader in your school community!

The Rural School Leader

There Is No Typical Rural Leader

One of the challenges of rural leadership—and counterintuitively, one of its opportunities—is the diversity of roles and responsibilities encompassed in the job of the head honcho of a rural school system. Across the country, many rural superintendents also serve as principal. Some superintendents may oversee a principal or two while being in charge of the fiscal functions of the district. In some areas, the superintendent shares the responsibility for certain district- or school-level functions with a lead teacher. Whatever the configuration, one thing is certain: there's no such thing as "typical" when it comes to rural education leaders. Just as rural communities vary from one to another, the shape of shared leadership depends on the context of the system. Often, the skills of the individuals in the system determine who fills what role—and sometimes a role is thrust upon someone by default because there's no one else available.

No matter the background of the educator leading a rural school community, it's highly unlikely they came to the job knowing everything they needed to know. College-level programs often fail to convey the holistic view of leadership needed for success in such a role. And while no one expects preparation programs to teach it all, letting these leaders flounder while they grow and refine their skills can lead to frustration, anxiety, and burnout. This chapter fills in some gaps for both novices and veterans by focusing on some of the most prominent aspects of rural school leadership, suggesting useful tools, and discussing how to amplify your advocacy efforts. To draw a distinction between district-level and school-level leadership, we will use the term "superintendent" for those aspects of rural leadership that deal with responsibilities tied to the district office, and "principal" to refer to leadership roles on a school campus.

The Rural Superintendent

When I am asked how I "do it all" in my role as superintendent/business manager, my immediate response is that I live by my calendar—thank goodness for Google! Many aspects of the superintendency are the same for large and small, rural and urban districts no matter where they are located. However, some areas bring unique challenges to the position, chief among them the multitude of demands and responsibilities placed on a rural leader. Shepherding state and federal requirements, managing local politics, and ensuring effective teaching and learning are just a few broad categories in which such demands fall. In contrast with larger districts, where multiple departments and personnel handle these varied and often siloed responsibilities, rural settings usually lack this depth of human capital. In fact, rural organization charts are often fairly flat!

Nevertheless, we can identify some commonalities across most rural superintendencies. Let's take a closer look at these aspects.

Serving at the Will of the Governing Board

One of the professors involved with my doctoral work said something about school leadership that stuck with me: "You are only one vote away from either having or not having a contract, and you should remember you work at the will of the board." To be an effective rural leader, you should have a thorough comprehension of the main responsibilities of the school district's governing board:

- **The governing board represents the community.** Because the board is elected by local citizens, they are obliged to consider the desires of the electorate. It is their responsibility to attend to community input when they make decisions. School leaders' interactions with the board must be based on an understanding of the district's strengths and weaknesses so that they can make recommendations relevant to the community's resources, personnel, and student needs.

- **The governing board sets policy.** Whether in response to legislative action, state board of education decrees, or other policy drivers, the board is responsible for establishing expectations for district operations. School leaders must ensure that these policies are carried out in the manner in which they were intended. Get to know the policy manual! The guideposts found therein often can prevent lack of control or direction.
- **The governing board makes decisions about hiring and firing but directly oversees only one employee.** Even in small rural and remote districts, the only employee the board manages is the leader they have selected to take on the superintendent responsibilities. Boards in rural areas sometimes struggle with "staying in their lane" with regard to management responsibility. School leaders must be aware that a lack of clearly defined roles in this area can lead to conflict that is detrimental to the effective and efficient running of the organization.
- **The governing board monitors the district's fiscal performance.** No matter the size of the budget or how it is expended, the board is accountable for ensuring that taxpayer dollars are spent responsibly on the needs and goals of the school community. From approving routine budgets to facilitating major procurements, the board oversees the financial health of the district. School leaders must be familiar with policies that govern the district's fiscal obligations, which can be challenging. Many rural education leaders lack a financial background and have had very little training in education accounting and planning in their preparation for the field. The best advice that I received during my superintendent internship was to make friends with the financial manager of the district. Close attention to and deep understanding of the district's fiscal requirements are crucial to being a successful school leader.
- **The governing board assesses the performance and progress of the school system.** The board's multifaceted assessment includes data from student academic performance, financial audits, personnel performance reviews, and levels of community satisfaction. School leaders must be well versed in each of these indicators, able to communicate data to the board, and ready to recommend appropriate actions to improve the system. Such communication ensures that the board can see the big picture of the district so that they can keep it running smoothly and moving forward—often by making hard decisions.

Because school leaders constantly make decisions on behalf of the board, it is good to have a working knowledge of the roles each entity plays. Figure 1.1 outlines a standard division of responsibilities.

FIGURE 1.1

Roles and Responsibilities of Governing Boards and Superintendents

Role/Responsibility	Governing Board	Superintendent
General	Governs the district	Manages the district, advises the board
Policy	Adopts	Recommends, implements
Board meetings	Responsible for	Assists in running
Budget/finance	Adopts, monitors	Prepares, administers, monitors
Instruction	Establishes criteria, approves	Recommends, oversees
Personnel	Approves or rejects based on established criteria	Interviews, recommends, evaluates, develops
Community relations	Creates positive image	Assists with image, communicates
Labor relations	Provides guidelines, ratifies contracts	Monitors process
Student services	Adopts policies	Recommends, implements, directs
Facilities/food service/transportation	Develops and adopts policy	Implements policy, writes procedures, recommends

Source: Adapted from Idaho Public Charter School Commission, 2013.

Ensuring Fiscal Responsibility

A major aspect of the role of superintendent relates to assisting the governing board with their fiduciary task of spending taxpayer dollars efficiently, effectively, and legally. This responsibility may be daunting for rural leaders who have little or no background in school finance. When I was offered the superintendent job in Stanfield, Arizona, where I would oversee budgeting, directing grants, and all other fiscal aspects of running the district, one of the first things I did was to ask the previous superintendent if she was willing to mentor me to address my lack of business background; she graciously acquiesced. I remember having to admit not knowing basic accounting information, which was humbling, but I now know that I am certainly not alone in having to overcome the challenge of dealing with school finances as a rural leader.

Most education leadership preparation programs do include some component of finance studies, but they are typically only one-semester, high-altitude overviews of the mechanics of education funding, the human resources aspect of budgeting, and maybe some of the politics that surround the flow of monies to schools. What I needed to know was how to manage funds—cost containment, reallocation of resources, how and where to make cuts, and long-term plans for enrollment fluctuation. Knowing how to strategize around district funds is vital to rural school leadership—so I learned. The following are some best practices that help me and other rural leaders to be effective fiscal agents.

Know how your state's funding system works. Without a sound operational knowledge of how your district's funding is determined and allocated by the state legislature, it is impossible to plan ahead. Budgets operate concurrently; at any given point in the fiscal year, I am working with three annual budgets—current, prior, and proposed. I cannot project or close out budgets if I don't know where the revenues are coming from or what expenditures I can plan. In addition, I am mindful that my recommendations to the board regarding tax levies have direct implications for the community. I strongly encourage new rural leaders to develop a working knowledge of school finance, even if they are not directly responsible for such decisions. Being able to speak to the board, the community, or the staff about the district's fiscal operations is an important skill to acquire. If there are no local experts to network with, look for workshops or contact your state business officials organization to connect with resources that can help.

If possible, increase funding by enrolling students from outside the district attendance zone. In my rural district, where enrollment is declining, we register almost any student who walks through the door. Arizona is an "open enrollment" state, but even before legislation was passed to expand that opportunity for students and their families, out-of-district enrollments were the only way to maintain or even build our population. It may sound slightly opportunistic, but the only way we can increase our funding is by serving more students. Almost 20 percent of my district's students live outside our boundaries; their inclusion makes a huge difference in the budget. It also makes marketing to attract new families an important part of my job as superintendent.

Master effective personnel management. Predicting staffing needs and patterns and responding proactively is key to a district's operational bottom line. The first year that I was a superintendent I had to eliminate some positions to operate within the parameters of the projected budget. While not an enjoyable process by any stretch, cutting staff, combining duties where appropriate, and tapping into contracted service providers and shared service arrangements were all ways to increase the efficiency of the budget. Key to effective personnel management is the recruitment and retention of quality staff, which will be highlighted in Chapter 2.

Get savvy with spending. Whether through using purchasing cooperatives, regional service centers, or agreements with surrounding districts that create economies of scale, being bullish on spending is a must. The first and most important place a rural leader can run into trouble is mismanagement of the district's finances. Being able to report to the board and the community where funds are expended and why can go a long way to establishing credibility in leadership. Because district budgets are subject to public review, consider hosting financial workshops to help community and board members understand the process and your execution of it. Effectively controlling the funding you manage is key to being a successful administrator.

Turn the lights off. You would think, being located in Arizona, my district would have taken advantage of our almost daily sunshine by installing solar panels. It's a shame we haven't, since that would certainly reduce how much money we spend on electricity! To look for cost savings, I had an energy audit done on our facilities. The results inspired some measures to improve energy efficiency such as replacing outdated ballast lighting with LEDs, replacing older HVAC units, and expanding our preventative maintenance plans beyond just a hurried checklist completed at the end of each year. Other practices to reduce energy consumption include automated timers for lighting, governor mechanisms on heating and cooling units, and water usage reduction. These initiatives seem like small things, but they can add up to big overall savings.

Know your federal programs and grants. Federal funding and grant opportunities support a variety of programming at both the district and building levels. For example, legislation regarding funding for English language learners and immigrant students (Title III), disadvantaged students (Title I), effective teacher preparation (Title II, Part A), and Indigenous students can facilitate opportunities for students and staff that might otherwise be out of reach for your district. Connect with your state department of education, which typically serves as the pass-through organization for these monies, to learn more and to take advantage of any available training and support for obtaining and managing these types of funding.

Expand your options. Strategies to increase district revenues or reduce expenditures include the following:

- Use outside vendors or consultants to fill gaps in background knowledge. My office works with an accountant to augment my more limited financial knowledge with professional expertise in budgeting and fiscal management.
- Become a member of various organizations and associations connected with school finance. Two that I find helpful are the Government Finance Officers Association (www.gfoa.org) and the Association of School Business Officials International (https://asbointl.org). I also belong to my state's school business officials association. Networking within these organizations can also connect you with other resources and avenues of support.
- Find a mentor knowledgeable about school finance to meet with on an as-needed basis.
- Conduct an audit of the district's various operations, including transportation, food service, human resources, energy use, and purchasing. Use the results to identify and mitigate areas of concern to prevent unnecessary expenditures.
- Develop a relationship with your legislative representatives and conduct advocacy work in the area of school finance.
- Implement an equity audit to ensure that funding is being spent in a way that provides equal opportunity and access for all students in your district.
- Train other staff responsible for portions of the budget (e.g., facilities manager, food service director) and ensure they have access to needed status reports on revenues and expenditures.
- Check the return on investment for all the programs and resources your district uses. Are the resources having a positive effect on desired outcomes for your student and staff populations? If not, consider restructuring to maximize the impact of your limited funding.

No matter how you plan and execute fiscal policy and procedure, remain mindful that the process needs to be done in collaboration with the community and staff and should be transparent. Multiple opportunities for input and regular communication on what is being considered, what is being done, and what the outcomes are will help ensure your district thrives.

The Rural Principal

There is no more difficult leadership role in a school organization than that of the principal. Whether rural, urban, elementary, middle, or high school, the on-site education leader needs to be all things to all people in the school environment—hard work on any given day! While rural principals share many commonalities with their urban counterparts, they also face unique challenges related to their context. Many of my conversations with rural principals center around a universal theme: they wear many hats that they may not have been prepared to don (including, in some cases, that of superintendent). These varied responsibilities generally fall into two primary categories: instructional leader and manager. In rural school settings, where schools are often smaller and have fewer resources than their urban counterparts, balancing and mastering the responsibilities of these dual roles becomes even more critical.

Because I came to superintendency from a principalship, I found the instructional leader part of my job easy in comparison with my other duties. In a nutshell, instructional leadership is the actions school leaders take to improve teaching and learning. These actions may look different in rural settings for several reasons. First, rural schools tend to have fewer resources to draw on for day-to-day curriculum implementation and assessment, requiring more leader involvement. Teachers may also need school leaders to procure different types of instructional support. Having fewer teachers in the district can hinder collaboration and networking between grade levels and content areas. Rural instructional leaders may need to actively seek out opportunities to share ideas and resources with others. This could involve building relationships with other schools, partnering with community organizations, or leveraging online platforms to connect educators from diverse regions.

Equally pressing are the critical operations of keeping the school's lights on and ensuring staff are paid on time. Savvy managers set themselves up for success by being proactive whenever possible in balancing the time commitments of management with those of instructional leadership. To paraphrase one of my professors, it's vital that you don't let the urgent get in the way of the important. Implementing processes and protocols around tasks like verifying payroll hours, signing off on purchase requisitions, and submitting required grant reports is key to being able to perform these tasks at high levels. Also vital is ensuring that any new tasks are fully understood, which underlines the importance of training and support for new leaders. This is where my own gaps in knowledge were the most glaring—and where I spent most of the first two years of my superintendency bulking up my practice. We will take a deep dive into some strategies to assist with this balancing act in Chapters 3 and 4.

Having been both an assistant principal and a site-level principal in my rural district of Sierra Vista, Arizona, I had some advantages that many of my peers did not. The district was large enough to provide administrative support for professional development, budgeting and procurement, and human resources (HR), as well as a level of insulation between the school site and the governing board. Good, bad, or indifferent, assistance in these areas gave me the luxury of being able to focus on the students and staff of my school rather than having to address all the challenges of the day-to-day running of the district as a whole. Many rural schools that I have come to know in the last decade feature a leadership organizational chart that is very flat and thin. In my current district, I am not only the superintendent but also the business manager, federal and state grants director, and HR director. Our principal (luckily, I have one to work with) takes on some district-level responsibilities as well, including serving as special education director and planning and implementing professional development for certified and classified staff. She is visible on buses, in the cafeteria, and at sporting events. She and I meet on an almost daily basis to plan, review data, and evaluate goal progress. Occasionally we even commiserate with one another! The level of working knowledge required for us to be effective in our myriad roles is vast. We each approach our role as generalists; we have to know how the system works to efficiently and effectively run the school and support district efforts. We'll explore the different aspects of rural principalship time management further in Chapter 4.

The Rural Advocate

As a rural school leader, I am the voice for the students in my community. I believe I have a duty to ensure that policymakers and influencers at all levels of the legislative process understand the importance of rural voices. Rural advocates face unique political issues that their urban counterparts may address differently or not at all. One such concern was the capacity of my district to continue to provide high-quality classroom instruction despite declining enrollment, loss of funding due to the approaching end to a voter-approved budget override (which implements a secondary property tax to fund education), and a central office staff of four. In my first three years as superintendent, I had to trim almost $1 million from the maintenance and operations budget (previously $5.5 million annually), cut staff and nonessential programming, and freeze pay increases to combat the severe financial reduction. Although the governing board has again called for overrides several times in the last decade, they have not been approved by voters. When these issues directly affect our staff and students, it is one of my responsibilities to tell the story of my district and share how the state's funding structure creates inequities for rural students. And to be clear, funding is not the only area of concern.

The unique needs of rural education are often overlooked, perhaps because "only" one in five American students attends school in a rural area (NCES, 2017). It is essential to elevate rural voices to include them in policy discussions at all levels. Unfortunately, little attention is spent on rural public education issues, to the point where most research and subsequent decisions are considerably urban-centric. Being heard regarding state initiatives, funding discussions, and other areas of district concern is a priority for me. I know that if there is no rural representation at policy meetings, urban perspectives will most likely be the only viewpoints considered—often with detrimental consequences for rural schools. It is imperative rural leaders work collectively on funding and education issues; they must take part in the process of considering education-related bills at all levels of government.

Relationships Matter

One thing I learned early on was the importance of nurturing relationships to support successful advocacy efforts. As I explored how best to become an effective advocate for my district, I tapped into the expertise of a superintendent colleague who excels in advocacy work. His framing: all politics are local. (Coincidentally, my state rural association approaches policy work in the same way). There are multiple areas of concern within education policy, from state statutes to state board of education policies to executive actions to federal regulations. Our influence is strongest with the *people* who make the decisions. Whether they are legislators, bureaucrats, or policy advisors, we can start to change education policy through our interactions with those decision makers. When we reach out to our policymakers with our help and support and share our rural perspective, we can establish a positive line of communication that secures our place at the table when decisions are made.

The Arbinger Institute's Influence Pyramid™ (Figure 1.2) is a framework that depicts the broadening effects created by different approaches to change. Most of your advocacy efforts will fall in the category of helping policymakers get it right—and a lot will involve relationship building. As education advocates, we have to start by being OK with knowing that differences of opinion and approach are part of life. We must also make an effort to get to know those at the policymaking table, both the ones we want to focus on and those who are their known and trusted allies. Beginning with relationship building is critical for advocacy work. We want to know *what* officials think, and we want to understand *why* they think the way they do. If I know that a particular lawmaker has a child with special needs and previously had a negative experience navigating services in their home district, I can have a better appreciation for the bill they proposed on fiscal consequences for schools that are not

FIGURE 1.2

The Influence Pyramid

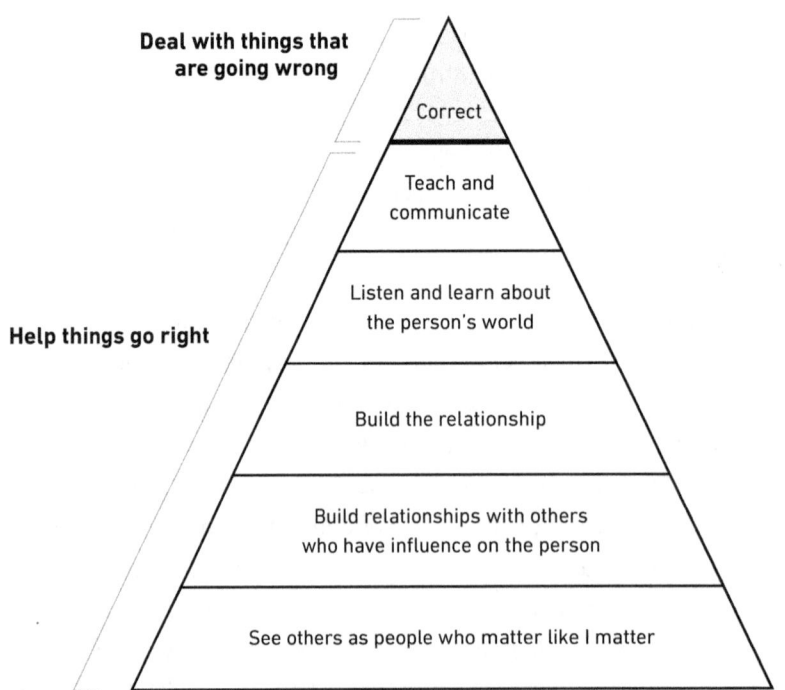

Source: From *The Anatomy of Peace: Resolving the Heart of Conflict,* by the Arbinger Institute, 2006, Berrett-Koehler Publishers. Copyright 2006 by the Arbinger Institute. Adapted with permission.

responsive to meeting IEP goals in a timely manner. With that understanding in place, I can better communicate why such legislation might negatively affect the special education program in my rural community.

Educating policymakers on latent consequences to rural schools is where the true power of advocacy work resides. But when legislation that I would consider to be harmful has already moved forward, I implement the "Correct" step from the top of the pyramid, perhaps by penning an op-ed piece detailing the concerns I have, speaking out against the legislation at a committee hearing, or contacting other legislators who may be able to stop the bill. Keep in mind that correction is a last resort, and must be done in a way that preserves your relationship with the people you wish to influence.

Being an Effective Rural Advocate

Your lived experience as a rural leader is the best tool in your advocacy toolkit. You can share knowledge that elected officials and others need to consider when they are deliberating on a vote. Why will certain policies work in an urban area but not in a rural context? You know the answer and can provide details with both facts and anecdotes. You are the expert who can connect the dots between policy and place in a way no other leader can. So after building relationships with policymakers, what are the next steps in your advocacy efforts? Here are some things to ponder:

- Know why you are advocating for a particular issue and what the consequences of a particular bill would be for your school community.
- Know the policymaker—learn about their background, their assigned committees, and their areas of expertise and interest.
- Find common ground with policymakers in your shared belief in the importance of education—even if opinions differ as to the best way to provide it.
- You can't advocate for something that you don't understand. Do the homework needed to speak intelligently on any advocacy issue, including the opposing point of view.
- Know the policymaker's position on an issue. If it's not clear, ask and be open to listening to the answer. Good advocacy work can and should include making an effort to understand where you might be able to provide a different point of view.
- Keep your advocacy work laser focused on issues with a high impact on your students and community. Your time and effort are precious; don't

squander your political capital by speaking to every issue on the table. Limit each encounter with the policymaker to two or three issues and illustrate your story with concise data.
- Keep your talking points and your requests short and simple while providing clarity on how the issues impact you so as not to waste time for either the policymaker or yourself.
- An advocacy visit is not a time for a debate! Remain calm and nonjudgmental. You are expected to take a stand on the issues at hand, but you should also be open to others' points of view.
- Advocacy is a year-round endeavor. Your first advocacy meeting should not be the only time a policymaker sees you. Work throughout the year to get to know each other.
- Don't rule out meeting with officials who are not aligned with your position. The whole point of advocacy work is to highlight what works for rural schools and communities—they need your voice, especially in this context!
- Offer your expertise to assist with writing or refining bills or policies. Most lawmakers do not draft their own legislation. You can bring an idea or proposal to be considered, review proposed legislation and provide insights on positive and negative outcomes for rural schools, or speak in support of or against legislation in a committee hearing.
- Most policymakers are not educators, so they rely heavily on staffers when considering education policy. Set yourself up as a resource for these staffers, invite them out to see your school, and send them resources and information. Meet with them if the policymaker is not available. Over time, being an ally and an expert voice in the field—one with a specific rural point of view—will boost your influence on their work.
- Even if your meeting doesn't go as planned or you don't get what you ask for, be sure to thank the policymaker for their time. Keep the door open for future conversations!

Assessing the Impact of Policies and Regulations on Rural Education

Are advocacy efforts worth carving out time in your very stretched calendar? I believe they are one of the more important functions of a rural leader! A very informal straw poll that I did with rural superintendents in my state revealed that the majority feel that both federal and state policies often overlook rural schools and their students. This may be because most policymakers and influencers do not live in rural places and therefore have limited understanding of the unique needs of rural people.

A few years ago, I invited the executive board and management of an educational nonprofit located in Phoenix, Arizona, to hold their quarterly board meeting on my campus. We planned a tour led by students, classroom visits, and a meet-and-greet with the administration. Less than a handful of the 20 attendees had any kind of rural background or understanding. The rest had never even been to a rural school! Stanfield is an hour away from downtown Phoenix, so we aren't as remote as many rural schools. And yet if these individuals involved in advocacy work for *all* Arizona schools lacked acquaintance with the rural context, how effective were their efforts for students who attend rural schools? "I just didn't know there were schools like this" was heard over and over as we gave the tour and answered questions. The bottom line is people who are making or influencing rural education policy need to spend time in rural schools to gain a fuller understanding of the issues.

There are also concerns related to federal grant funding. For example, Title I funding to address educational quality for low-income students is allocated using a formula that favors larger districts. Even though more than 85 percent of students in my district receive free or reduced-price lunch, because our total population is small, we receive less funding than a neighboring district with a 50 percent free and reduced-price lunch count and twice as many students. Title I is a noncompetitive grant, and we receive the allocated amount provided we are in good status with all grant requirements. However, an increasing number of federal competitive grants are offered for a variety of program focuses each fiscal year. As a U.S. Department of Education School Ambassador Fellow, I have been a reviewer for several such grants, and I can say without a doubt that I would not have the time or capacity to apply for most of them. Gathering the required documentation, program narratives, and other application requirements is a hardship for most rural schools, given that staff are often already at their limits. Therefore, larger urban and suburban districts with greater staffing capacity are typically the recipients of these funds.

Stronger Together

The rural setting can be isolating—even in a school district! In Arizona, 55 districts are considered single-site local education agencies (LEAs). These districts, including mine, are typically small, cover elementary grade ranges, and can often be remote. In such districts, educator affinity groups found in larger urban districts are hard to maintain or nonexistent. What this has highlighted for me, especially during the pandemic, was the need to intentionally connect with colleagues to exchange ideas, challenges, and resources. Especially if you are new to your position as a rural leader, I strongly encourage you to join one or more existing rural education support networks, many available at no or low cost.

Ad Hoc Support Systems

In March 2020, the U.S. education community as a whole was thrown into unprecedented (I grew tired of that word!) circumstances when the COVID-19 pandemic required schools to conduct the business of teaching and learning in a way that had never been done before. My principal and I labored over how to provide digital learning to our students, most of whom did not have broadband internet access; how to keep teachers engaged and active even from home; and how to continue to support students' basic needs, such as food and counseling services. I was able to meet weekly with other superintendents in my county using virtual platforms over the next few months. It was helpful to hear what plans others were considering, what safety protocols were being instituted, and what the myriad reports needed for our state department of education entailed. Most of this planning and reporting fell to me as the superintendent, as my principal had her hands full figuring out how to sustain teaching in a community with limited broadband access. Without the support of my colleagues, our plans would not have been as successful.

I assumed that if I was struggling with how to ensure everyone had what they needed to keep going, while at the same time take care of myself, other rural leaders were struggling as well. With the assistance of Grand Canyon University's Canyon Professional Development division, two of my colleagues and I started a Rural Education Leaders Network that offered two things: (1) professional development around just-in-time strategic planning, and (2) the opportunity to talk to peers about what was going on in their communities and how they were approaching barriers and challenges. The first year saw participation from 25 leaders around Arizona. It went so well, and the feedback was so positive, that we launched a second year in collaboration with the Small School Districts' Association of California and expanded our reach to the southwestern states of California, Utah, and Nevada. The second year drew in 65 leaders to network and participate in virtual sessions focused on John Maxwell's *The Five Levels of Leadership* (2011). Now in its third year of operation, the Rural Education Leaders Network (RELN) is offered in 16 western states and has almost doubled its membership. The bottom line is that rural leaders need each other! The synergy that happens when professionals talk about their day-to-day challenges and successes is a powerful thing that can be rare in a rural setting. The RELN is only one of many such opportunities. Look for communities of practice in your state or region through your state associations, higher education institutions, or your Regional Education Laboratory. And if you can't find one, start one in your area! A silver lining of the pandemic was the way rural places connected virtually with each other in the absence of face-to-face opportunities. Start small and go virtual!

National education associations are another means of connecting with peers. For example, the National Association of Secondary School Principals (NASSP) offers an online community of practice specifically for rural principals that meets regularly to provide support and information to members and nonmembers. You can find out more about the NASSP's Rural School Leaders Network at www.nassp.org/leadership-networks/rural-school-leaders-network.

Rural Associations and Organizations

Organizations at the local, state, and national levels can offer ways to get involved with rural education policy work, network, and gather information to support your advocacy.

- **Local Level**
  - Most counties have an Education Service Agency (ESA) or Board of Cooperative Educational Services (BOCES) of some kind. They may be able to support a partnership with other rural schools in your area by offering a meeting location, bringing in resources and technical assistance, or providing opportunities for networking and training. If this kind of arrangement isn't in place in your area, reach out to start one! Even quick check-ins allow rural leaders time to talk with one another.

- Local service organizations like Rotary Club or Elks Club can be a way to connect with the community. Hearing from club members outside the education community can supply valuable context for some of the issues and barriers that affect rural schools. Local chambers of commerce can serve in the same capacity.

- **State Level**
  - Forty-two states have a rural education association of some kind (National Rural Education Association, n.d.). State associations often provide a variety of information, training, and technical assistance. Most have some kind of annual conference that brings the field together for networking and professional development.
  - Rural resource centers are also typically run at the state level and associated with an institution of higher learning. There is no standard type of center—all offer resources and support unique to the rural leaders and schools in their state. Currently, 20 rural resource centers operate throughout the United States. Contact the universities in your state to see if they sponsor organizations that specifically focus on rural education.

- **Regional Level**
  - The U.S. Department of Education's Regional Education Laboratory (REL) Program comprises 10 regions across the country that partner with educators and policymakers to support meaningful change. They work with LEAs and state education agencies (SEAs) on decisions about education policy, programs, and practices in pursuit of positive educational outcomes. Currently, the REL program is authorized under the Education Sciences Reform Act of 2002 and administered by the Institute of Education Sciences. Twenty percent of all funding must be targeted to assist rural education in each region. For more information, visit https://ies.ed.gov/ncee/rel.
  - The Rural Schools Collaborative is a nonprofit organization headquartered in Illinois with a focus on building sustainable rural communities by working to connect place, teachers, and philanthropy. Twelve Regional Hubs operate in 30 states to facilitate collaboration on projects and grants and highlight the efforts of rural teachers. For more information, visit https://ruralschoolscollaborative.org/regional-hubs.

- **National Level**
  - The National Rural Education Association serves as a rural advocate at the national level with both the U.S. Department of Education and Congress. They also interact with the White House on a variety of issues concerning rural students and schools. Additionally, they provide professional development opportunities to members at an annual national conference and support research on rural schools, which is disseminated in a quarterly publication. For more information, visit www.nrea.net.
  - The National Rural Education Advocacy Coalition represents several organizations including the National Rural Education Association, the American Association of School Administrators, and a number of state rural education associations. Each year they release a legislative agenda focused on rural issues and work with the Department of Education and legislators to advance the rural education perspective. For more information, visit www.nrea.net/nreac-legislation.
  - The American Council on Rural Special Education advocates for enhanced services for children with exceptional needs in rural places. For more information, visit www.acres-sped.org.

- **Other Federal Resources**
  - The Rural Education Resource Center of the U.S. Department of Education offers a variety of programs, upcoming events, news, and grant information. I use the center's website to gather information to support my advocacy work at both the state and federal levels, and I recommend checking it regularly for updates. For more information, visit www.ed.gov/rural-education.
  - The National Agricultural Library of the U.S. Department of Agriculture (USDA) has resources on a host of relevant topics, including community development, rural health services, housing, and environmental justice. As the hub of a typical rural community, the USDA may be able to provide support and information on efforts that involve not just the school but the community at large, with the rural leader serving as a facilitator to move policy and action forward. For more information, visit www.nal.usda.gov/legacy/ric/rural-citizen-services.
  - The Department of Education's 10 RELs, referenced above, are another resource for the rural advocate. One of the key missions of the REL

Program is to assist rural schools by providing training and technical support, conducting rural education research, and reporting research findings to the field. Twenty percent of the REL budget must be spent on rural initiatives and programming. As a member of the REL 15 Rural Community of Practice, I meet regularly with LEAs and SEAs to investigate current rural issues facing schools and determine how SEAs can offer support. This community of practice has been not only a source of high-quality research and technical information, but also an avenue for networking across the four states covered. (The RELN, mentioned earlier, was formed from these relationships.) For more information, visit https://ies.ed.gov/ncee/edlabs/projects/rural.asp.

The many diverse responsibilities that fall onto the shoulders of the rural leader can often include tasks the leader is not fully prepared to address. From working with a governing board, to managing the fiscal duties of the district, to being a vocal advocate for the school and community, to ensuring an effective community of support is in place, leadership in a rural district is multifaceted. Just like with teaching, you'll never experience the same day twice!

Although rural school leadership may involve wearing many hats, it is a rewarding endeavor that is closely tied to the success of the community being served. Ensuring that multiple supports are in place, starting with the governing board, and roles are clearly defined can have a positive impact on your success as a rural leader learning the ropes while also balancing the duties of instructional leader and manager.

Rural school leaders across different communities often must overcome similar barriers. One of my mantras is "Rural innovates out of necessity!" If the answer to a problem is not readily apparent, rural leaders must find a creative solution. The following chapters highlight various rural school leadership challenges and some trailblazing solutions unique to rural settings to address them. Context matters; while some solutions seem tailor-made for one rural school, they may not be practical or even possible in another. Some chapters may apply directly to your current circumstances; others might not be as relevant but may spark some proactive planning. Either way, the resources and ideas shared are ones that have made a difference for rural leaders on the ground—and I hope they will serve you well, too.

2

Rural Teacher Recruitment and Retention

No doubt about it, teaching is hard work! It's also amazing, uplifting, and the most important work on Earth. There is no greater joy than connecting with a student around learning. Public education in the United States has gone through many changes since the 1700s, when the Founding Fathers proposed the creation of a formal system of education to achieve their goal of an educated citizenry (Center on Education Policy, 2020). The desired outcomes of students' educations, teacher qualifications, and the impact of societal reforms and standardization on schools have all shaped the demands placed on the current teacher workforce. Possibly in response, the number of teacher candidates in university and other preparation programs has dropped considerably. According to the U.S. Department of Education's Title II report (2017), the number declined from 725,000 in 2009–2010 to 441,439 in 2015–2016. That's an astounding 35 percent fewer potential teachers coming into classrooms across the country!

In 2018, Richard Ingersoll and colleagues analyzed the transformation of the teaching workforce over a 29-year period. Their report laid out some startling findings related to efforts to recruit and retain teachers:

- The growth in number of teachers employed (64 percent) has outpaced the increase in student population (24 percent) due to several factors, including the demand for smaller class sizes and the need for more English learner (EL), special education, and science, technology, engineering, and math (STEM) teachers.
- One in 10 teachers leaves the profession after their first year of employment (i.e., before gaining enough experience to be an effective educator).

- The turnover rate for teachers of color is significantly higher than for any other demographic.
- Schools that experience the highest rates of teacher turnover tend to be low-income and located in either rural (28 percent turnover) or urban (19 percent turnover) areas (Ingersoll & Tran, 2023).

During the summer of 2022, the American Association of School Personnel Administrators (AASPA) hosted a national summit focused on the teacher shortage. The white paper that was subsequently produced highlights both findings and solutions that are worth considering when addressing the scarcity of applicants at the local level (Heynoski et al., 2022). The authors of the paper first presented an analysis of root causes of the shortage through six lenses: political, economic, social, technological, legal, and environmental (PESTLE). Figure 2.1 presents the questions addressing each factor and lists some key issues to consider. While the aim of the national summit was to target the lack of teachers in the field on the whole, the PESTLE analysis—and the solutions it inspires—could be applied to any school site. Rural leaders can tailor this framework to fit their unique context.

The PESTLE analysis highlights the fact that the factors influencing the lack of educators in the pipeline are systemic and long term. District responses often center around such solutions as increased compensation or dual enrollment programs, some of which may be effective. However, AASPA encouraged members to take a deeper look into the issues and redesign their approach to talent acquisition (Heynoski et al., 2022). They recommend five shifts that outline systemic actions that can be taken by a variety of stakeholder groups to attract new applicants to the profession and keep those who are already in place:

1. **Reduce barriers to careers in education while preserving standards of excellence.** Career pathways exist across the country, but barriers to those pathways need to be addressed. Some possible steps at the local level are to guarantee that educators conducting clinical experiences with them will receive a contract on completion, sponsor visas for overseas candidates, or offer tutoring support for licensure exams.
2. **Design comprehensive capital management systems.** Educators always need more resources, but allocations should be based on a set of policies and procedures that operate effectively from recruitment to retirement. Implementing human resources (HR) practices that align with the district's mission and vision; conducting "stay" interviews, ensuring effective HR department management; and providing a long-term, comprehensive onboarding program for new staff are examples of beneficial capital management.

FIGURE 2.1

PESTLE Analysis

Environmental Factor	Key Issues to Consider
Political: What role do local/state/national politics play in shaping education organizations? (Impact of policies, rules, regulations, and funding)	• Controversy over social issues (e.g., racial diversity, gender expression, curriculum content) • Education funding • Local control • Elections at all levels • Tax policies • Support for education
Economic: How does the performance of the economy impact education organizations? (Impact of the economy on finances)	• Educator salaries • Cost of preparation and certification, including unpaid clinicals • Lack of career trajectory • Inequity in funding for different locales (rural vs. urban) • Inflation, unemployment rates, interest rates • Increased competition for student enrollment • Increased competition for educator candidates
Social: To what extent does the social environment and community demographics influence education organizations? (Impact of beliefs, norms, and demographic trends)	• Public perception of teaching profession, negative media coverage • Declining enrollment in teacher prep programs • Challenges experienced by educators of color • Shifting community demographics (socioeconomic status, race/ethnicity, refugee/immigrant status, special needs) served in schools • Mental health needs of students • Increasing task expectations with no additional compensation
Technological: How does the rate of technological development and innovation affect education organizations? (Impact of technological advances and innovation)	• More connected society • Growing virtual schooling options • More technology skills required • Variance of virtual access • Limited educator preparation for technology integration • Automation and emerging technologies
Legal: How do changing legislation and industry standards impact compliance requirements for education organizations? (Impact of current and proposed legislation or standards)	• Unfunded mandates and their fiscal impact • Variation in licensure requirements by state, lack of reciprocity, and inefficiencies in certification process • Variation in alternate pathways to licensure • State pension restrictions for retiree re-employment • District restrictions for employee leave • Employment legislation, health and safety policies (including pandemic response)
Environmental: What influence does the surrounding environment have on education organizations? (Impact of the physical environment and environmental policies)	• Location of population centers and influence on applicant pool • Poor working conditions (lack of resources, poor infrastructure) • Concerns over school safety and violence • Educator perception of lack of preparedness • Lack of educator support, mentoring, coaching • Pandemic demands placed on educators

Source: Heynoski et al., 2022.

3. **Establish transparent and equitable total rewards systems.** Efforts to increase educator pay should be accompanied by attention to staff's "total rewards," including all associated benefits such as medical insurance, payments into the state retirement system, growth

opportunities, tax incentives, and staffing flexibility. Districts can align their offerings with employee needs and wants in response to survey data, create flexible staffing models, and regularly evaluate pay equity, making adjustments if necessary.

4. **Strengthen educators' sense of purpose, belonging, and connection.** Staff wellness structures can and should be broadened to ensure that employees are engaged and connected to the workplace and feel like they are invested in meaningful work. Staff should have opportunities to contribute input, experience a positive work culture, draw on support and mentoring, and connect with the community at large to further partnerships and increase educator impact.

5. **Deliver exceptional employment experiences.** The public's perception of the teaching profession is at an all-time low, and one way to turn it around is to start from within. Educators who are excited about their chosen career path are excellent vectors for a positive public relations campaign. Local leaders can further their cause with intentional attention to improved employee experiences such as treating staff members with top-notch customer service, promoting work-life balance with flexibility and support, regularly gathering feedback on what is and is not working, and helping teachers become education ambassadors through referral programs. (Heynoski et al., 2022)

Challenge: Openings with No Applicants

Being a teacher in a rural school comes with many upsides—appealing geography, opportunities for outdoor recreation, and a slower pace of life, to name a few. Rural schools typically have smaller classes, which means a smaller workload, greater control over curriculum and instruction, and the opportunity to create engaging lessons based on student needs and local assets. However, there are challenges as well. Rural educators are often responsible for teaching multiple subjects, some of which they may not be prepared to teach. The scarcity of professional learning communities and collaboration, a perceived lack of privacy, and the influence of small-town politics on the classroom are other concerns. And then there is the smaller tax base, lack of diversity (although that is changing), restricted accessibility to resources like healthcare, generational poverty, and limitations on opportunities to provide students with rich experiences beyond the community. Given these significant barriers, finding candidates for rural teaching positions is a challenge.

Solutions: Recruitment Strategies

As I mentioned previously, it has become harder and harder to attract applicants to my rural area. However, it's not about getting applicants interested in becoming a Stanfield Roadrunner in particular. It's also an issue stemming from leaks in the teacher pipeline that have sprung across the nation, resulting in teacher scarcity. Out of necessity, rural leaders have had to grow more adept at cobbling together a full contingent of educators for their classrooms. Let's look at some ways the rural education community has leveraged different stakeholder groups and supporters to both attract teachers to jobs and then endeavor to keep them under contract.

As I write this, we are starting the new school year and have welcomed students back into our buildings. In my single-site district, we employ 25 certified teachers when we are fully staffed. Currently, we have three openings that are not yet filled; there would have been more had we not created a multiage 4th/5th grade classroom and contracted with an online school to provide middle school social studies instruction. We also had to convert library time into computer coding class and add the instructional aide housed there to the "specials" rotation due to a lack of a PE teacher. The bottom line is we are making it work while continuing to seek candidates for these openings.

I am not the only one that has had challenges with attracting teachers. Unfortunately, rural communities often serve as the "canary in the coal mine," and they began struggling with teacher shortages on a proportionally larger scale years before urban areas. Even before the pandemic, rural leaders were discussing the difficulty in getting applicants in large numbers—or at all. Some districts can draw on test scores, location, pay scale, or reputation to entice viable candidates, but others are desperate to just fill a position. Following are some strategies that leaders can consider to recruit applicants to vacancies in their rural communities.

Strengthen Your Human Capital Management Plan

A well-structured recruitment and retention plan is essential in the current job market, where competition for applicants has never been greater. Current HR best practices include establishing a more comprehensive, year-round plan for attracting, retaining, and sustaining a full contingent of staff called a human capital management system (HCMS). You can evaluate your district's approach to HR by using a self-assessment tool developed for the U.S. Department of Education that identifies 56 quality indicators in six areas: general system design; recruitment, selection, and placement; induction and mentoring; professional development; evaluation; and recognition and rewards. Access the tool online at https://bit.ly/HCMS-Assessment-Tool.

Engage with Social Media

Social media is a must when it comes to communicating about the opportunities that rural communities offer. Messages shared on various social media platforms can promote your rural school as well as familiarize the public and potential applicants with your district's vision, mission, and values. Use social media to celebrate successes of both staff and students, highlight events, and of course, share job postings alongside testimonials from current employees (see Figure 2.2 for more ideas). Get to know the various platforms, and focus on no more than five to target either the group you are trying to attract or the local community.

Postings should be consistent, include your district brand, and align with the vision and mission of your school and district. Schedule your posts to ensure your channels aren't accidentally neglected, which will also enable you to concentrate on making proactive rather than reactive posts. Keep posts short and include visuals as often as possible; one tool that can help with creating attractive graphic content for no or low cost is Canva (www.canva.com). Also consider posting in different languages, depending on the demographics of the local community. Finally, link the district and school websites in your personal social media feeds to drive traffic to your website.

FIGURE 2.2

What Should I Post?

1.	District and school current and upcoming events	6.	School activities and programs
2.	Employee recognitions	7.	Holiday recognitions
3.	Job postings	8.	Student success highlights
4.	Newsletters and other school communications	9.	Student artwork or writing
5.	Community information and events	10.	New employee welcomes

Keep in mind that the district is responsible for posts and comments on its social media platforms, so you must be strategic about granting posting access and transferring responsibility when employees change roles. It's also a good practice to have a disclaimer on your social media site, along with a statement regarding usage expectations.

Create Marketing Videos

Rural districts are increasingly developing promotional videos featuring both administration and currently employed teachers to attract applicants. A visual that highlights opportunities and advantages for prospective candidates is valuable, and a series of videos detailing the assets of the school community posted on the school or district website can be an excellent recruitment tool. Be sure that any students appearing in the videos have a media release on file (and know who doesn't so you can respect their privacy while filming). Not sure what to put out on video? These ideas can help start the process:

- **School or district overview.** What makes your school unique? What should people know about the school, its history, and its traditions?
- **"Meet the Staff."** Depending on how many employees you have, this could take a few weeks or all year. Have staff members introduce themselves, talk about the work they do for the school, and share something personal about themselves. A 30-second introduction can go a long way to creating connections between staff and the school and local communities.
- **Classroom happenings.** Classrooms are a continual source of video content! Highlight fun projects, student interviews on what's going on in their classroom, and "A Day in the Life" opportunities.
- **Extracurricular events.** Sports, after-school clubs, field trips, parent nights, and other activities that take place outside the classroom make great content. Not only do they give a glimpse into what is going on at the school, they might inspire parents to get more involved!
- **"I Am a Rural Teacher."** Showcase your teachers by having them explain why they choose to teach in a rural setting in addition to what they value about teaching in general. Encourage them to share classroom updates and examples of the learning going on in their rooms.
- **Regular updates.** A "Monday Message" or "Friday Shoutout" by administration is a good way to keep the community informed about what is happening on campus. These updates don't have to be long: a

two-minute video is long enough to share information and make connections with the school community.
- **Parent showcases.** Ask parents or grandparents to highlight what they appreciate about the school and the community. Especially in rural areas, they may have attended the school as a student. Have them talk about their past experiences.
- **Live streaming.** Consider setting up a livestream for events like graduations, student assemblies, or plays. When accessible to the general public, these events can extend connections to distant friends and family and broaden awareness of your school.

Be Transparent About Rurality

Many job seekers who apply to rural school openings are not from rural communities and have no experience with living and working in a rural place. In states like Alaska, where the majority of teachers are hired from out of state, unclear expectations about what life will be like in rural and often remote communities equates to high rates of turnover, year after year—at an annual cost of approximately $20 million to the state (Petersen, 2019). When structuring any type of recruitment plan, highlighting community assets in a realistic and comprehensive manner will go a long way to ensuring that candidates are truly interested in experiencing a rural school setting. I strongly recommend using *Teaching in Rural Places: Thriving in Classrooms, Schools, and Communities* (Azano et al., 2020) for insights into what it means to be a teacher in a rural community to spark discussions with job seekers or new hires.

Facilitate "Grow Your Own" Programs

The Grow Your Own (GYO) movement has become a staple in the rural leader's pantry of ideas for filling teacher vacancies. More and more, the focus has turned to drawing on local resources to solve the alarming lack of outside applicants. While many such models have also started in urban districts, the main tenets of these programs grow out of rural needs.

To be effective, GYO programs must address three main areas: lowering prospective teachers' costs by reducing or eliminating tuition burden; recruiting from classified staff and the local community, including paraprofessionals, parents, and retirees; and supporting certification requirements with test preparation or waiver requests (Master & Doss, 2022). It is also important that these programs commit to securing high-quality instruction and maintaining high expectations for program outcomes.

In 2022, the Clarksville–Montgomery County School System (CMCSS), located north of Nashville, Tennessee, partnered with Austin-Peay State University, Nashville State Community College, and Lipscomb University to create a Teacher Residency Program that is the country's first apprenticeship approved by the U.S. Department of Labor. This GYO model provides teacher candidates with highly structured training concurrent with full-time employment in a classroom setting, free of tuition and textbook expenses (CMCSS, n.d.). Scrutiny and attention to these types of programs are opening doors to funding that will make them even more sustainable and attractive for recruits.

Other successful GYO programs follow different trajectories. The University of Montana Western provides an online option for teacher candidates to gather the needed coursework for certification (Rispens, 2022). And at Montana State University–Northern, a "running start" dual enrollment program was created to provide high school students an accelerated career track (Montana State University–Northern, n.d.). Teachers of Promise Pathways partners with local school districts to work with students in grades 10–12 to recruit them to teaching through local certification efforts. Students earn both high school and college credit and qualify for paid tuition through a state-funded program.

Becoming an education preparation provider with state approval for certification issuance is a GYO model that allows the teacher candidates to do all coursework and clinicals through the district where they will eventually take a teaching position. Jaime Festa-Daigle, director of student achievement for Lake Havasu Unified School District (LHUSD) in Lake Havasu City, Arizona, describes her district's approach below.

Voices from the Field: Jaime's Solution

Lake Havasu City, Arizona, is known for several things. From 1968 to 1971, Robert McCulloch transported the London Bridge piece by piece from England to the newly founded city and rebuilt it over the Colorado River. Kawasaki tested the first Jet Skis on the lake in the early 1980s. And Biggie Smalls and MTV highlighted Lake Havasu City's spring break celebrations in 1995. In other words, Lake Havasu City is known for its recreation and tourism.

Its school district is known, however, for its support and development of National Board Certified Teachers (NBCTs). The first

Lake Havasu NBCT certified in 2001; since then, 32 teachers have earned their certification. In addition, LHUSD was named as a National Board Accomplished District in 2019. LHUSD's focus on accomplished teaching and teacher leadership provided the district the capacity to create our own teacher preparation program.

Like many rural districts, LHUSD has had difficulty recruiting and retaining teachers. Resources are tight, and finding housing for new staff can be difficult. For years, LHUSD focused on recruiting novice teachers from states like New York, Michigan, and Ohio that had cold winters and more teachers than teaching jobs. For a time, this strategy was effective. But LHUSD invested in these teachers by providing quality induction and mentoring programs, and after a few years, many would return to their home state. As more districts traveled out of state to recruit, LHUSD was unable to find enough teachers willing to make the move to the sun-drenched city.

However, as a close-knit community, LHUSD hired many former Lake Havasu High School graduates, some who went to school to become a teacher and some who did not. Faced with statewide teacher shortages, Arizona began allowing alternative teacher preparation programs of varying quality and cost to potential teachers to be approved by the state board of education. As a longtime NBCT, I knew that I could use the resources we already created to develop a quality teacher preparation program that fit our needs. I knew that what we offered was higher quality than many prep programs that cost a lot of money and offered little more than a certificate for teachers at the end.

We had recently rewritten our teacher evaluation to align with the National Board for Professional Teaching Standards Core Propositions. This would be the foundation of our program. I worked with teacher leaders in the district to identify what was essential for teachers to learn. We focused on early literacy, serving students with different needs, classroom management, and professional skills. We ensured that teachers who took this path would have access to multiple levels of mentoring and support. We invested in coaches to work with teachers to develop their skills and help them reflect on their practice. I also partnered with our local community college to identify four key courses to offer as part of the program, knowing that our teachers would benefit from the knowledge that a partner institution could provide.

We were able to recruit from within the community and grow our own teachers. These new recruits were connected to our community and had a vested interest in staying. They learned about the importance of accomplished teaching from the get-go. Our goal is to support teachers through three years of induction, with their final year focused on reflective practices. We then support teachers in earning their National Board certification, as we know our NBCTs are much more likely to stay with us.

Although Lake Havasu will always be synonymous with boating, we also want it to be synonymous with an excellent school system that is dedicated to developing and retaining accomplished teachers who serve our community.

—Jaime Festa-Daigle, director of student achievement,
Lake Havasu Unified School District, Arizona

Rural school districts are not the only ones devising GYO strategies to combat the lack of teacher candidates. In Arizona, the Department of Education's Teacher Recruitment and Retention division is responsible for providing programming, grant funding, and technical assistance to schools across the state. The division collects and disseminates educator workforce data and has launched several initiatives to help address the shortage statewide with a Teacher's Academy. They have also worked to incorporate several alternative pathways to teacher certifications, such as internship programs, and have expanded teaching certification reciprocity with other states. Be sure to check with your SEA to determine if they are also poised to assist your rural community with securing applicants for open positions.

What else can the resourceful rural leader do? Here are some ideas to consider when looking at ways to attract both teachers and prospective teachers to your rural district:

- **Proactively create employment contracts for student teachers or residents at your site.** The assurance of future employment will make the process of getting certified more attractive to potential staff members.

- **Assist employees with applying for loan forgiveness programs.** Specific grant funding from the federal government can often be obtained for teachers who commit to a certain amount of time in a rural school district (typically five years). Check with your state's department of education for specific information.
- **Retain applications of candidates who were not hired in case a future opening aligns with their skills.** Provide feedback on why they weren't selected for a particular position, but let them know you will keep them in your pipeline to engage with them if the opportunity arises.
- **Establish an employee referral program.** Offer current staff members a "finder's fee" stipend for any successful referral to an open position. This type of bonus also goes a long way in setting up a positive impression of the district within the community.
- **Use Title II-A funds to offer stipends to teachers who take hard-to-fill openings, such as those in special education or mathematics.** Consider using those same grant funds to pay a relocation stipend to candidates who aren't local to the district.

Solutions: Retention Strategies

This year, our school's principal had three certified staff members resign from their positions within two weeks of the beginning of the school year—including one on the night before we were set to return to work! Recruitment of teachers is only one half of the discussion. Retention is probably even more important, because losing employees results in a loss of fiscal investment in hiring, placement, and training. You really can't talk about one without bringing up the other. In most of the research on this topic, retention means that a teacher stays with their school for a minimum of three full years. What are some of the ways rural schools can retain their staff?

Provide Comprehensive Onboarding and Support

When I first started teaching over 30 years ago, onboarding at my rural school included pairing me with the more experienced teacher across the hall who taught the same grade I did. If I needed anything, I went to her for help. We have grown beyond that approach to engaging our new staff and are now much more intentional about helping educators to settle into their new role—although a coaching or mentoring piece is still integral to the process. A rural school that might have a shortage of available staff, however, could turn to online coaching as a way to fill the gap. Sharing coaches between schools and districts is another way to provide support when personnel aren't plentiful. Here are some other things to keep in mind while connecting new staff with the school community:

- **Bring new hires to campus right away to participate in a school activity or event.** This type of introduction will help them start making connections with current staff.
- **Create a Welcome Team specifically for onboarding new staff members.** The team can work together to engage new staff, with a particular individual assigned to the newcomer as an ambassador—the go-to person for answering logistical and other workplace questions.
- **Provide a list of key personnel and their areas of responsibility.** The list will help address any issues or concerns that might arise for the new employee.
- **Provide ongoing and consistent opportunities for socialization.** Outside-of-school contact will help employees feel like they are part of a team.
- **Set up monthly forums to provide information on policies, procedures, goals, improvement plans, and so on.** These meetings, which should be hosted by school leadership and can be virtual or in person, give new staff time to ask questions and get clarity on what is going on in the school community. They can also serve to highlight key personnel and programs new staff may interact with, like IT or special education.
- **Identify and advertise the various growth opportunities within the school and district as a pathway toward leadership.** These could include positions like lead teacher, department chair, instructional coach, or other openings in which teachers develop their own leadership potential while expanding the site's distributive leadership capacity.

Incorporate Flexible Staffing Models

One of the benefits that I have found in my rural community is that educators are invested in the school community and stay engaged for a longer period of time. Three of our teachers are retirees who returned to work after a few years because they knew we had a need that we were unable to fill. Some of our substitute teachers worked for the district previously as full-time teachers.

But another option that has worked well to fill the gaps in our needs has been employing part-time educators in a flexible staffing model. These staff members work for a portion of the day or week and typically do work that would be conducted by an interventionist or coach. We also benefit from the part-time contributions of a grant program liaison who works a 30-hour week with another business in the community. Implementing flexible schedules and incorporating part-time employees are worth considering. Following are some structures to consider:

- **Co-teaching.** Sharing one classroom between two part-time teachers is not a new concept, but it has recently become more attractive. Co-teaching could be structured with a daily schedule or week by week. The advantage is that both teachers could "substitute" as needed. Eliminating the need to provide medical benefits would result in additional cost savings.
- **Multiclassroom leadership.** In this model, which emerged from the pandemic and the teacher shortage, a highly effective teacher leads a collaborative team in a grade level or subject area. The team includes between two and eight staff members (e.g., teachers, paraprofessionals, teacher interns). The teacher leader teaches part time; is responsible for planning, data disaggregation, and modeling; and serves as the teacher of record. This adaptation of a GYO program allows for flexible staffing if needed. Arizona State University's Next Generation Workforce (https://workforce.education.asu.edu) and Opportunity Culture by Public Impact (https://opportunityculture.org) both have more information on the variety of possible scheduling structures.
- **Remote work.** Some functions of a school or district can be performed at any location. Examples of managerial tasks that can be accomplished by a remote worker with access to broadband include conducting one-to-one online testing, disaggregating assessment and other data, and following up with parent contacts. Having offsite employees perform these duties would allow onsite staff to focus on more student-centered activities. Even a situation in which an offsite teacher works with an onsite classroom aide is an option when there are no applicants for subject-specific positions in the upper grades.

Benefits of flexible staffing include lower salary and benefit costs, opportunities for flexible employees to fill in gaps to allow for full-time staff to focus on their own responsibilities, and less disruptive turnover. It may also enhance the desirability of your school system over those with more rigid staffing models, and can therefore be used as both a recruitment and a retention tool.

Conduct Stay Interviews

Traditionally, exit interviews are used to gather information on what a district could have done differently to retain a resigning educator. However, feedback from an employee who is walking out the door is not a reliable source of actionable information. In contrast, stay interviews can yield applicable data that can be leveraged to focus leadership efforts on reducing the need for exit interviews. Figure 2.3 offers some sample questions that you could use; limit the interview to five or six of them. Being strategic about who you interview is key to getting the needed data. Targeting those highly effective staff who get positive student outcomes will yield usable information. Also consider meeting with teachers who are valuable to the school system and whose loss would leave a large gap. These listening sessions should be conducted one on one and structured as open-ended, honest dialogue. As with all gathered data, it is vital to use the information gained to refine or adjust policies and procedures. Honor your staff's time and contributions by being transparent about how the data collected are being used to improve the system.

You can learn about setting up stay interviews from the following websites:

- Office of the Maricopa County (AZ) School Superintendent, Human Capital Management Systems page: https://schoolsup.org/reil
- Ohio Department of Education, Human Capital Resource Center: https://ohiohcrc.org/stay-interviews

Pivot to a Four-Day Workweek

One tool for both recruitment and retention used by rural schools for many years is the four-day schedule. Originally, a four-day workweek was implemented as a way to save district funds by operating for fewer calendar days in a school year, but increasingly, it is being advertised as a work-life balance measure for teachers. The number of schools moving to a shortened week has increased from 250 in 1999 to more than 1,600 in 2019, with over 70 percent of those in rural areas (Barshay, 2022). Research on the four-day week in rural areas has found that the shortened week and the traditional week show the same amount of learning growth, and in fact, the shortened week benefited rural students overall due to a decrease in the number of bullying incidents (Morton, 2023). It is worth exploring whether restructuring the traditional school week would assist with filling job openings in your district.

FIGURE 2.3

Sample Stay Interview Questions

Questions	Considerations
What do you look forward to when you come to work each day?	Answers will vary, but trends may come to the surface; dig for responses more elaborate than "My students" in an effort to get more usable information.
What do you dislike about work every day?	Any trend that surfaces is an immediate actionable item.
When was the last time you considered leaving the district? The teaching profession?	Especially with your top performers, this question can highlight the risk of losing teachers who would leave hard-to-fill gaps.
What were the circumstances that caused you to consider leaving?	Employees' responses can provide you with specific information to create a more satisfying working environment for them.
Would you recommend this district to other educators seeking employment? Why or why not?	Teachers who are excited to work with a school are the best spokespeople; those who are not can have a detrimental effect.
What would tempt you to leave this school district?	Responses could be internal to the school setting (e.g., school culture) or external (e.g., lack of career advancement opportunities in the current setting).
What is the best part of your job?	Trends may emerge that you can use to inform marketing for the school or district.
What part of the job would you eliminate today if you could?	Trends can emerge that can be addressed by elimination or support.
What talents do you have that are not currently being used?	Answers can address what future opportunities the educator might be interested in and can serve to match current school needs with educator strengths.
Do you feel that you have clear goals and objectives in place?	Answers will target where leadership can improve on communication regarding school or district improvement plans and supports for educators to meet stated goals.
As your principal/superintendent, what can I do more or less of?	Look for trends and know that trust is required for an honest response.
How would you like to be recognized for the work that you do?	Responses can help structure more meaningful recognitions for current and future staff.
Do you have the tools and resources to do your job? If not, what is missing?	Having the right resources can make a difference in how well educators are able to do their work.
What professional development (PD) has benefited you the most? What PD do you still need?	Trends in responses can assist with developing the school PD calendar and target areas for support.

Source: Questions adapted from Verlinden, 2022.

Open Up to Other Options

What else can resilient rural leaders do to increase educator retention rates? Following are some more ideas to consider when looking to preserve your school's most valuable resource—your employees!

- **Strengthen the skills in your human resources department.** Not only should your HR representatives be familiar with the district's policies and procedures and state and federal workforce requirements, they should be tasked with (and trained in) providing a variety of support to staff. This includes educating staff about benefits, sharing professional development opportunities, supporting career growth, and removing barriers to employment or employment advancement.
- **Offer a contract completion bonus in addition to a signing bonus.** If your district faces contract breakage during the school year, promising a completion bonus may lessen the disruption of midyear resignations. Leaders can use Elementary and Secondary School Emergency Relief (ESSER) or Title II-A grant funds for this type of retention tool.
- **Compensate for lower base salaries with affordable medical coverage for employees and their families.** Affordable medical care benefits are especially attractive to retired educators who have returned to work. Additionally, rural schools with school-based clinics may be able to offer basic health services to their employees and their families at no or low cost in a convenient location.
- **Cover the cost of supplementary coursework.** As mentioned previously, rural teachers are often responsible for multiple subject areas. Covering the cost of coursework to ensure the teacher is well prepared to instruct in all of their assigned subjects not only makes them a more valuable resource for the school, it also demonstrates the value the school places on them.
- **Offer onsite child care.** Child care is a valuable service that can make a big difference for families. Rural areas often lack affordable, convenient care. The availability of onsite child care also makes it easier for staff to participate in extracurricular activities as coaches or sponsors. Investigate state licensure requirements for facilities and care providers if you are considering providing this benefit.

Multiple research studies have pointed out that teachers are the greatest single influence on students' educational outcomes. The time you spend on planning and implementing a well-thought-out, comprehensive recruitment and retention plan is unquestionably worth the effort. And ultimately, your students will reap the rewards!

3

The Rural Principal

A recent report released by the Wallace Foundation (Grissom et al., 2021) notes that the influence a principal has on students' educational outcomes is second only to that of their classroom teacher. Principals (who might, in rural settings, also be district superintendents) are called on to be generalists tasked with a multitude of responsibilities, from daily site operations to establishing school culture and climate to ensuring that students are getting the best education possible.

Most research on the principal pipeline, or the pathway to prepare educators to be school leaders, has been conducted in urban settings; keep in mind that rural principals face unique challenges. Nevertheless, to mitigate some of the difficulties in recruiting principals, the Wallace Foundation suggests policy considerations that could make the position more attractive (Mitgang, 2003):

- Understand that issues driving a principal shortage are complex and require a change in conditions, incentives, and regulations.
- Address working conditions, salary, and other incentives to make the principalship more enticing.
- Review hiring practices and eliminate barriers to getting the right candidate for a school. Researchers often found a disconnect between desired attributes and the hiring process.

Challenge: Limited Resources in the Face of Increased Responsibilities

New school leaders face common challenges. Research conducted in Great Britain, Europe, and the United States by the National College for School Leadership (Hobson et al., 2003) identified seven:

- Feelings of professional isolation and loneliness
- Dealing with legacy, practice, and style of the previous leader
- Dealing with multiple tasks, managing time and priorities
- Managing the school budget
- Dealing with (e.g., supporting, warning, dismissing) ineffective staff
- Implementing new government initiatives, notably new curricula or school improvement projects
- Problems with school buildings and site management

These challenges are often heightened in a rural setting, where the principal is responsible for the entirety of the task in addition to the daily running of the campus, student discipline, parent meetings, teacher evaluations, and unanticipated events such as late buses or sick employees. If the school office is marginally resourced with staff, the principal usually takes on the many tasks that no one else can address. This can very quickly lead to burnout.

Rural principals often have more wide-ranging task lists than their urban and suburban colleagues (Preston et al., 2013). These can include addressing local, state, and federal mandates that are often unrealistic in a rural setting, leading to stress and burnout. One such example is federal reporting for American Rescue Plan fund expenditures. Unlike larger schools with personnel capacity to meet reporting requirements, rural schools with limited staffing often need to rely on the principal to complete this work. The reports are the same, but the administrative burden in a rural setting is more onerous because staffing capacity is smaller.

A thorough understanding of the challenges related to the rural context goes a long way to devising solutions to the problem of hiring rural school leaders. Knowing where potential pain points reside—and considering how to ease them proactively—can help a school community looking to fill a principalship in their local school district.

Understanding Rurality

Numerous studies (Cruzeiro & Boone, 2009; Montgomery, 2010; Schuman, 2010) highlight the importance rural superintendents and governing boards place on the idea that a potential principal candidate should have a historical connection with the local community. The "fit" they are looking for includes familiarity through having lived there, or at least having lived in a similar rural area, and thus understanding the community's history, values, priorities, and culture. Being able to fall back on that understanding helps a newly seated administrator when differences of opinion on community-school issues arise.

Living in a rural community as an educator is a many-layered endeavor. A small rural town dynamic can be complex, with a variety of relationships and connections that can be both strengths and potential barriers. This complexity can be daunting for a principal who has never lived in a rural place (Knutson & Del Carlo, 2018). Adults who work with students in a rural school setting will also typically play other roles in their lives. Parents and extended family members who live locally further extend the network. This interconnectivity can lead to ill-defined borders between the school and the community at large. A lack of privacy, suspicion engendered by an "outsider," and expectations for involvement beyond the school day can be difficult circumstances for new leaders seeking to gain entry into the community fold. Being a rural principal is a lifestyle, not just a job (Preston et al., 2013), and the high level of visibility, along with the demands on a leader's time, can be a barrier.

The upside to these complex relationships is how strongly the rural community is invested in the success of the school. It is much easier to build support and trust in a closely interconnected setting. Rural leaders, whether new to the rural way of life or not, should make a point to focus on building and nurturing these relationships. Being an effective communicator is foundational to that effort. The U.S. Department of Education (Office of Elementary & Secondary Education, 2019) suggests four strategies rural leaders can use in order to enlist members of the rural community as effective partners in school initiatives:

1. **Stay focused.** Most rural leaders do not have the depth of support found in larger districts and are often the only person leading initiatives or strategic planning. Focusing your communication will ensure that you can move the work you start toward completion.

2. **Streamline messages about school initiatives.** Avoiding the "one more thing" mindset when addressing the community is key to ensuring ongoing support for and understanding of work tied to the overall goals of the school.
3. **Engage a wide range of stakeholders.** The more people understand how rural education intersects with their interests and is mutually beneficial, the more likely they are to share resources and ideas.
4. **Don't miss any opportunity.** As part of the community, rural school leaders have many opportunities outside the building to share what is happening at the school and how community members can get involved. Having an "elevator speech" ready prevents an informal conversation with a stakeholder being a missed opportunity to educate the public and garner support for the school.

Role Diversification

I believe most newly seated rural leaders understand the concept of wearing many hats. However, when putting theory into practice, being all things to all people is often overwhelming. Every principal prepares for and understands the duality of being both an instructional leader and a manager. Adding in rurality, with many tasks competing for attention and not enough time to get to them all, requires a different level of dedication. Rural leaders typically have fewer support staff to assist with managerial duties and a flatter organizational structure, which means they often carry the burden of not only school-site but also district-level responsibilities. These can include fiscal and curricular decisions, community liaison tasks—even substitute bus driver duty! The heavy time commitment and background knowledge required lead to long days and weekend work to stay ahead. It's no wonder that many potential candidates look at a rural principalship position with wariness and that rural communities often see smaller applicant pools as a result.

Limited Access to Professional Development and Resources

Very few educational leadership preparation programs are set up to holistically address all the issues that might confront a rural principal. This lack of background knowledge can be overcome with focused professional development, but tracking down and accessing relevant programs can be challenging.

Rural principals often have limited peer contact, mentorship, or collaboration opportunities. Travel costs and lack of time can also deter principals from seeking networking and collaboration.

Further, rural schools typically experience constraints on resources, such as a lack of available funding due to a smaller tax base or higher operation costs for a district in a remote locality, which makes goods and services more expensive. These constraints also affect teacher recruitment and retention, maintenance of school facilities, and programming options, especially when paired with limited infrastructure and access to broadband. Although it's necessary to get creative with available funding, a novice principal may lack insight into how to develop a budget that, while lean, meets the needs of students and staff.

School Accountability

The principal is the primary factor that influences student achievement outcomes (Leithwood et al., 2004). Given the current emphasis on high-stakes assessments, the proliferation of school accountability measures, and, especially in light of the recent pandemic, an increased focus on both student and school improvement, principals have never been under more pressure to perform effectively. In many rural communities, schools face additional challenges caused by poverty, failing agricultural business, and declining enrollment that affect educational outcomes (Tieken, 2014). Any new initiatives must take into account the needs and interests of the community at large and of parents—and they are subject to influence from the same groups. In addition, the notion of change is a difficult sell in many rural places. Rural communities tend to be strongly rooted in traditions and continuity, and are therefore leery of major changes that might evolve from the imposition of school improvement measures.

Stress

Expectations of visibility and accessibility can be stressful for rural principals. Further uniquely rural stressors may include lack of employment for family members, geographical isolation, and the level and variety of demands placed on the principal. A rural school leader must be someone "who truly values a small town and can tolerate a high degree of visibility, who demonstrates that he or she wants to be close to the community and students, and who understands the educational challenges a small district faces" (Cruzeiro

& Boone, 2009, p. 7). Other qualities foundational to success as a rural principal include the following:

- Flexible and versatile
- Prepared to be called on to perform duties beyond typical administrative tasks, such as managing grants or filling in for absent teachers
- Able to shift roles and perform a variety of extra duties as needed
- Knowledgeable about the community and its culture and committed to getting involved (Cruzeiro & Boone, 2009)

Solutions for the Resilient Rural Leader

Rural districts suffer from a higher turnover rate in school administration, and administrators in remote rural areas are less likely to stay longer than one year (NCES, 2022a). The challenges faced by a new rural school leader may be unanticipated, and they may feel unprepared. When I first started my principalship, I needed to navigate many situations where I didn't even know how to start. New leadership is harder in a rural community because of the diversity of demands. How can resourceful rural leaders effectively face these challenges given the complexity of the job? Let's take a look at ways to address these concerns.

Strengthen Recruitment and Retention Strategies

Just as there is value in considering what options are available for attracting and keeping rural teachers, the same is true for rural leaders. Figure 3.1 provides some strategies and barriers for district leadership and board members to consider when seeking to fill a rural leadership position. The strategies and barriers are very similar to those identified in the previous chapter regarding teacher retention. Wood and colleagues (2013) found that the proximity of the rural school community to urban areas was a significant challenge, because competitive salaries were likely to draw leaders away from the rural area. They also noted that working conditions were not identified as a negative factor in leader retention; in fact, their research showed that the most successful retention strategy was a positive culture and a connection with the staff and school community that engendered a sense of belonging within the leader. This valuable information highlights the importance of building a culture and climate that focuses on engaging all within the building.

FIGURE 3.1

Rural Leadership Recruitment and Retention Strategies

Recruitment	Retention
Strategies • Grow Your Own programs • Competitive salaries and benefits • Housing relocation assistance • Include building-level staff in the process • Promote the rural area **Barriers** • Geographic isolation • Social isolation • Community culture • Working conditions • Proximity to higher-paying districts	**Strategies** • Formal induction and mentoring • Positive school culture • Access to technology • Stay incentives • Tuition/degree assistance • Community welcome/support **Barriers** • Geographic isolation • Social isolation • Salary limitations • Distance from professional growth opportunities

Make Visibility Work for You

There is an expectation in a rural school community that the principal be highly visible and widely available. Engagement in local activities and happenings goes a long way to establishing trusting relationships, which are key to success. Principals can expand their efforts not only by being present during noninstructional hours, but also by encouraging active parent participation in school events.

Being strategic about visibility is worth considering. My board president was happy to share a list of people I needed to get to know within my first few months in the Stanfield community. I needed to consider not only who the school supporters were but also who the detractors were. Which longtime residents held sway in the community? Who could, and would, undermine what was being done? Knowing who influenced the community's goals and priorities—and how they exerted that influence—was essential to my work as a new leader in the community. For example, getting to know the business owner next to the school campus was extremely beneficial. He owns several planes and does crop spraying for the local farms. Right after I started, a very rainy monsoon season resulted in an explosion of mosquitos on campus and an epidemic of mosquito-bitten students. The very supportive business owner was able to address the issue quickly with a weekend pesticide application at no cost to the district. He continues to be available for these services as a result of that relationship.

As different community members are introduced or made known to you, place them in one of four categories to determine your priorities for establishing contact and building relationships. Those with a high level of community influence can either be supporters of the school or detractors, as can those with a low level of community influence. To maximize your visibility and time, start by connecting with those community members in the high influence, high support category.

School leaders new to a rural community experience both professional and personal transition. While it might take time to establish relationships with community members, these relationships are vital to a successful tenure. Starting your role with open communication and visibility and taking the time up front to get to know the community, its history and key citizens, and its values and goals will pay off in the long run. In the school setting, make an effort to get to know your students and staff, a process often made easier in a rural setting where buildings contain fewer people. Principal Sam Hess of Mill Street School in the Orland Unified School District in California shared an introduction strategy that he used when he first arrived in his district. He recorded a quick video introducing himself to staff and the community and asked them to set up a time to meet with him one-on-one once he finalized his move to his new home. Even a brief visual like this can start you on the path to establishing communication.

Your first task is to determine which stakeholders you need to reach out to. Stakeholders are any groups or members of the community who either have an interest in the school or are involved with or affected by what happens at the school. To help identify who is a stakeholder, answer the following questions:

- Who has an interest in the function and progress of the school and district?
- Who has a vested interest in the students and families the school serves?
- Who has something to contribute to the school, whether tools or information?
- Who already has a solid understanding and is supportive of what is happening within the school or district, and what should they know to maintain that support?

- Who is a detractor of the school or district, and how much information do they have about what the school is doing?
- Who are the different stakeholders and groups within the community established as needing to be involved? Who is missing that needs to be brought on board?

Once you identify potential stakeholders, be strategic about your engagement by prioritizing who you will speak to first. A framework shared by the Reform Support Network (2020) will help to guide your engagement with almost any community-based stakeholder along a continuum from *inform* to *inquire* to *involve* and then to *inspire*.

1. **Inform.** Use a variety of platforms and methods to provide information to the school community and all stakeholders. These can include the school website, social media, videos, presentations, and newsletters.
2. **Inquire.** Gather feedback from the school community regarding changes to programming, policies, or procedures. Use tools like surveys, focus groups, or listening sessions. Include all stakeholder groups in the inquiry to gain an understanding of diverse perspectives.
3. **Involve.** Establish opportunities to work with key stakeholders for two-way communication in a variety of groupings. These might include parent-teacher organizations (PTOs), a school site council, and advisory groups made up of business, civic, and faith-based leaders. All stakeholder groups in the community should have representation and involvement.
4. **Inspire.** Work to bring in the voices of a large coalition from the community to increase the number of stakeholders who fully understand any change initiatives. Inspire these stakeholders to actively solicit support from the community at large so that they become invested in the proposed changes.

Getting to know the community and its stakeholders is vital to creating an open line of communication that can facilitate connections and lay the groundwork for support for change initiatives that might need to be considered. Here are some key points to keep in mind:

- **Find out how the community wants to be engaged.** In Stanfield, a large number of people do not have broadband internet access. Therefore, while we do use social media, we also text community members to communicate information. How did we know this was their preferred method of contact? We asked through a survey! A simple survey is a great way to ensure your communication is targeted in a way that involves the largest number of community members possible.

- **Be transparent about what is happening, and be consistent about the message.** If there is a way to either livestream or record meetings for later viewing, do so. Engagement, especially across a large geographical area like many rural communities, should not be restricted by the meeting location.
- **Do background research to understand the full scope of the issues, including what has been tried, what outcomes were gained, and who was involved.** The more detailed knowledge you possess, the more focused your conversations with stakeholders can be. Know what questions need to be answered or addressed.
- **Use existing structures when possible rather than creating new ones.** If parent groups like PTOs or site councils already exist, start with them, as they are already invested in the work of the school. If an ad hoc group needs to be created down the line, members of the group will understand why and will be more likely to accept any outcomes or decisions.
- **Use plain language when talking about the school, programs, or other aspects of the school.** If necessary, create a handout with jargon words defined.
- **Listen and allow all to contribute before giving an opinion or a recommendation.** Especially when the support of stakeholders is important, allowing them to voice their input makes the process and its eventual outcome more robust and relevant.
- **Consider any special needs the community might need met to fully engage.** Do you need to use an interpreter (spoken, close-captioned, or signed)? Are there ADA (Americans with Disabilities Act) requirements to address?
- **Follow up with consistency.** In any stakeholder engagement, follow-up is essential. Not only does it help keep everyone informed on outcomes and timelines, it also shows that you value stakeholder input. People who know their participation matters are more likely to continue to engage with the school and its leader. Use a variety of platforms (e.g., social media, website, newsletters) to share the outcomes of your engagements.

Grow Your Own: A Rural Principal Pipeline Model

Just as it was with teachers, the Grow Your Own model of leadership development in a rural school setting has been increasingly effective for districts with few or no applicants for leadership openings. In my 13 years at Stanfield, the school has seen four different principals. Two stayed for only one year, partly because of the unanticipated demands of being a rural leader, and partly because they did not live in or nearby the community. This turnover caused a huge challenge for continuity and raised concerns around who might apply next for the opening. Fortunately, the current principal is a member of the community who has a long-term interest in the school's success. We are currently in the process of "growing" her into a superintendent/principal leadership role—a move that will benefit the school and community by ensuring consistency, maintaining the established culture and climate, and allowing the continued implementation of change measures for growth that have been set in place. I know that I and the governing board are lucky to have a viable and effective candidate who already has the needed background, experience, and certifications.

In the past, I have worked with potential candidates to complete needed coursework for administrative certification and placed them in lead teacher or assistant principal positions to give them experience. To this end, I cannot overstate the importance of a collaborative working relationship with higher education institutions. These teachers were able to complete their degrees because the institutions worked with us to provide working partnerships that supported their skill development. The traditional GYO model for the principalship describes the leader having "moved up through the ranks" after starting as a teacher or even a paraprofessional. However, in a rural setting, the path might need to be shorter due to a lack of available steps between the classroom and the administrative office.

Key features of a successful GYO rural leadership program include the following:

- A solid working relationship with an institution of higher learning that can meet the programming needs of rural learners, including virtual learning options for those in remote areas
- Curriculum covering a wide range of topics including school finance, technology, strategic planning, and federal grants, with specific focus on the rural context

- Screening processes for potential leadership candidates that assess both readiness and willingness to stay in the community for a set period of time in exchange for district funding of certification tasks
- Allocation of flex time for full-time employees who are also in the leadership program
- A cohort model, drawing from both the school district and the geographical area, that fosters networking and support
- Just-in-time, ongoing professional development opportunities that complement coaching and mentoring from expert practitioners
- A strong focus on managerial and relational skills in addition to educational leadership practices

Enomoto (2012) identifies five "aspects" foundational to a solid GYO program for future leaders: (1) content knowledge and development of skills; (2) application to school standards, support, and systems; (3) opportunity to grow a network with other leaders in the field; (4) conversations with experienced site leaders; and (5) reflection for continuous learning. In addition, consider looking to well-structured and successful GYO programs for rural leaders such as the following for inspiration:

- In Ohio, a business-education leadership preparation program at The Ohio State University focuses on developing leaders for underserved schools, most of which are in rural areas. The BRIGHT Fellowship pays for a living stipend as well as an executive MBA for participants completing a yearlong leadership residency. The residency includes leadership coaching and student-teaching experience. At the end of the program, newly licensed leaders are required to spend three years in a school district leadership role. Learn more about the program at https://bright.osu.edu.
- The Northeast Leadership Academy (NELA 2.0), hosted by North Carolina State University, focuses on principal preparation specifically aimed at rural schools. It includes coursework toward a master's degree and license, targeted professional development in instructional leadership and management, and executive coaching. Frameworks, outcomes, and deliverables are available for review at https://nela.ced.ncsu.edu/about-nela-2-0.
- In Texas, the Dallas Independent School District created a few programs for leadership development housed in its Leader Excellence, Advancement and Development (LEAD) division that both work with the

university system and maintain a focus on mentoring new leaders during and after their coursework, as well as creating an effective distributive leadership framework. Learn more about it at www.leaddallasisd.org.
- The Principal Preparation for Excellence and Equity in Rural Schools (PPEERS) program in North Carolina is a research-practice partnership supported by the Institute for Partnerships in Education. Participants complete a master's degree in school administration and obtain their principal licensure after two years, following a framework that was co-designed with district partners. Learn more about the program at https://ipie.uncg.edu/partnerships/principal-preparation-for-excellence-and-equity-in-rural-schools.

Include Rural Contexts in Higher Education Programs

In the last decade, some higher education institutions have developed courses to fill gaps related to rural contexts in principal preparation programs. However, research has shown that students who were required to participate in clinicals or internships in rural places acquired a deeper understanding of rurality (Rosenkoetter et al., 2004). These types of programs go beyond the GYO model to focus on preparing future rural leaders with established coursework. Topics such as place-based education, school finance, advocacy, and community relationship building have started to appear throughout the country.

While the number of online courses on these concepts is increasing each year, some institutions have established programming that is worth investigating. The University of West Alabama features a doctoral program specifically for rural education with two tracks, one for organizational change and leadership and the other for teaching and learning. Both tracks include coursework tailored specifically to the rural setting. More information can be found at www.uwa.edu/academics/collegeofeducation/departmentof curriculumandinstruction/ruraleducationdoctorofeducation. While not providing a full rural-focused program, the University of Maine offers an elective class on rural school and community leadership (see https://online.umaine.edu/online-master-of-education-in-educational-leadership). Postsecondary and graduate course offering in rural leadership is an area that is experiencing growth, and it is one that is ripe for even more attention.

Build a Network

On any school campus, the principal is an island in a sea of teachers. That isolation is magnified in a rural setting, with limited collegial resources for support. Therefore, it is essential that newly placed rural leaders be provided with some type of coaching or mentoring. Relationships between new and seasoned leaders can be set up formally, but there is just as much value in informal connections.

The benefits of a coaching relationship are many, among them guidance and support that can lead to greater self-confidence, having a trusted peer to serve as a sounding board, and the sharing of background knowledge that can help build critical skills needed to effectively carry out all the responsibilities of a new principal (see Figure 3.2 for a more extensive list). In larger school systems, these mentors can be found within the district, but rural leaders may need to be more creative to find inspirational connections.

Effective mentoring programs share some commonalities that make the experience richer for both the principal and the mentor:

- Support from the superintendent, which shows the district values the process and is committed to its success
- Training for the mentor (conducting a needs analysis, communication skills, feedback skills) and the principal (goal setting, reflective practice)
- The right fit between participants, with attention paid to matching the type of rural environment as closely as possible to incorporate the mentor's background and experience
- Clearly defined goals and expectations for outcomes and for how the mentoring is facilitated
- An understanding that participants are investing in a mutually beneficial relationship that should go beyond just answering questions to effectively leverage the skills, background, and experience of the mentor

FIGURE 3.2

Areas for Mentorship

Professional	Personal
• Using data to inform decisions • Dealing with parents and community members • School budgeting and finance • Legal issues • HR requirements, hiring, improvement plans • Culture and climate building	• Safe space for dealing with frustrations • Assistance with strategic planning • Active listening • Encouragement • Support for risk taking

Source: Smith, 2007.

A potential barrier to a rural mentorship program is the lack of administrative depth in many rural communities, which means the mentor has to come from somewhere outside the school system. There are several ways to address this gap in personnel. Setting up cross-district mentoring with a neighboring school system's principal makes it possible to have both in-person and virtual mentoring sessions and is the easiest way to establish a mentoring program. Another option is for the principal to work with a superintendent, either active or retired, who has previously served as a rural principal, preferably within the last five to eight years. If the demand for mentors is large in your area or region, consider creating a pool of mentors who can work with several principals at a time. If you opt for this approach, consider holding regular training sessions with all principals in the program to discuss broader topics such as school finance or culture and climate building. Also consider finding mentors using established rural networks such as the National Rural Education Association, Regional Education Labs, or other resources described in Chapter 2.

Take Care to Take Care

Leadership can be an isolating and lonely position, and in a rural setting the stresses that come with a lack of built-in support can be much more difficult to deal with. On top of one's "island" status, scrutiny from the community and the on-call nature of being a rural leader can be draining. Rural principals are expected to not only be engaged with the school but also actively participate in the community. This can lead to overwhelm and burnout. Leaders must find healthy ways to deal with these stressors and equip themselves to handle the many challenges that come with rural leadership.

According to a RAND survey of principals in 2022, 85 percent of school principals in all locales were experiencing job-related stress at the time. Teachers reported stress at rates lower than that, and other industries were more than half as likely to report being stressed. Also concerning were the rates of burnout and depression (Steiner et al., 2022). These statistics show that educators are coping with serious challenges to their well-being as they emerge from the COVID-19 pandemic.

There are many facets to protecting your personal wellness as a rural leader, and it's imperative that you actively make the effort to do so. Below are some reminders of ways to enhance your own well-being:

- Connect with other people.
- Practice mindfulness, meditation, deep relaxation, and breathing.

- Exercise.
- Follow a healthy diet.
- Stay away from or cut back on alcohol, cigarettes, and drugs.
- Participate in counseling sessions with a licensed professional.
- Laugh.
- Take up a new hobby.
- Write in a journal.
- Get a therapeutic massage.
- Reduce or eliminate social media time.

Paying attention to how stress is affecting your daily work, relationships, and job satisfaction can provide some early warning signs of problems that you need to address. As I tell my staff, "We can't fill the cups of others if ours is empty."

◘ ◘ ◘

Given the influence principals have on all aspects of a school's educational outcomes, being thoughtful and intentional about how new leaders are brought in, how they are supported in their assigned duties and professional growth, and how they are embraced by the community at large can make a difference in both their success and their retention. It starts with relationship building, both inside and outside the school walls.

4

The Effective and Efficient Rural School Leader

In today's school climate, school site administrators are expected to be effective instructional leaders in addition to managing student affairs, operations, and staff. Instructional leadership can be defined by a set of behaviors that the principal displays for both student and staff learning, setting high expectations for performance outcomes. Blase and Blase (2000) identify several behaviors that principals employ to meet this expectation, including making instructional suggestions to teachers, providing feedback, modeling effective instruction, supporting collaboration, providing professional development, soliciting opinions, and praising effective teaching. Fullan (2002) notes that, as agents of change, principals must have the capacity to deal with rapidly changing environments.

As previously mentioned, the landmark report released by the Wallace Foundation confirmed the importance of the principal to student outcomes (Grissom et al., 2021). In fact, because of the scope of their influence, principals affect larger numbers of students than classroom teachers. The power of the principalship lies in the ability to create a learning environment where teachers can grow and refine their pedagogy and students can learn. Figure 4.1 distills the varied skills and behaviors leaders need to refine to improve their effectiveness.

All four areas of leadership work together at all times in a delicate, and sometimes messy, balance toward the ultimate goal of positive student

FIGURE 4.1

Time to Lead

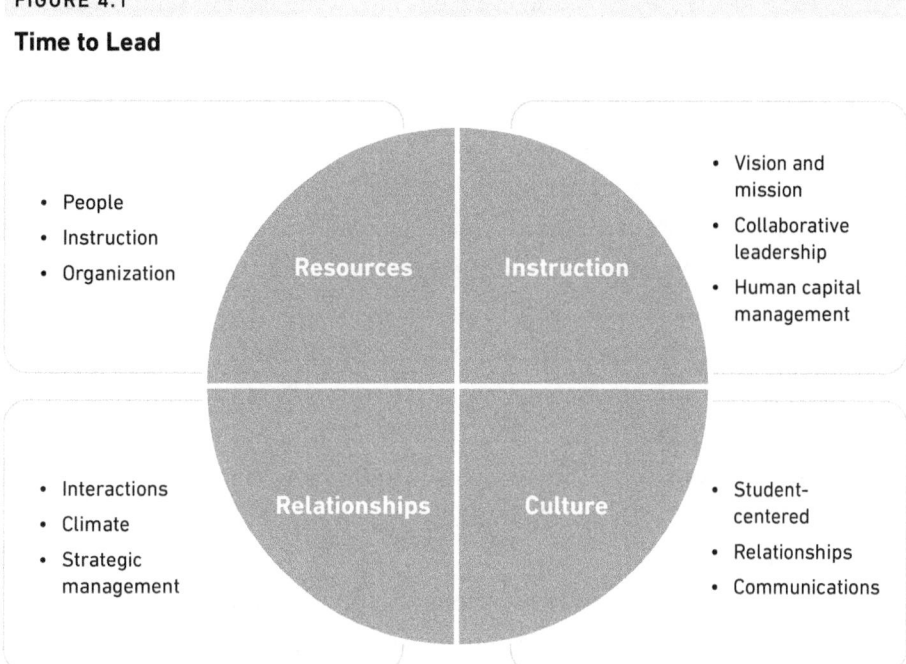

outcomes. Each has instructional leadership and site management components built in. Leadership skills include the ability to develop staff by supporting their pedagogy and building strong working relationships while still managing resources, using data to drive decision making, and creating strategic plans. Leadership behaviors are actions that build a positive climate while facilitating instruction-focused collaboration and strategically managing personnel and resources. An effective leader of learning creates a results-oriented and reflective environment that is aligned with the vision and mission of the school while effectively managing daily behaviors and tasks effectively. Finally, school leaders need to build a student-centered culture that is individualized and grounded in relationships among stakeholders, as well as communicate with stakeholders in a way that empowers staff to do what is necessary for student growth.

Challenge: Effective Instructional Leadership

Instructional leadership in a rural setting can be quite challenging. It requires a comprehensive understanding of effective teaching and learning practices as well as the ability to adapt to the unique needs of the school community. This crucial role encompasses multiple facets:

- **Setting a clear vision.** Successful instructional leaders establish a clear educational vision and goals for the school, aligning them with district and state standards and guidelines.
- **Curriculum development.** Leaders actively participate in the development, implementation, and evaluation of the school's curriculum, ensuring it meets the needs of all students.
- **Instructional support.** Leaders provide guidance, support, and professional development opportunities to teachers to enhance instructional practices.
- **Data analysis.** Leaders analyze student achievement data and instructional practices to identify areas for improvement and make data-driven decisions.
- **Classroom observations.** Leaders regularly provide one-on-one or group coaching sessions to support teachers in implementing effective instructional strategies.
- **Collaboration and teamwork.** Leaders foster a collaborative culture among teachers and encourage them to share best practices and engage in professional learning communities.
- **Parent and community involvement.** Leaders actively engage parents and the local community, building strong partnerships to support student success.
- **Teacher evaluation.** Leaders conduct evaluations based on defined criteria, providing constructive feedback and guidance for professional growth.
- **Continuous improvement.** Leaders guide the school in a continuous improvement process, regularly assessing progress, adjusting strategies, and promoting a culture of innovation.

And the list could go on!

Challenge: Efficient Management

It can be difficult to manage efficiently when there are so many different roles the rural leader must fill beyond academics. Often, the urgent demands of staff shortages, lack of substitute teachers, managerial tasks such as grant reporting, and other functions take priority. Rural school leadership is a constant juggling act of dual roles of instructional leader and manager—especially in a rural setting, where there are fewer people to handle tasks.

Rural leaders may have to think differently about who to task with assisting and supporting their various responsibilities. Principals who have better time management skills spend more time in classrooms and more time as the instructional leader (Grissom et al., 2015). Those who come into rural leadership from outside the rural setting face a large learning curve that they may be underprepared or unprepared for! Ensuring longevity for rural leaders means assisting in skill development necessary for success.

Solutions for the Resourceful Rural Leader

As a doctoral student at Northern Arizona University, I had a professor who consistently emphasized the importance of being visible to the individuals you are leading. He had started as a rural administrator in a few communities around Arizona, ending up in Chandler as superintendent. His words of wisdom were, "Do your 'people-work' before your paperwork. People-work while they are in the building, and paperwork when they leave." This was sometimes a difficult goal to reach. I often had to dedicate time during the day to the multiple managerial tasks of running the district's business office, grants, and HR department. However, it is possible to ensure that your "people-work" is being done as well. Being an effective and efficient manager takes planning and organization. Intentionality can help with finding the time and space for instructional leadership *and* the work of running a rural school—with a lot less stress. Let's take a look at some ways to manage all those hats rural leaders wear!

Focus on Instructional Leadership

While there are common aspects to instructional leadership across the board, the distinctive characteristics of rural schools often necessitate different approaches. Here are some recommendations in key areas that rural leaders should consider to improve their effectiveness:

- **Embrace the local community.** Build strong relationships with local community members, parents, and stakeholders. Attend community events, engage in open dialogues, and seek input on educational priorities and goals. For example, organize town hall meetings or establish a

community advisory board to involve community members in decision-making processes.
- **Address transportation barriers.** Rural areas often face transportation challenges. Ensure that all students have access to quality education by working with local authorities, parents, and transportation providers to establish efficient bus routes or explore alternative transportation options such as carpooling initiatives.
- **Foster partnerships.** Collaborate with local businesses, organizations, and higher education institutions to create opportunities for students. For instance, establish partnerships with local farms, businesses, or trade schools to offer internships, mentorship programs, or vocational training opportunities that align with the rural community's needs.
- **Leverage technology effectively.** Recognize that technology can bridge geographical gaps in a rural setting. Invest in reliable internet access, digital tools, and online resources to provide quality educational experiences. For example, offer virtual field trips, online courses, or videoconferencing to connect students with experts and educational resources beyond the local area.
- **Support teacher development.** In rural areas, teachers often face isolation and limited professional development opportunities. Provide ongoing support and mentorship to teachers by organizing professional learning communities, virtual workshops, or expert presentations through videoconferences. Additionally, facilitate opportunities for teachers to share best practices and collaborate with colleagues from other rural schools.
- **Adapt curriculum to the local context.** Acknowledge the unique characteristics and strengths of the rural community when designing curriculum. Incorporate local history, agriculture, or other relevant subjects to make learning meaningful and culturally relevant for students. For instance, integrate lessons on sustainable farming practices or local ecological systems into science curricula.
- **Personalize instruction.** Recognize the diversity among students in rural schools and implement strategies to meet their individual needs. Use differentiated instruction techniques, small-group instruction, or individualized learning plans to cater to students with varying abilities and interests. For example, offer project-based learning opportunities that allow students to explore topics related to their local environment or community.

- **Provide comprehensive support services.** Due to limited access to services, rural students may require additional support. Collaborate with community organizations, health care providers, and social services to offer counseling, mentoring, or tutoring services. Consider using telehealth options to provide mental health support to students when in-person resources are limited.
- **Encourage community involvement in schools.** Promote volunteerism and community engagement in the school setting. Invite community members to share their expertise as guest speakers, organize career fairs, or involve the community in extracurricular activities. For example, establish a mentorship program where local professionals provide guidance and career advice to students.
- **Advocate for equitable funding and resources.** Rural schools often face financial constraints and resource disparities. Advocate for equitable funding at the district and state levels to ensure that rural schools receive adequate resources to support student learning. Communicate the specific needs and challenges of the rural community to policymakers and community leaders to prioritize educational investments.

Keep in mind that these recommendations are general ones; the specific needs and characteristics of each rural setting will vary. As an instructional leader, it is crucial to continuously assess and adapt your strategies based on your local context and the evolving needs of your students, teachers, and community.

Practice Distributed Leadership

By necessity, rural schools rely on a collaborative environment where everyone pitches in to ensure that students have what they need, when they need it, and that the school is meeting its purpose. Due to smaller staff numbers, rural leaders may take atypical measures to involve staff in goal setting, professional development, and shared leadership responsibilities. Tapping into the strengths of the staff means first identifying what expertise each individual brings. This "side-by-side" style of leadership, as opposed to leading from the front, makes the running of the school much more successful. It also allows leaders to develop the capacity of those who may decide to move their career toward a leadership role.

Typically, a rural school leadership team has schoolwide representation. Members of the team are usually selected based on their background and expertise, not how long they have been at the school. What role(s) team members take on depends on the needs of the school, the strengths each member brings, and where the leader needs support. However, following are some items that leadership teams tend to focus on:

- Digging into student data to ensure that progress is being made in all grade levels and subject areas
- Planning and leading collaboration time, both by grade level and subject area, to support and refine teacher practice and provide opportunities for feedback and reflection
- Identifying areas for professional development for some or all staff members
- Engaging in strategic planning for initiatives and other areas of improvement

Distributed leadership is not just about assigning people tasks to carry out, it is focused on a collective effort to create a culture and climate conducive to student growth. According to the results of a study in rural Georgia, some important considerations can have an impact on the success of a shared leadership structure: the positional leader has to be willing to give up control of some leadership responsibilities; a collaborative culture must already exist; the vision and mission of the framework have to be shared by all; student achievement has to be the focus for all leadership practices that are deployed; and practices like routine faculty meetings need to already be in place (Setchel, 2008). Without these foundational pieces, the framework will most likely be less successful.

To establish a distributed leadership framework, there are some things to keep in mind. First, be sure to develop the skills of all members of the leadership team by rotating responsibilities such as setting the agenda or leading the meeting. Once those tasks are assigned, step out of the way. While it might be difficult to let go of control, micromanaging not only prevents someone from learning by doing, in the long run, it also makes more work for the micromanager! Trust your team members to get the job done, even if it may not be the way it's been done before. Also, allow for feedback and reflection as they develop new leadership skills to keep the leadership team on track to improve and make your overall job easier. Don't forget to celebrate together when the team does well. Just like students, staff performing a new or different function need to hear when they are meeting the mark.

Use Figure 4.2 to assist with planning your distributed leadership framework. Responses to the key questions listed can help determine next steps and

FIGURE 4.2

Distributed Leadership Planning Guide

Issue	Key Questions to Consider	Other Elements
Purpose	• What is the primary purpose for implementing a leadership team (reduce principal workload, provide teacher expertise, etc.)? • Is there a shared vision for leadership? If so, what is it? • Has there been communication about the vision of distributed leadership? • How will the team determine if the site is ready for distributed leadership? • What roles will team members take on, and how are they defined?	
Structure	• What structure would promote the work of the team? • What structures are already in place (department chairs, instructional coaches, etc.), and how could they support the team's work? • Will team members be nonevaluative or evaluative, and how will that change the approach? • How will collaboration time with the team be structured (before/after school, release time, virtual, common planning time)? • Will team members be certified staff only or will classified staff be included? • What will the selection process be for team members? Who will be involved with selection or replacement? • What budget must be allocated and for what?	
Training	• How will team members be trained on leadership skills? • How will the faculty be trained on distributed leadership? • What kinds of professional development and supports will be provided for team members? Faculty?	
Ongoing supports	• What will successful team outcomes look like? How will data be collected to verify? What data will be used? • How will faculty be informed of team discussions, plans, goals? How often? Using what method(s) of communication? • How will team members be replaced? Cycled? • What could go wrong, and how can problems be mitigated? • How might relationships between teachers and the site leader be affected?	

be a starting point for discussions about the why and how of this leadership concept. Please note that these questions assume the creation of a leadership team of some kind. If there are other factors, like negotiations or governing board policies that might need to be taken into consideration, include them in the "Other Elements" column to ensure they are discussed as part of the planning conversations. Keep in mind that the language used matters, and it can make a difference in how the framework is developed and how it is received.

There are many resources to review to support those starting the process. Here are a few that would work in a rural setting, as they are adaptable and provide some foundational pieces to consider:

- Northwestern University's James Spillane is a leading researcher on school leadership. He has curated a variety of materials for Northwestern's School of Education and Social Policy Distributed Leadership Study website (https://distributedleadership.northwestern.edu). The site hosts a variety of tools, presentations, and current research.
- A report titled *Transforming Schools* (Bierly et al., 2016) lays out five principles to consider when planning for and launching a distributed leadership initiative. A heavy focus on the roles and responsibilities for all who are taking on leadership tasks is discussed. The report also identifies some best practices and gives site examples. Find out more at https://media.bain.com/Images/BAIN_REPORT_Transforming_schools.pdf.
- The Wallace Foundation has done extensive work around principal leadership. Their collaboration with Learning Forward on *The Principal Story Learning Guide* has an excellent chapter on cultivating leadership in others at the school. The website also features a learning module complete with learning activities that takes between four and five hours to complete. Find out more at https://learningforward.org/toolkits/the-principal-story-learning-guide.

Use Decision-Making Tools

School leaders can make hundreds of decisions over the course of a single day. Some decisions are small, easily made, and low-impact, such as the color of paper used for a parent form. Some require input from stakeholder groups and multiple data analyses because they will have a significant impact on the school community, such as the hiring of a new superintendent. However, all decision making follows the same steps:

1. Identify the decision that needs to be made.
2. Collect any necessary information or materials.
3. Identify all possible alternatives.
4. Crosswalk alternatives with gathered information.
5. Make a choice from among the possible alternatives.
6. Take action.
7. Assess results and take additional action if necessary.

Rural leaders often have to take the lead, gather information, deliberate, and act on their own to deal with a vast and varied host of issues. Using established frameworks and tools to guide the decision-making process can help clarify what needs to be done faster and more efficiently.

Analyze root causes. In every larger dilemma that needs to be addressed, it's important to understand the start or origin of the issue. The two tools described below, which can be used by both groups and individuals, can assist in root cause analysis, which can then lead to better decisions.

- **Fishbone Diagram.** This tool is widely used to show cause and effect. Once you identify the problem, brainstorm all possible underlying causes and record them as "branches" stemming from the issue. Next, break down each cause into the things that led to those conditions. This step is essential for problem solving, as it can help uncover steps to take toward fixing the main concern. Once you have investigated all main causes, you can create an action plan with clear priorities.
- **5 Whys.** This tool helps narrow down information gathered by starting with a problem and then asking "Why?" five times. Break each response down into as many reasons as you can generate. Once the whys have been named and analyzed, create an action plan to address each one.

Find possible alternatives. Once the problem has been dissected, it is much easier to create alternative solutions to the problem. These tools can be used individually or with a group.

- **Mind Maps.** There are many structures for mind maps, but all help capture thoughts and ideas discussed during a brainstorming session on how to solve the dilemma being analyzed. The easiest way to create a mind map is to start with the problem at the center, branch out with key words or phrases, and then attach things to consider further.

- **Six Thinking Hats.** Developed by Edward de Bono (n.d.), this tool allows a wide variety of viewpoints to be laid out for consideration and facilitates full participation from all members of the group. Each of the six different-colored hats represents a focus or perspective to think from: white, facts and logic; red, emotions and feelings; yellow, positive outcomes; black, negative outcomes; green, creative ideas; and blue, management and organization. Determine which team member will "wear" each hat and provide a visual representation for the rest of the group to remind them of each role. One way to encourage an even deeper dive is to rotate the hats once everyone has contributed to allow for as many perspectives and ideas as possible.

Analyze the options. Once possible alternatives have been identified, each needs to be evaluated. Especially in a rural setting, some generated ideas will not be feasible. Running through an analysis of the desirability and risks of alternatives can help narrow down or eliminate options.

- **Pro-Con T-Chart.** The easiest and probably most recognizable analysis of alternatives is a T-chart divided into halves, with pros listed on one side and cons on the other. Brainstorming all aspects can help an effective alternative emerge. If more detail is desired, add a third column to capture implications or things to consider.
- **SWOT Analysis.** A SWOT analysis, frequently used in education, consists of a chart with four quadrants labeled "Strengths," "Weaknesses," "Opportunities," and "Threats." The option is analyzed by breaking down its characteristics and possible consequences into these four categories.

Prioritize. One of the most important things to consider when managing decisions is the urgency of a task and how to prioritize its completion. As a new rural leader, I often found it difficult to determine what was the most important activity to accomplish—everything seemed urgent!

- **The Pareto Principle.** Based on the 80/20 rule, or the law of the vital few and the trivial many, the Pareto principle states that 80 percent of outcomes derive from 20 percent of causes. Identifying the characteristics of the 20 percent that are having the most significant impact can place a leader in a better position to prioritize decisions. Once you have

identified multiple issues to address, assign each one a value on a scale of 1–10, according to time spent, budget impact, or another metric that makes sense to you. Based on those values, determine which are in the top 20 percent of the group, and make those your priority.
- **The Urgent–Important Matrix.** This method can be used to facilitate your workflow. Classify each task on your list as urgent or not urgent, and important or not important (see Figure 4.3 for an example).
  - *Urgent/Important—Do.* These are critical tasks that must be completed by the end of the day; you should have no more than three or four in this quadrant. If they start stacking up, consider moving them or parts of them to the Delegate quadrant.
  - *Not Urgent and Important—Schedule.* These tasks are important, but there is some time to work on them before their deadline. When all urgent items are completed, these should be next in line. Beware of procrastination of these items, as they can quickly become urgent if they are not addressed when they are small and manageable.

FIGURE 4.3

Urgent–Important Matrix Example

	Urgent	Not Urgent
Important	**DO** • Complete report due tomorrow • Communicate with the board on a student issue • Respond to the media on a school activity for the evening news	**SCHEDULE** • Register for next month's conference • Complete contribution to the school newsletter • Conduct walkthroughs of classrooms
Not Important	**DELEGATE** • Update the agenda on the website for the next board meeting • Take photos of student work for social media • Collect attendance data for grant report	**ELIMINATE** • Plan vendor luncheon for a company we don't use • Clean out desk drawer • Organize filing cabinet

- *Urgent and Not Important—Delegate.* If possible, give these items to someone else to complete. These often appear on your list as a result of someone else asking for assistance with their urgent task, but taking them on risks your own urgent items not being completed as needed. If you are doing someone else's work, who is doing yours?
- *Not Urgent and Not Important—Eliminate.* Tasks that don't affect overall operations can be done when there is time. They are not a high priority for completion and usually are not timebound. Plan for these items, which can be time wasters, by putting them on your calendar, setting a timer, or using an unanticipated "free" 15 minutes.

I want to share an example of my district taking a systematic approach to decision making. About six years ago, it became apparent that we needed to purchase a new language arts curriculum. The problem solving started when we collected student outcome data that were not showing the growth we wanted to see. To determine what was going on, the staff created a Fishbone Diagram. It became obvious fairly quickly that an outdated curriculum and variability in its use across the campus were huge factors in the disappointing data. We dove further into the issues by doing the 5 Whys exercise, which led to great conversations around fidelity of implementation, lagging professional development, and missing components in the program's classroom materials. We also considered the need to incorporate technology, as we had made the move to a one-to-one platform under our technology plan. Examining the problem through the lens of these structures took finger pointing and blame out of the equation and made for a more productive discussion.

We used Pro-Con T-Charts to look at possible curriculum solutions. Once we narrowed our choices down to two potential publishers, staff did an in-depth SWOT analysis to reveal any concerns that we would need to address. Again, these frameworks removed personal preference and bias from the discussion and ensured that the materials that we eventually purchased were the best option for setting up our students for success. These specific decision-making tools are not the only ones out there, but I have found them to be the easiest to use.

A few words of caution: using a systematic approach to decision making reduces the likelihood of quick decision making resulting in negative outcomes. However, there are some potential drawbacks to a structured approach. First, while it's important to get feedback and include stakeholders in the decision-making process, at the end of the day, the leader is the one who has to make the final decision—and this should be made clear from the start. Second, as leader, you should be mindful of not shying away from conflict and discomfort during the decision-making process. A fair amount of discomfort means that all ideas and viewpoints are being considered and that the final outcomes will most likely be supported by most. Another concern is the appearance of being indecisive when looking at all angles of a dilemma. This can be mitigated by setting a timeline for the decision and sharing it with stakeholders. Finally, even with a strong process in place, you might make the wrong decision. Try to figure out where the mistakes were made, and then use that information to guide future decision making.

Maintain an Open-Door Policy

As both principal and superintendent, I have established an open-door policy for all members of the school community. My goal is to encourage people to come in to discuss issues and concerns, ask questions, or give feedback about anything happening on campus. This allows me the opportunity to increase collaboration, build relationships, and solve problems quickly and efficiently. While there are some times in my schedule where I truly need to be behind a closed door with a time-sensitive task, for the most part, this method of communication works. At the very least, it prevents things from becoming larger problems due to a lack of attention while they are small. Figure 4.4 lists some tips for managing an open-door policy in a way that promotes ongoing communication without sacrificing productivity.

An open-door policy is just one communication tool that can help rural leaders sustain ongoing and frequent communication with all stakeholders in the school community. Here are some ideas to keep in mind when creating, refining, or improving your efforts to engage on a regular basis with staff, parents, and the rural community at large.

- **Plan means of both formal and informal communication for all stakeholder groups.** In addition to meetings, information, ideas, and goals can be posted or disseminated at places where people gather, such as a local store, the post office, or the community center. Share contact information in case people want more details.
- **Attend community gatherings and meetings such as fundraisers, local or county fairs, and board of supervisors meetings.** Being

FIGURE 4.4

Open-Door Policy Dos and Don'ts

Do	Don't
• Set parameters by being clear that when the door is open, visitors should feel free to stop in. If the door is closed, they should make an appointment or come back later. • Ask for solutions to accompany all problems that are presented. • Set up frequent check-ins with staff if daily interruptions become an issue. • Involve other staff members (school counselor, HR, etc.) as appropriate. • Keep appearances in mind. Meeting with the same person or group frequently can lead to gossip or perceptions of favoritism.	• Be completely unavailable. Set up a signal, such as a knock, to be used in case of an emergency. (Be sure to define what constitutes an emergency!) • Interrupt when the other person is speaking or get distracted by technology. Be engaged. • Fail to act as quickly as possible when presented with an issue or concern. • Let your day get knocked off track by discussions that require more time than you can give. Be sure to set up a follow-up meeting to allow for in-depth conversation if needed. • Underestimate the importance of time, both yours and your staff's.

available for informal conversations is a great way to stay connected to the community and strengthen the bonds between school and the local area.

- **Prepare materials and information ahead of time so you can respond to questions, concerns, or issues.** Pay attention to connecting school and district concerns to happenings at the regional or state level as well as the local level. Ensure that materials are concise and easy to understand.
- **Connect with other school communities in the area to share information quickly and efficiently.** This may be accomplished through one or two people who travel to the different communities or a group that creates common talking points so that all stakeholders in the region get the same information.
- **Use social media and websites strategically for one-way communication of necessary information.** Always include a method for following up with a person to continue the communication.
- **Be transparent with initiatives and decisions made by the school or district, and outline how stakeholders were involved.**

- **Find ways to engage with a variety of community leaders to share information from the school or district.** Know that in a rural community, word spreads quickly! Be sure everyone who needs to know the information is reached so no one is left out of the process. Being the direct source is important.
- **Keep school staff informed about what is being shared out so they are also engaged in community discussion.**

Facilitate Volunteerism

One way that parents, family members, and other members of the community engage with a school is through volunteering for different activities or tasks. In rural areas, removing barriers to volunteers' desire to be part of the school community and support teaching and learning can be challenging. Transportation issues or commuting distance can impede rural volunteerism. Working with faith-based organizations or local businesses is one way to mitigate transportation difficulties. In my community, we have used school buses to transport regular volunteers and have connected with local businesses to set up dedicated volunteer days, with employees given release time to spend at the school working with teachers and students. In a setting where more hands are always needed, finding creative ways to invite more community members into the school not only engages them, it also helps lighten the load!

Optimize Your Circadian Rhythm

Managing how time is spent every day is essential for the rural leader. Time management tools, tips, and tricks are easy to find, and most are easy to use. The hard part is in the fidelity of implementation! However, when used effectively to maximize time on task, these strategies can lead to improved productivity in getting the manager side of the principalship accomplished and freeing up more time for being out on campus and in the classroom as the instructional leader. Put simply, time management is the thoughtful and disciplined use of time targeted toward both improved workflow and increased productivity.

Are you an early bird or a night owl? Research on when people are at their most productive shows that it varies—a lot! Identify when you do your best work, and use that time for your tasks that require the most focus. Plan the rest of your workday around that two- or three-hour block. Don't know where to target? Take a week and notice when you are most energized and less likely to be distracted. Once you have your productive time scheduled, be sure to minimize interruptions, close your door, and turn off your email notifications. If you have someone working with you, ask them to support you by alerting walk-in traffic that you are not available. If you let the staff know your plans, they can schedule meetings and other interactions with you for a different part of the day. In a perfect world, your productive time would be at a set daily time, but rural schools are not always predictable. The more that you can protect that block though, the more those important required tasks can be accomplished in an effective and efficient manner.

Schedule All Work

Mark Twain said that the secret to getting things done is to get started. As a rural superintendent, there are always a multitude of tasks, meetings, paperwork, and other activities that require my time throughout the day. When asked how I keep things straight, I usually reply that my Google Calendar makes the difference. Not only is it on my desktop, but I can also access it on my phone when I am out of my office. Whichever calendar platform you use, there are ways to ensure that your time is being managed to allow for maximum productivity and free up time for instructional leadership tasks.

Do you know how you spend your time and what is taking up your calendar? Before making any changes, track your activities for a two-week period. To get the best overall view, log your activities in 15- or 30-minute intervals. By the end of the tracking period, you will have a good idea of where your calendar can be streamlined. You may find that you are doing a number of things that are not necessary or that could be accomplished in a more efficient manner. As a teacher, I used to dread meetings with administration that could have been accomplished in an email rather than taking up 30 minutes after school. Once you identify the clutter in your daily schedule, you can set up a daily or weekly calendar that allows you to focus on what is most important and necessary. Here are some ideas to get you started after your schedule audit:

- During the summer, add all personal and professional nonnegotiable school year events (vacation, governing board meetings, in-service days) to your calendar so that other items can be plugged in around them. If possible, work with stakeholder groups to set up the annual calendar before school even starts.

- Put activities that occur on a recurring basis on the calendar at the start of the year. These could be leadership team meetings, teacher observations, walkthroughs, end-of-quarter celebrations, or state testing windows. Even if dates shift, it's easier than starting from scratch!
- Use the color-coding feature of your virtual calendar. I code personal items in a different color (orange) than district meetings (red) or school activities (purple). This strategy helps me look over the week and see where I will need to be or what tasks I will be performing at a glance.
- Set reminders for managerial tasks such as payroll approval, Monday Message release, and voucher processing, and color-code those items as well.
- Print out a daily calendar at the start of the day so that you can track and reschedule activities and tasks as required.
- Use the Pomodoro Technique to plan out your daily schedule. With this technique, invented by Francesco Cirillo, you use a timer to spend 25 minutes on focused work on only one task with no interruptions, and then take a 5-minute break. After four such intervals, you take a 30-minute brain break to recover and re-energize. If this technique works for you, be sure to assign that 30-minute break to a task that does not require intense focus, such as visiting a classroom.
- If you need to attend multiple meetings in a day, stack them back to back in an effort to avoid the loss of time that can take place as you get back into the flow of work. Determine how much time you really require between meetings, and plan ahead to gather any necessary materials. Decide if you might need to address any items immediately following a meeting, and if so, schedule time to do so. To stack meetings consistently, always respond to a request for a meeting with a specific time that works for your calendar.
- Deliberately set up days on the calendar to be out of the office and not available. Spend these "walkabout" days specifically in classrooms, in the cafeteria, and on the playground. Let staff know the purpose of the schedule and have the office protect the time from drop-ins and parent calls by communicating why you are unavailable. I scheduled walkabout days monthly as a principal, and it was time well spent as an

instructional leader. Try scheduling daily time to be in classrooms on a rotating basis and protect that time in the same way, if possible.

- Every Friday (or Monday morning), I review the next week's schedule to know what is coming up. I also gather any needed paperwork or other materials and mark them with the task and date so that everything is ready when the assigned task comes up for action. I also attach digital materials to events in my virtual calendar if possible. Set up a time at the end of the week to plan out next week's tasks. Finish the more difficult things at the beginning of the week so the remainder of the week can flow. Getting more time-consuming and challenging tasks out of the way can make for a less stressful week. Consider keeping Mondays free of any interruptions such as meetings so that you have time to focus.
- If you have someone who helps manage your calendar, meet with them on a regular basis to discuss open periods that can be given to things that come up that require attention. My secretary and I meet at the start of each day and review my calendar together. She then knows when my day has openings and when my door needs to be closed, and can assist with daily traffic and phone calls. This 15-minute meeting is essential for keeping my time organized.
- Most devices and software programs have a "do not disturb" function. Some even have a setting to block out specific periods of time, like your most productive period of the day. Ensuring that there are no disturbances when you need to focus on a task can maximize your productivity and efficient use of time. Don't forget to use your autoresponder for emails!
- Take a "two birds, one stone" approach. When setting up your weekly calendar, look for tasks that could be paired or that will complement one another. For example, if you need to attend a parent engagement event after school and you must also collect survey data for a grant report, pair those tasks for efficient use of your time and effort. This could also be done with tasks that can be carried out simultaneously. I often listen to webinars and podcasts on my one-hour drive to work. I can take a phone call while doing a facility walkthrough. These simultaneous tasks are different from multitasking, as their combination doesn't affect your ability to provide the appropriate level of focus.
- Beware of the multitasking myth. While some say rural leaders have to multitask in order to get everything done, research has shown that the

better option to produce a quality product is to focus on one activity at a time. Tasks that require a lot of attention are not candidates for the "two birds" approach. If you have a tendency to multitask, make a concerted effort to remove other projects and distractions from your work area (your phone is a likely candidate, as is your email).
- Email is one of the biggest time traps in an office environment. Block off specific times of the day to review and respond to emails, and then train people to expect a 24-hour turnaround rather than a 24-minute response. Outside that email block, turn off email notifications so that they do not distract you from the work at hand.
- Create a to-do list and update it throughout the week. Your to-do list can be virtual; there are many apps you can use to track items that need to be addressed with deadlines and cross them off after completion. The Notes app on my phone is a great way to record additions to my list when I am out of my office. My preferred tracking system is a legal pad, with tasks added on a rolling basis and crossed off when they are finished. For longer-term items I use large sticky notes that I can refer to as needed and take notes on when information comes up. Be sure to include work time for the tasks on your list in your daily calendar! I have learned that if I don't dedicate time in my schedule, a task can easily get pushed off and then not completed. Don't forget to include personal activities on your to-do list as well.

The importance of being organized with a solid management plan as a foundational component of a rural leader's success cannot be overstated. Ensuring that tasks are completed efficiently, resources are used effectively, and goals are met allows leaders the time and space to do the work of supporting teaching and learning as the instructional leader. It is a balancing act—one that recognizes that both instructional leadership and school management are vital to achieving success in a rural school setting. When they are both implemented well, the result is a school that is a successful learning environment for students.

5

Access in Rural Communities

Challenge: Limited Resources

Rural communities tend to have limited options for resources and services. The World Bank quantifies these limitations with the Rural Access Index (RAI), which measures the proportion of the population that lives within two kilometers of an "all-season" road; the RAI is a clearly understood global development indicator that is conceptually consistent across countries (The World Bank, 2022). People who live in rural places understand that doing so comes with a scarcity of access to a multitude of goods and services, among them health care, emergency response services, utility and other infrastructure, employment, and even geographical accessibility. All of these and more are issues that leaders of rural school communities must understand and try to mitigate in some way.

The Digital Divide

The COVID-19 pandemic highlighted the lack of reliable broadband for students in rural areas to learn from home. According to the Pew Research Center, between 2016 and 2021, the number of broadband users in rural areas grew by 9 percent, although only 72 percent of rural users reported in 2021 that they had high-speed internet access at home (lagging behind suburban and urban users at 79 and 77 percent, respectively; Vogels, 2021). While the digital divide between those with access to high-speed internet and those without has been narrowing in recent years, most of these expansions have been in urban communities. Rural areas still lag behind, raising concerns not only in education, but also in the fields of health care, emergency response, and workforce development. It has become increasingly evident that reliable broadband access is an essential utility, and that connectivity infrastructure is necessary for all communities. In an era where 8 in 10 middle-level jobs require some level of digital proficiency (Bradley et al., 2017), rural leaders are smart to be concerned about how to provide internet access to their students.

Broadband can be accessed in different ways, including a fixed subscription or a mobile subscription. The location of the rural community is a factor in the feasibility of bringing broadband to residents. In areas where the school is closer to infrastructure, fixed broadband is a cost-effective way to provide the service. However, the difficulties of running fiber to remote locations that may also have geographical challenges like rugged terrain means that most solutions have been mobile, with towers and relay systems used to tether the rural area to internet access. Despite the considerable amount of federal dollars that has been allocated to providing connectivity to rural areas, many locations still lack access to high-speed internet.

Recent studies on access to both the internet and devices found that rural students also face a usage gap, with technology being used for lower-level thinking activities like remediation and drills rather than research, connection with others outside the classroom, and computational thinking (Hohlfeld et al., 2017; Warschauer & Matuchniak, 2010). Also of concern is the number of students who must share an internet device when they are at home—typically a smartphone on a monthly cellular data plan that quickly reaches its data limit (Moore et al., 2018).

Food Deserts

Living in a rural area can contribute to food insecurity, and the rates of having limited access to food are higher in rural communities than in urban areas (Feeding America, n.d.). In 2021, the USDA reported that 1 out of every 10 rural households is food insecure, with Black and Native American individuals experiencing double the risk of white individuals (Coleman-Jensen et al., 2022). Lack of secure food access linked to poverty will be discussed in Chapter 6, but it is also tied to issues around transportation and distance to a food source.

A study conducted in five states by Feeding America (n.d.) on rural concerns around access to food found that reasons for food insecurity were very consistent:

- Unemployment and underemployment in rural areas, in addition to seasonal work, made purchasing food a struggle.
- Distance to food resources was far, making them difficult to obtain.
- While able to buy in bulk at box stores or supercenters in places that were a distance away, "filler" foods closer to home were more expensive and there was a limited selection.
- Food assistance programs like SNAP were not close enough to be a reliable resource.

Food deserts exist throughout the country. In my rural school community of Stanfield, Arizona, the local market, previously owned by the family of our governing board president, closed after a Walmart Supercenter opened in the next town over. In many rural towns, local grocery stores fall victim to larger conglomerates that offer better prices and more variety. But there is often little or no public transportation to get to the larger stores, which means that people with transportation challenges are further burdened.

Medical and Other Health-Related Gaps

As in urban and suburban places, influences on health outcomes include how individuals take care of themselves, community and environmental factors, and access to health care. However, residents of rural areas experience additional concerns. According to the Rural Health Information Hub (RHIH; 2022), these include economic factors, remote locations and a lack of dedicated transportation, lower educational attainment, and cultural and social differences. Rural residents also have more difficulty finding health care providers, especially specialists. Only 15 percent of the U.S. outpatient physician workforce are family practitioners, but those doctors provide 42 percent of the health care in rural areas (American Academy of Family Physicians, 2014).

According to the Insurance Institute for Highway Safety (IIHS) and Highway Loss Data Institute (HLDI), more than half of all crash-related fatalities happen in rural places, despite the total vehicle miles traveled in rural areas being less than a third of those traveled across the country (IIHS & HLDI,

2023). This is most likely due to a lack of emergency responder capacity in rural communities. Rural areas also have higher incidence rates of diabetes and heart disease and an additional 22 percent greater risk of injury resulting in death (Myers et al., 2013).

Finally, youth in rural places have a suicide rate nearly double the rate in urban communities, due to both poverty and the stigma of asking for help, with two-thirds of those incidents involving a firearm (Rath, 2015). Many suggest that this statistic is a result of the fact that mental health providers are more likely to live in urban areas, placing a transportation demand that rural residents are unwilling or unable to meet.

All of these factors add up to the unquestionable reality that health care is a concern for rural leaders, who often step up to provide services to both students and staff members as part of their duties. The lack of both general medical care and trauma center availability means that the school may be the only accessible provider of any kind of health care.

Housing in Rural Areas

When discussing educator recruitment and retention, many rural leaders note that the lack of affordable housing is a barrier to securing new staff. According to the Housing Assistance Council (2021), affordability is the biggest housing challenge in rural America—even more so than inventory and location. In rural areas that used to host now-defunct industries like mining, very few new homes are being built, contributing to the overall rural housing shortage. At a hearing before the Senate Committee on Indian Affairs, Senator Lisa Murkowski noted that half of prospective educators offered a contract in Alaska did not accept it due to a lack of available housing (U.S. Government Printing Office, 2004). In fact, in one rural school, the principal slept in a janitor's closet and a special education teacher slept on a rollaway bed in her classroom, while other teachers shared a single home. When housing is available, it often needs significant maintenance and modernization. And Alaska is not the only state facing these issues.

School Facilities and Preventive Maintenance

Even rural schools with solid leadership and classrooms fully staffed with effective teachers can see teaching and learning suffer if the buildings housing them are deteriorating or inadequate. As I know from firsthand experience with the heat of an Arizona August, students don't learn well when they don't have air conditioning! When I talk with rural leaders from around the country, one of the most frequent issues raised is the condition of their facilities and the lack of access to resources to repair them. Whether the problem is outdated electrical wiring or plumbing, inadequate technology infrastructure, asbestos abatement concerns, or the overall age of the buildings—or all of the above—many rural schools are in desperate need of repair. Add to that the fact that the cost of facilities and preventive maintenance typically falls to the district, in rural places where funds from property taxes and bonds are not easy to access, and rural leaders face a no-win situation. Many states do not provide facilities funding, and if they do, it may not be sufficient to fill the district's needs. Litigation under the argument that children in all locales should have equitable and adequate access to a quality education has been one way for districts to remedy the situation. In terms of equity, a "level playing field" should mean that all school buildings are held to a high standard of upkeep, whether located in a wealthy community or one that is unable to raise taxes for facilities. On the other hand, "adequate" means that the state should provide the resources necessary to meet state education goals, which include facilities. Whether through sales tax, general obligation bonds, lotteries, or other state-directed funding streams, states have an obligation to ensure that their students, including those in rural places, are learning in facilities that are in good repair.

Solutions for the Resilient Rural Leader

Many of the issues surrounding lack of access in rural school communities are things that the school or district cannot solve alone. Partnerships and collaborative funding application are essential to equalizing opportunities for all rural students and their families. Because the school is often key to these partnerships, rural leaders can take the lead in finding and developing solutions to the resource challenges facing the community as a whole.

Bolster Digital Equity

Most rural schools have been able to provide technology devices for students to learn online while at school. However, many homes are not connected to the internet, leaving students without access to online learning from home. There are many examples of leaders being creative about connecting rural schools with the "middle mile," as well as helping students with the "final mile." The middle mile refers to the segment of telecommunications that connects the internet service provider to the local exchange. Typically, the middle mile consists of fiber optic cables, microwave relays, or other technologies that can provide connectivity to schools and other entities. The final mile is the part of a network that provides service to the end user in their home or business—usually the most expensive and challenging part of the network, susceptible to distance and outdated technology.

Before embarking on any digital equity plan, gather a coalition of willing stakeholders who can expand your pool of resources. They may already be working on the connectivity issue. Consider contacting the following individuals and organizations:

- Local school governing boards, staff, and parent groups
- Community organizations and centers
- Local business leaders and chambers of commerce
- Local municipalities, boards of supervisors, county and state governmental entities
- Social services such as housing, local aid
- Libraries and other rural school districts
- Hospitals and health care providers
- Institutions of higher education
- Banking institutions
- Commercial internet service providers, local, independent, regional, and national
- Elected officials
- Faith-based organizations and nonprofits

After identifying potential stakeholders and partners who are also interested in addressing broadband access concerns, find out what the gaps and needs are related to community connectivity. A needs assessment like the one described in Chapter 9 can be modified to help identify what technology resources are already available, what services can be leveraged, and what human capacity is already in play that could be brought in to make the planned project a success. Depending on the needs of the individual community, the focus of this assessment could include a review of service availability, reasons for nonusage, required up and down service speeds, or affordability.

In any discussion about rural connectivity and lack of access, one of the main concerns is funding. Rural schools typically do not have the budget to pay for bridging the digital divide by themselves, no matter what that looks like in the context of the community. However, there are a number of potential funding sources to consider when planning a project. At the state level, you can contact the broadband office, who can provide guidance on expanding broadband access as well as technical assistance. BroadbandUSA has an online guide that lists all current federal funding available for broadband builds (https://broadbandusa.ntia.doc.gov/resources/grant-programs). Local and regional internet service providers may also be a source of information on any future projects and potential financial backing. Other grants and dedicated resources include the following:

- **E-Rate.** The Universal Service Program for Schools and Libraries, also known as E-Rate, helps institutions get connected to digital services by discounting costs. For schools, funding is dependent on both the location and the percentage of low-income students served. Discounts can be anywhere from 20 to 90 percent of the costs for infrastructure like access points or routers and monthly service fees. Additional funds have been set aside in recent years to modernize and upgrade connections to industry standards. Many rural schools have used E-Rate to build fiber optic lines directly to the school or upgrade their network to provide more bandwidth. To learn more about accessing E-Rate funds, visit www.usac.org/e-rate.
- **The Community Reinvestment Act (CRA).** This often-overlooked funding source is available from banks that receive insurance from the Federal Deposit Insurance Corporation under a law enacted in 1977 to prevent redlining and to encourage banks to work with all sectors of the community, including low- and moderate-income individuals and businesses, to meet their credit needs (Office of the Comptroller of the Currency, 2014). As part of their insurance agreement, banks are obligated to give back to the community through grants, volunteering, and community investment. Banks can meet their obligations by assisting with and investing in digital equity initiatives. To learn more about ways the CRA encourages banks to connect with and support their communities, visit https://fedcommunities.org/four-ways-cra-encourages-equitable-community-investment.
- **REAP.** The Rural Education Achievement Program (REAP) is authorized under the Every Student Succeeds Act and consists of two

formula-based grant programs: Small, Rural School Achievement grants (SRSA) and Rural and Low-Income School grants (RLIS). These two programs are specifically designed to meet the unique needs of rural schools that lack the human capital to apply for competitive federal grants or that receive formula-based grant allocations that are too small to have an impact on the overall purpose of the grant program.

- RLIS targets rural school communities that have large numbers of low-income students. The grants are administered through the applicable state education agency.
- SRSA targets very small rural districts. Funds are awarded directly to the district from the federal government.

Both REAP grants can be used to support Title I-A, II-A, III-A, and IV-A grants. Additionally, SRSA can be used in 21st Century Community Learning Centers programming, and districts can consolidate Title II-A and IV-A funding for allowable expenses to expand program impact. RLIS funds can be used for parental involvement activities, while SRSA funds cannot. REAP funding eligibility can be determined by the district's National Center for Education Statistics Locale Code or a state's designation of rural. To find out more about REAP funding and to determine your district's eligibility, visit https://oese.ed.gov/offices/office-of-formula-grants/rural-insular-native-achievement-programs/rural-education-achievement-program.

One successful digital solution model is an initiative of the Arizona Rural Schools Association (ARSA) called the Final Mile Project (2022). Although most schools and libraries throughout the state have access to strong fiber optic infrastructure (largely funded by the E-Rate program), some rural areas still struggle with home access—the "final mile" described above. The project focuses on bringing connectivity to homes from anchor locations using a decentralized "to and through" model that incorporates towers that have a seven-mile radius capacity (see Figure 5.1).

Identified projects throughout Arizona have worked with ARSA advisors to put out requests for proposals (RFPs) from regional internet service providers. Many of these projects have rural utilities service funding from the U.S. Department of Agriculture (USDA) to keep total costs low. Monthly rural broadband services fees can be very expensive, so one of the RFP requirements

FIGURE 5.1

Final Mile Project Map

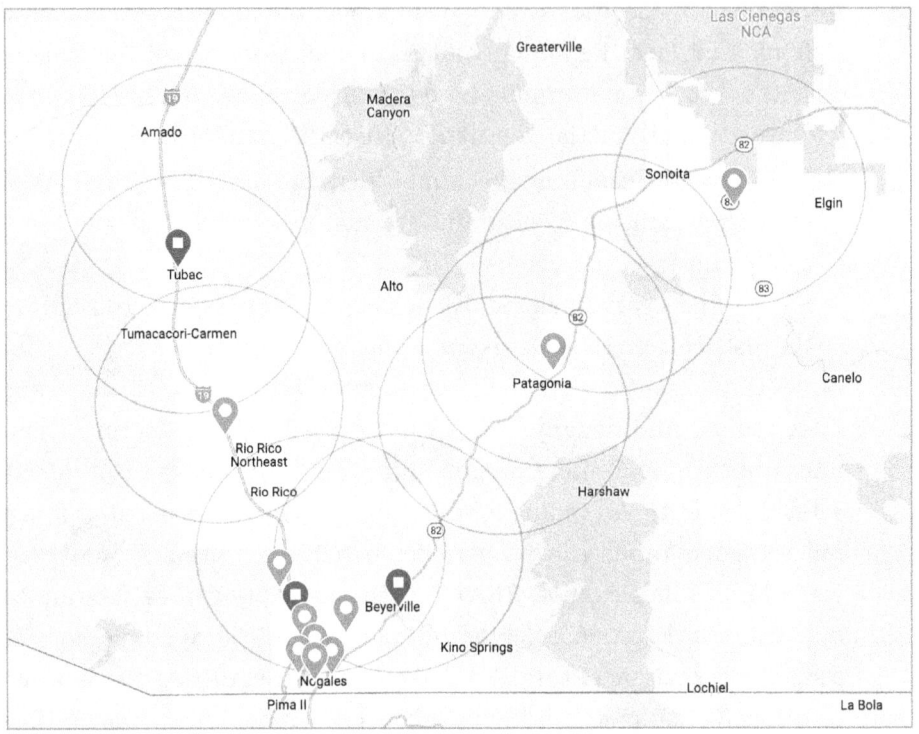

Map showing southern Arizona locations of fiber-linked nodes made possible through the Final Mile Project. Households within a 7-mile radius of each site are able to access broadband internet service.

Source: M. Eaton, State E-Rate Director, Arizona Department of Education. Used with permission.

is very low-cost basic service charges for basic home internet usage. Additional upgrades and other packages can be purchased by individual households as desired. Learn more about the Final Mile project at www.finalmileproject.com/The-Project; the "to and through" model is described at www.shlb.org/policy/research/to-and-through.

Another solution you can spearhead is to work with interested stakeholders to create a digital equity office through the local government. This type of community collaboration can focus efforts by establishing a strategic plan for digital access, becoming a clearinghouse for possible solutions for connectivity, and keeping track of progress toward goal attainment. Another benefit to this type of office is that knowledge of and relationships within the community can be leveraged when evaluating providers for infrastructure or digital services. A digital equity office can be a bridge between the local community and state or regional offices that lead the same type of work. Some of the responsibilities a digital equity office could take on include the following:

- Monitor gaps in access in the rural area and liaise with internet service providers to establish affordable infrastructure and service. The rural leader can be a partner in gathering these data from students and their families.
- Coordinate digital literacy skills training, possibly in collaboration with the local school district.
- Represent the rural community's interests and maintain ongoing communication and outreach with stakeholders, potentially with assistance from the rural school leader.

Something else to consider is the development of digital literacy skills for students, staff, and families. Even in rural communities, jobs are becoming more technologically advanced, and basic understanding of technology and computational thinking skills are essential. Digital literacy skills can be taught even if the community as a whole suffers from limited internet access. One way is to physically take the training into the community. There are a number of vendors that provide mobile hotspots for buses that can be driven to various locations in the rural area. Training could also be hosted at the public library or at a local business partner's location and facilitated by a local educator or a member of the community. Another idea to consider is a no-cost facilitated training called a learning circle. Learning circles are study groups that utilize either open-source or participant-created resources and are open to all within the community. Peer 2 Peer University (www.p2pu.org) offers a platform to participate in or host learning circles on any topic you wish.

In rural communities where the distance from the middle to the final mile currently precludes home access, consider staging access locations within the community as a stop-gap measure. These types of school–community partnerships have been deployed successfully across the country. Create a community map for students that directs them to the businesses or community places where they can do homework, conduct research, or take advantage of other internet-based resources. These arrangements have the additional advantage of providing foot traffic to the community location.

Additional digital equity resources are available in some or most rural places. While there is no one-size-fits-all approach to bridging the digital divide, many available supports can be adapted to a specific rural community. Investigate what nonprofits or federal programs are available in your area to learn what technical assistance they can provide. You don't have to be a technological wizard to bridge digital gaps in your area! You just need to start the process. Here are some places to help with that:

- **BroadbandUSA.** Housed within the National Telecommunications and Information Administration, BroadbandUSA helps local, tribal, state, industry, and nonprofit organizations looking to expand broadband connectivity and promote digital inclusion. They offer a host of resources and toolkits, a national broadband availability map, state-by-state program and point of contact information, and current news about funding sources and grants. They also implement the Broadband Equity, Access, and Deployment Program, Enabling Middle Mile Broadband Infrastructure, and the Tribal Broadband Connectivity Program, along with other federal grant programs, many of which focus on underserved rural communities. Find out more at https://broadbandusa.ntia.doc.gov.
- **Connect Americans Now.** This Microsoft-supported coalition of more than 300 organizations and companies across a broad sector of industries, including education, promotes mixed technology solutions, one of which is the use of white spaces in TV signals, to connect rural students to the internet. They also focus on digital literacy skills training. Find out more at https://connectamericansnow.com.
- **Connected Nation.** A nonprofit organization, Connected Nation develops and provides tools, resources, and templates for planning technology initiatives at the state and local levels. They also focus on supporting the creation of public–private partnerships that can be targeted toward specific areas and produce a podcast by the same name. Find out more at https://connectednation.org.
- **The Schools, Health, & Libraries Broadband Coalition (SHLB).** This coalition focuses on obtaining access to broadband for schools, health care providers, libraries, and other anchor institutions. SHLB participates regularly in advocacy efforts at the Federal Communications Corporation, the Capitol, and the White House. They maintain a variety of resources for community leaders, including policy updates, host regular informational webinars, and encourage and facilitate networking among SHLB members. Find out more at www.shlb.org.

Tackle Food Insecurity

Many rural students and their families rely on the school for meals, and rural leaders can take steps to help them with reliable access to food. Many students receive both breakfast and lunch through the federally funded National School Lunch Program (NSLP). Almost 30 million students took part in NSLP offerings in the 2021–2022 school year (up more than 10 million from the previous year) (Food Research & Action Center, n.d.). While most schools operate a federally funded meal program, there are some additional ways that rural leaders can secure student nutrition:

- **School breakfast program.** For many students, school breakfast is truly the most important meal of their day. Many who live in a food desert may not have had access to food since the previous school day. To ensure that all students are able to eat breakfast, consider extending the hours that food is available to students so that those who arrive late still have a meal to start their day. Implement a schoolwide "breakfast after the bell" or "breakfast in the classroom" program. Also consider a second-chance breakfast an hour into the school day for those who were not able to eat the first breakfast.
- **After-school snacks and meals.** During supervised after-school activities or events, schools that participate in NSLP and meet the federal guidelines of 50 percent free and reduced-price lunch recipients can provide a snack for all participating students. These offerings can also include a larger dinner meal.
- **Summer meal programs.** There are many ways that a rural school can run a summer meal program, including developing a delivery service to bus stops or setting up locations away from the school site where families can access meals. This expansion of noncongregate meal options would eliminate many barriers for rural families. Casa Grande Elementary School District in Arizona not only delivers meals through their bus stops, they also publish the times that buses will be at each stop and allow families to sit in the air-conditioned bus while they eat their meals. You can also consider extending program hours to offer families more time to get to the serving locations. Offer activities in conjunction with food to make the program more attractive for families. Superintendent Stuart Packard and the Buttonwillow Union School District in

California not only provide meals during the day, but also serve dinner to families while providing activities for the children to participate in after they finish eating.
- **Food bank expansion.** Partner with area food banks to provide more robust choices, hours, and locations for access to food, and consider locating a food bank on campus. This eliminates the need to arrange transportation. Minimize or eliminate paperwork requirements to participate in food bank services. Paperwork is a barrier for many families who don't have access to the required documentation, may not speak or read the language used on the forms, or are reluctant to submit any documentation for fear of governmental oversight.
- **Program coordination.** Understand how food assistance can be braided among multiple programs and recognize that more support might be needed during the weeks between SNAP or other benefit programs, especially at the middle or end of the month. For example, not only do many Stanfield families participate in SNAP, they also frequent the local food bank at the church next to the campus. This assistance is blended with the Community Eligibility Program under which our food service operates for the NSLP, allowing all students to eat breakfast, lunch, and snack at no cost. The more programs that students and families can engage in to gain reliable access to meals, the fewer children go without food during and after the school day.
- **Inclement weather plans.** Weather can impact families' ability to access food security programs, both in the heat of summer and in the cold of winter. Have a plan to be responsive to those who might need a different level of support to get to food access locations under certain weather conditions (Haynes-Maslow et al., 2020).
- **Backpack programs.** Roll out backpack programs, which provide healthful food for students to take home, for weekends, holiday breaks, and the summer with the support of a school–community partnership. Look to stakeholders in the community who are already doing this work, such as food pantries or faith-based meal providers.
- **Food desert mitigation.** Ironically, many rural agricultural areas are considered food deserts. Start a farm-to-school program either by having the school purchase fresh fruits and vegetables directly from local farmers or by starting a school garden. The USDA provides grant funding to support these types of programs; funds can be used for training,

equipment, or implementation. A secondary advantage to this type of program is that foods that have local cultural value can be secured at more affordable prices.

Arrange for Health Care Alternatives

As the hub of their rural community, schools are often charged with looking after the health of the students and staff they serve. That care might also extend to the local community. Whether through a healthy living initiative, a school-based clinic, or a community partnership in support of nutrition, schools can serve as an important resource within the community. Rural leaders can instigate a variety of health-related activities that can make a difference. Some examples follow:

- **School-based health clinics (SBHCs).** Creating a school-based location for services such as medical, dental, or mental health care can benefit all stakeholders. In 2017, there were 2,584 SBHCs across the United States, with nearly a third of them located in rural areas (Love et al., 2019). It stands to reason that when services are available on the school campus, a greater number of students will access them. School-based clinics can be run through partnerships with nearby medical centers or hospitals and can be structured to allow access for family and community members, either during or after the school day. Costs for starting an SBHC are dependent on available facilities and any necessary modifications to fit the needs of the clinic. You might be able to support ongoing costs using federal funding (e.g., Section 330 of the Public Health Service Act, School-Based Health Center Capital Program), Medicaid, or state funding.
  - *Medical care.* An SBHC will not replace the care of a school nurse, who serves all students in the school, but it can open access to many who might not otherwise receive primary health care, screenings, or other services.
  - *Dental care.* Students with oral health concerns are much more likely to be absent from school; in fact, it's one of the leading causes of chronic absenteeism (Healthy Schools Campaign, 2015). Oral health care is a service that can easily be provided on a school campus. School-based dental services like cleaning, fluoride varnishes, or sealants can help students prevent cavities and train them in oral hygiene. Teledentistry, whereby a dental technician comes to the school to

provide basic care and then consults with a dentist remotely to diagnose any issues and provide intervention, is also an option. Mobile units are another way to get services to students and the community. These vehicles are set up with a full-service chair and equipment and can facilitate dentists in providing initial treatments.
- *Mental health care.* As previously stated, mental health concerns are diagnosed at higher rates in rural areas than urban areas. This can be problematic, as limited access to providers in rural communities means that families must either travel to services or forgo them altogether. You may be able to establish an onsite space for local providers to service students or community members. Telehealth services for mental health can be provided at the school when in-person services are not possible. Because each state is regulated differently, you will have to research policies for coverage and reimbursement as well as licensure requirements for the mental health professional. You will also need to address how HIPAA privacy standards will be met.

- **Community access.** Resources and facilities that lead to healthy lifestyles, such as gyms or wellness organizations, are often not available to residents of rural communities. The school can play a part in promoting good health for all stakeholders by working with partners to provide access in the following ways:
  - *School facilities.* Allow community residents access to the school's facilities (gyms, track, fields, weight rooms) when the school day is over.
  - *Adult sports.* Facilitate adult sports leagues that practice and play on the school campus after hours and on the weekends.
  - *Physical recreation.* Create opportunities for communal physical activity like walking clubs, yoga sessions, running clubs, or other recreational group activities using school resources.
  - *Clinics and screenings.* Work with local or regional medical care organizations to sponsor health clinics, immunization drives, mammogram support, or other itinerant medical services.
  - *Wellness exhibitions.* Sponsor a wellness fair or wellness days that involve the community at large in collaboration with school staff and facilities.
  - *Topical health trainings.* Collaborate with community partners to offer parent training on a variety of health-related subjects such as good nutritional choices, infant care, and emergency response (e.g., CPR).

Arrange Housing for Rural Educators

I often hear rural leaders say that the issue of housing is an influential factor with regard to concerns about teacher pay and retention of current staff. Many rural places have no housing available for teachers and their families. A study by the Learning Policy Institute found that almost 25 percent of former teachers—and not just rural teachers—would return to the classroom if housing were provided (Podolsky et al., 2016). Homes that are available are often either priced out of range of a teacher's salary or not in habitable condition. One of the focuses of the USDA is the Rural Housing Service, which oversees a few programs that focus on building issues in rural communities. Here are a few areas that the service can help with; more detailed information is available at www.rd.usda.gov/about-rd/agencies/rural-housing-service:

- **Single-family housing programs.** These programs provide direct loans to low- and moderate-income rural families.
- **Health and safety repairs.** Funding through grants or loans is available to rural families to fix up homes that are not habitable.
- **Multifamily housing programs.** Loans are provided to assist with rental payments for very low-, low-, and moderate-income rural residents. Funds may also be used for facility improvements.
- **Low-income housing tax credit (LIHTC).** The LIHTC program provides tax credits for the acquisition, rehabilitation, or new construction of rental housing for lower-income families.

A teacherage—a residence for teachers—used to be part and parcel of rural school employment, but over the last century, as we have become more mobile and able to drive to get to work, that practice has faded away. However, in response to the lack of housing in rural communities, many districts are going back to the idea of constructing and maintaining teacher housing. In New Mexico, the Public Education Department was awarded $80 million to build family homes in districts in the northern part of the state that educators can rent at low rates (Velazquez, 2022). In rural eastern Texas, the Marfa Independent School District converted a vacant administrative building and a retired barracks into apartments for teachers (Ridlen Bowen, 2022). In Montana, where 96 percent of school districts are considered rural, the Colleges of Education and Architecture at Montana State University collaborated on building tiny homes that could be placed on district property and used as teacher housing (Schmidt, 2019). In Vail, Arizona, the school district purchased land and built 24 tiny homes for teachers to buy at a low cost or rent for a period of time (Mejia, 2019). The problem of housing shortages cannot be solved by the district alone. Collaborating with community partners, state entities, and nonprofits may be required to offer effective solutions in a given rural area. Following are some factors to consider when seeking feasible options:

- **Housing allowance.** Consider building a stipend for housing into the standard teacher contract, if there are available local homes in the area that are priced outside of a teacher's budget capacity. The stipend could also take the form of rental deposit assistance, such as first and last month's rent or security deposit.
- **School-owned land for staff housing.** In many states, public land is available at low or no cost for both affordable and mixed-income housing development. In addition, in an endeavor such as providing staff housing, the district would be exempt from zoning rules, allowing for a broad range of housing options (Sturtevant, 2019). This type of initiative could also include repurposing vacant or underused district buildings for staff homes. Some districts that have taken this approach have partnered with nonprofit organizations such as Habitat for Humanity or local businesses. It may also be feasible for districts to lease and manage school-owned land to a developer or nonprofit.
- **Teacherages.** Housing specifically intended for teachers is also an option. Whether by purchasing established property, such as a hotel, or by building tiny homes, providing housing at low rates for teachers has been a game changer for many rural school districts.
- **Banking relationships.** Local or regional banking institutions may be interested in a partnership to ensure staff can obtain affordable loans or alternative financing. Referring staff to a community partner benefits both the district and the local community.

Focus on School Facilities Maintenance

There are a variety of barriers to a rural leader being able to access support, fiscal or otherwise, to maintain facilities. States often require a minimum number of students for new construction and may not have a mechanism to condemn buildings that are no longer viable. The life span of buildings and capital projects may be an underestimated factor in funding decisions.

Arguably, few states keep accurate and current assessments of the condition of school facilities, especially those in rural areas. When funding is available, rural schools are often given short shrift and deemed ineligible for complete repair, having to make do with projects like a half-sized basketball court rather than a full-sized athletic facility (Lawrence et al., 2002).

When assessing the needs for facilities maintenance in a rural district, you should start with a preventive maintenance plan (PMP) to keep current facilities in the best working condition possible. Most states have a state office of facilities that can be a resource for devising a well-structured PMP, but some generalizable best practices follow:

- Facility issues can be directly correlated to deferred maintenance, inadequate funding, undertrained staff, or poor staff practices. Employing well-trained, prepared maintenance staff can reduce replacement, overhead, and utility costs and lower labor costs.
- When assessing facilities, include stakeholders at the local and state levels, especially if there are major concerns about viability. Including stakeholders from the start can facilitate the decision-making process for funding or help in other areas where opposition might delay progress.
- Collect data on all facilities and systems to ensure all decisions are based on reliable information. This includes documentation that system or facility failure is not a case of mismanagement but truly an end to the system's useful life, and therefore should be eligible for funding to renovate or replace it. Data should include the following information:
    ○ What facilities are in use? How old are they? What is their condition?
    ○ Are facilities and systems working as designed and as they need to?

  A baseline audit is integral to all current and future PMP efforts. Consulting with a third party to do an audit may benefit the district if trained personnel are not available. Remember, safety should take priority over all other considerations.
- Know the four levels of school facility maintenance:
    ○ *Emergency maintenance.* An issue that needs to be immediately corrected to ensure the health and safety of those on campus (e.g., a ruptured gas line).
    ○ *Routine maintenance.* An issue that needs to be addressed but is not urgent and can be taken care of when there is time (e.g., removal of trash from a classroom).

- *Preventive maintenance.* An issue that is scheduled on a regular basis to ensure facilities remain in good working order (e.g., cleaning carpets).
- *Predictive maintenance.* An issue that is monitored for possible occurrence based on specific parameters and factors in conjunction with preventive maintenance (e.g., a sensor on the cafeteria refrigerator that alerts staff to technological updates or malfunctions). Typically this involves monitoring software.

Renovate or replace? That is often the question when it comes to older rural school facilities, and the answer is influenced by the amount of available funds and the desire of the local community to potentially take on a tax burden. Public input from all stakeholder groups should be a part of the decision-making process, along with collaboration with local and state governmental agencies and planning and zoning departments. Even with the approval of all these groups, moving construction forward may not be feasible, and rural leaders have to consider their options for providing working facilities that don't require either state or local funding. Here are some suggestions:

- Team up with a local or regional contractor to address some of the major issues facing the facility for low cost or even pro bono.
- Work with the school's career and technical education (CTE) program to include school facilities maintenance in their curriculum as teachable projects.
- Start a community foundation that can work with the school to raise funds for any projects that need to be addressed. This type of foundation not only provides fiscal support, it can also help elevate awareness of issues for local taxpayers, which may lead to future support in an election.
- Investigate state grant programs that might be available, typically through either a formula-based or competitive process. In many states, rural schools enjoy priority rating for these types of grants.
- Determine if the school meets the qualifications to be added to the National Register of Historic Buildings, which may allow for the allocation of federal dollars for reinvigoration. Places to look for national funding sources include the National Park Service, the Foundation of the American Institute for Conservation, and the Getty Foundation. A comprehensive list of all federal grants can be found at www.grants.gov. You may also be able to access state funding through your state's historic preservation office.

Address Disparities in College and Career Readiness

College attendance rates for rural students have struggled to keep up with those for urban students even though the groups demonstrate the same levels of academic performance. As previously discussed, the flight from rural communities by young adults is often linked to education attainment opportunities, but the rates of postsecondary program enrollment are lower overall for rural students. Some of the factors in this disparity may be ones that rural leaders can manipulate, such as the scarcity of advanced placement and dual enrollment courses. According to Gagnon and Mattingly (2016), 93 percent of urban and suburban districts offer these course options, compared with only half of rural districts, which means that students from rural areas are not as prepared to enter college.

Factors outside the control of the school leader, such as socioeconomic status, also come into play. Many rural students do not have family members who have attended postsecondary institutions, so they don't have a mentor to help navigate the enrollment process. The rising cost of obtaining a degree, putting it out of reach for many rural students, is also a concern. Without mentoring and financial support, many qualified rural students simply don't apply to college.

Following are some suggestions that rural leaders can implement to bring college attendance rates in line with those of the larger population:

- **Create systems of support.** Pair students looking toward college or other postsecondary opportunities with mentors. Not only can mentors provide encouragement, they can also share institutional knowledge to help students access specific programs they want to pursue. Programs that have a strong college-going focus, such as AVID (www.avid.org), can also be implemented schoolwide.
- **Diversify the curriculum.** Offer a wide range of fine arts courses such as music, theater, and art that can expose students to opportunities beyond high school. While many rural areas are seeing a revitalization of local culture, still more have deficits in this area the school can assist with. If there is a shortage of human capital to teach these courses, tap into the local community to find people or organizations to help broaden and expand the school's curricular offerings. These community partners can provide another pathway for students to see college as a valid option.

- **Provide access to digital resources.** During the pandemic, many rural areas geared up their broadband access efforts and can now leverage that connectivity by offering advanced placement and dual enrollment courses remotely. These courses can be either synchronous or asynchronous, depending on the needs and capacity of the district. The ability to access a virtual teacher to lead a class in a higher level math or a foreign language has been a sea change for many rural students. There are a variety of platforms and programs available, each with different budget impacts. One such program is the Arizona Student Opportunity Collaborative (https://azsoc.org), which offers appropriately certified teachers for a growing number of courses at the middle and high school levels. Through online materials and synchronous lectures, to a local teacher using created curriculum, to independent modules with support from a teacher as needed, the collaborative has filled gaps in many rural areas across the state.
- **Help families with paperwork.** Although this suggestion might seem so basic as not to be worth mentioning, walking high school students and their families through the Free Application for Federal Student Aid (FAFSA) and college application process is an easy way to start rural students on the road to college and career. Use social media to remind students and families of approaching deadlines.

  For students not planning to attend postsecondary institutions, bring in business members from the community to help them connect with and work through industry certifications or other training programs. If invited, many will take the time to come to the school to discuss their programming, financial assistance, and other areas of concern. Some may have ties to summer programming that will help students with college and career readiness.
- **Invite alumni to speak with students.** College graduates from the local community—recent and not-so-recent—can serve as role models that show rural students what their future could look like. Invite former students to return to give a commencement speech or to be a guest for the day hosted by a specific teacher. Knowing someone from a similar background has been successful can give rural students the confidence that they can do the same.
- **Connect students with college access programs.** Investigate college access programs that have a national presence and can serve your

students. There are currently eight Federal TRIO Programs, supported by Department of Education funding, to consider for fit within your school community. Designed to provide services for individuals from disadvantaged backgrounds, low-income students, and first-generation college students, among others, TRIO grants can help with funding projects to boost college attendance. One program, Upward Bound, provides precollege support such as academic instruction and tutoring, counseling, work-study programs, and cultural enrichment for first-generation or low-income students. Gaining Early Awareness and Readiness for Undergraduate Programs (GEAR UP) is a program that offers both state and partnership grants for training middle and high school students planning to enter college. Finally, the Student Support Services program funds precollege tutoring in academics as well as counseling assistance for students to get through the college application and financial aid process. Look to see if any of these TRIO programs are available in your local or regional rural area.

You don't have to look hard to find examples of rural schools that have successfully raised their postgraduation success rates. Here are three that have had phenomenal growth in this area:

- **East Wilkes High School, North Carolina.** Located in rural Appalachia, East Wilkes High School has implemented a dual enrollment program with Wilkes Community College and established a strong CTE program offering training in welding, agriculture, and culinary arts. As a result, the school's graduation rate increased from 75 percent in 2015 to 90 percent in 2019, according to the North Carolina Department of Public Instruction. Furthermore, a higher percentage of high school graduates are enrolling in college, with 61 percent of the Class of 2019 planning to attend a two- or four-year college (North Carolina School Report Cards, n.d.).
- **Baldwin County School District, Georgia.** For over 10 years, Baldwin County Schools have used a community schools model framework to support students dealing with poverty (Communities in Schools, 2020). Intentional outreach to the local community and fostering community relationships has led to both academic and nonacademic benefits for students, including tutoring, clothing, and health care. Across the district's eight schools, more than 4,000 students receive support of some

kind, and graduation rates went from 60 percent in 2010 to 92 percent in 2020 (Communities in Schools, 2020).
- **Fowler High School, Colorado.** In the rural town of Foster, Colorado, graduating classes for Fowler High School are small, but college-going rates are higher than the state's average. From 2019 to 2022, graduation rates were over 90 percent (with a slight dip after the COVID-19 pandemic), and each of those years saw between 58 and 81 percent of graduates enrolled in some type of postsecondary program (Colorado Department of Education, 2023). For generations, parents and the community have partnered to promote the benefits of a college degree (Gonzales, 2022). A cultural expectation of high school graduation and postsecondary education plans has made a difference in how students are prepared for life after high school.

Rural leaders may embark on their journey unprepared to be confronted with various issues of access. Tackling challenges like student food insecurity or affordable housing for teachers is not generally covered in typical educational leadership preparation courses! While many areas of concern, such as lack of broadband access, have been well documented, others are not as well known, despite the fact that they can have a tremendous impact on the ability of the school to fulfill its primary objective of teaching students. Understanding what actions to take to help mitigate these concerns is the first step in clearing the way for ease of access that can benefit all in a rural community. How awesome it is to be a leader who can have that kind of positive impact on your students and their families!

Rural Poverty

About eight years ago, my principal and I worked together on a couple of grants that would provide funding for a complete workout facility and an onsite clinic that could provide medical, dental, and mental health services to both students and the community; we won both. We also applied for and were awarded a Gold Award of Distinction—the first in our state—for our work on the Centers for Disease Control and Prevention (CDC) Whole School, Whole Community, Whole Child model, as well as the HealthierUS School Challenge award. We planted a community garden, started a cycling team, and worked to increase outreach and communication to our Tribal community on the Tohono O'odham reservation. When the National School Lunch Program instituted the Community Eligibility Provision, we knew we would qualify, as we had already been providing meals for all students at no cost.

Why was this work for our students important? We knew that the vast majority of our students were living in poverty. As educators, we saw on a daily basis the hardships that our students and their families struggled with to make it to school every day, let alone be able to do homework the night before. Many of those children lived in circumstances where there was no running water or electricity. We marveled that they consistently showed up!

Early in my tenure, while looking at our demographics for some required reporting, I discovered that our zip code was among the most impoverished in the state. Forty percent of our residents did not complete high school, and just

1 out of 10 has a bachelor's degree. The average household income is 20 percent lower than the poverty threshold, according to 2021 U.S. Census data (U.S. Census Bureau, n.d.). Medical and mental health services are not available locally, and many lack reliable transportation to access needed care. The concerns around food security are real—the only places to get food are the Circle K convenience mart or the newly reopened Stanfield Market, which offers a very limited selection of whole foods. Residents in the Stanfield area must travel, at a minimum, 20 miles away to either Casa Grande or Maricopa to access goods and services. Additionally, the migrant families we serve are highly mobile and are therefore in need of transitional services on a frequent basis. All of these factors mean that Stanfield Elementary School is a safe haven for our students, their families, and the community. The safe, healthy, caring environment we provide counters these children's daily struggle to learn and thrive.

Challenge: The Far-Reaching Negative Impacts of Poverty

There have been numerous studies on the impacts of poverty on students and their academic outcomes. As early as 1967, when President Lyndon Johnson commissioned a report titled *The People Left Behind,* which documented a rate of rural poverty at 25 percent, or double that of their metropolitan (urban) counterparts, we have known that rural children experience poverty at greater numbers than their nonrural peers (Institute for Research on Poverty, 2018). While poverty has a negative and often devastating effect on children in any locale, limited access to resources makes it much more difficult to connect rural families to needed services. Add to that the fact that poverty tends to be localized into areas or regions that then suffer higher crime rates, higher dropout rates, and higher unemployment (USDA ERS, 2022). Regions that show greater concentrations of poverty include the "Black Belt" and the Mississippi Delta in the South, Appalachia, and Native American lands in the Dakotas and the Rio Grande Valley (Institute for Research on Poverty, 2020).

In 2019, the nonmetropolitan poverty rate was 15.4 percent, compared with the metropolitan rate of 11.9 percent (NCES, n.d.a). Poverty rates among age groups also differ when comparing rural and urban locales, with a quarter of rural children under the age of 5 living in poverty as compared with urban rates of 17 percent for the same age group. In fact, for all children under 18, 5 percent more live in poverty in rural areas (NCES, n.d.a).

What these data do not show is how long these children have lived in poverty. Persistent poverty, or poverty over a long period of time, has huge impacts on students. Children in poverty often live in single-parent homes, with the parent in most of these rural homes being a female with low educational attainment and few employment prospects, making extraction from the cycle all the more difficult (Institute for Research on Poverty, 2020). This deep poverty, perpetuated across generations, is often linked with poor health statistics, lower academic outcomes, higher dropout rates, greater numbers of teen pregnancies, higher rates of food insecurity and homelessness, and other negative life circumstances. And unfortunately, rural children have also been disproportionately affected by the slower economic recovery rate in rural places during the last few recession cycles (Farrigan, 2014).

African Americans, Native Americans, and Hispanics in rural places are also more likely to be affected by poverty than those in urban areas. While persistent poverty, defined as living for two years or more under the set poverty threshold, is greater for people of color in all locales, it is higher for African Americans in rural communities (Institute for Research on Poverty, 2020) who tend to be more segregated in high-poverty communities than their urban counterparts (Lichter & Parisi, 2008). Rural people of color who live in poverty are poorer on average than poor rural whites (Huang & Howley, 1991).

The challenges experienced in under-resourced schools—absence of highly effective teachers, fewer higher-level course options, general lack of community support—have a profound impact when coupled with poverty, and the impact is even more significant when the poverty is concentrated in one area (Mattingly et al., 2011). Additionally, poverty makes it more difficult to mitigate negative school outcomes such as higher rates of dropout, disciplinary actions, disability identification, absenteeism, and lower reading and math achievement.

Homelessness

Another issue linked to poverty that has an impact on rural students is homelessness. Students experiencing homelessness have the lowest attendance rates, lowest academic outcomes, and lowest graduation rates of any subgroup—and these outcomes put them at the greatest risk of future homelessness (Shapiro, 2023). While the number of homeless students in rural and urban areas is similar, in rural areas, resources are very difficult to access, especially those that traditionally come through the schools. Rural homelessness is also more likely to be hidden (Morton et al., 2018). While the McKinney-Vento Homeless Assistance Act of 1987 mandates support for students without secure housing, these federal grant dollars do not always make their way to rural school communities, and even when they do, there may not be resources available to spend them on. Rural students are historically more underserved than urban students not only because of the lack of resources, but because of the scarcity of safe places for them to go. The dangers to students experiencing homelessness were exacerbated during the COVID-19 pandemic, because the adults who typically notice that students are displaying signs of housing insecurity no longer connected with students in person. That loss of direct connection led to an underreporting of students eligible for McKinney-Vento services (Fields & Surma, 2020). Often tied to homelessness is chronic absenteeism, which further negatively impacts students' ability to learn. Even with the provision of support like clothing and access to medical, vision, and dental care, the shortage of housing in rural places turns a potentially short-term concern into a long-term problem. Nationally, for every 100 families who qualify for subsidized housing, there are only 36 available units (Shapiro, 2022).

Adverse Childhood Experiences

The largest investigation of childhood abuse and neglect and household challenges was conducted from 1995 to 1997 by the CDC and Kaiser Permanente (Felitti et al., 1998). The resulting report identifies 10 traumatic events that can lead to negative outcomes for children who experience at least one of them. These events, collectively termed adverse childhood experiences (ACEs), include neglect, both emotional and physical; divorce of the parents; parental incarceration; physical, emotional, or sexual abuse; mental health concerns; substance abuse; and the death of a parent or primary caregiver. While ACEs research is not specific to rural children, there is a correlation between poverty and the number of traumatic events children might experience in their formative years (Crouch et al., 2020). In fact, some researchers are pushing to include poverty as one of the ACEs in future data collection. According to the CDC, these traumatic events have been experienced by 1 in 6 adults, contribute to half of the 10 leading causes of death, and, if mitigated, could eliminate almost half of the depression found in adults (CDC, 2019). In rural America, studies show that almost 60 percent of adults have experienced at least one ACE, and 15 percent have experienced four or more ACEs

(Chanlongbutra et al., 2018). Some of the solutions discussed in this chapter, including trauma-informed (TI) instructional practices, can make a difference for rural students who have experienced at least one ACE. The difference between urban and rural TI supports are the familiar challenges with access that rural communities often face. Often, planning for and implementing these interventions in a rural context require adaptations.

Solutions for the Resilient Rural Leader

The effects of poverty can be greatly diminished when the rural community pulls together to support the students in their schools. Each stakeholder group, including state and local entities, can and should play a part in creating learning environments that support the whole child. At the most basic level, the principal and teaching staff can implement high-impact instructional strategies that focus on monitoring individual progress, building vocabulary, and creating environments conducive to learning (Benton et al., 2022). School leaders should provide teachers with intentional and actionable feedback on pedagogy to strengthen instructional practices that benefit all students in the building. There are many resources that can provide support for school leaders in building and supporting teachers' skills, and they are too numerous to list here. However, the Supporting Students in Poverty with High-Impact Instructional Strategies Toolkit, created by the National Comprehensive Center, does an excellent job of naming strategies and providing resources for a deeper dive. You can access the toolkit at https://compcenternetwork.org/resources/resource/7542/supporting-students-poverty-high-impact-instructional-strategies-toolkit.

Many of the solutions that can help rural students living in poverty are tied to budget choices. For example, the federal dollars that can be accessed through the McKinney-Vento Act program, a part of Title I-A, are limited and must be managed through a liaison (see https://www2.ed.gov/programs/homeless/legislation.html or https://nche.ed.gov/legislation/mckinney-vento for more information). Project HOPE-Virginia has created a toolkit for liaisons and school administrators, available at https://education.wm.edu/centers/hope. No matter the programming you put into place in your rural school, you need to know what assets are available to be leveraged in your area. Chapter 9 will help with asset mapping information that is foundational to some of the solutions discussed below.

Apply for Rural and Low-Income School (RLIS) Programs

As part of the federal Rural Education Achievement Program (REAP), the RLIS grant program provides rural school districts with funding targeted at improving student achievement. Specific to this program is the requirement that a minimum of 20 percent of children served must be in a rural area and have family income below the poverty threshold. The grant is not competitive, although there is an online application. Lists of eligible LEAs are released on an annual basis and can be either downloaded from the RLIS website (https://oese.ed.gov/offices/office-of-formula-grants/rural-insular-native-achievement-programs/rural-education-achievement-program/rural-and-low-income-school-program) or your state education agency. The application of these funds can be very broad, tracking with expenses eligible for the Small, Rural School Achievement (SRSA) Program, with two exceptions: (1) unlike SRSA, RLIS can fund parent engagement activities, and (2) RLIS may not be used for extracurricular programs, while SRSA can.

Track Student Mobility with Other Districts

A study out of Penn State University found that students who live in poverty also tend to be highly mobile, shuffling back and forth between several school districts (Center on Rural Education and Communities [CREC], 2023). There are multiple reasons students may move, including housing costs or availability, loss of income, and domestic violence. Keeping track of students who move in and out of the district can put schools in a better position to respond to students' and families' needs. Such documentation can be kept by the school or district, but capturing and sharing student mobility data over time at the county or regional level would have more impact. Most students tend to stay within a small radius of a few neighborhoods (CREC, 2023). Open communication among neighboring districts not only helps track students, it also makes it easier to get records transferred more efficiently. The sooner a receiving school gets student information, the faster they will be able to start supporting the specific needs of students living in poverty.

Establish Mentorships

Mentoring programs are not a new concept. When I first started teaching middle school in the early 1990s, one of the foundational concepts of an effective middle-level curriculum included a daily advisory class period. Each teacher was assigned a group of students that stayed with them during the whole time the students were in middle school. Mentorship programming has since evolved to include frameworks like AVID and others that rely on the relationship between a caring adult and the student as a vehicle to explore opportunities and possibilities for the student, furnish a nonjudgmental sounding board, and encourage students to think beyond their current situation. Putting a mentoring program in place in rural areas needs to take the community's unique assets and barriers into account. There may be strong school-to-home connections, but limited access to resources makes it necessary to assess individual student and community needs and create a program from what is available. Currently, only 10 percent of nationwide mentoring programs serve rural places (Youth Collaboratory, 2018). Let's look at two examples of mentoring frameworks that can be used within a rural context to ensure all students who need or want a mentor have access to one.

The first model pairs older students with younger peers. These mentorships can be especially helpful during transitional years, such as moving from middle to high school. Both mentor and mentee can benefit from these arrangements. The primary focus of the pairing is on building the relationship in a positive way, rather than on deficits or what's wrong. Figure 6.1 outlines some best practices for setting up a student-to-student mentorship program.

The second model pairs staff with students. One way to establish intentional mentoring matches with staff is to list each student and have each adult place markers next to the students they know. Students who receive no markers are targeted for pairing with a caring adult within the school environment.

FIGURE 6.1

Peer Mentoring Best Practices

Relationship Building	Logistics	Considerations
• Asset building, not just tutoring • Mentors gain self-efficacy, leadership opportunities, positive contribution • Adult support and follow-up as needed	• Maximum two years' difference • At least 10 meetings over the year to build meaningful engagement • Consider transportation, time of day, school calendar, meeting location	• Training mentors is key to program success • Choose diverse mentors, not just high achievers • Need may focus on a particular area (e.g., foster care, college and career readiness)

Source: Kupersmidt et al., 2020.

Students considered at risk should also be a priority for pairings. Some training is needed to ensure that mentors know what is expected of them, and students who participate should also participate in discussions about what mentoring is and how it can help them.

Both mentoring models have pros and cons. Consider the following as you assess how a mentorship program would work in your school:

Pros

- Both can be implemented at no to low cost.
- Peer-to-peer program engages students who might not otherwise participate in a mentoring program.
- Positive outcomes include a more positive outlook on both teachers and school, as well as greater self-confidence.

Cons

- Outcomes may not have an impact on issues that originate outside of school, such as peer relationships or drug use (Herrera et al., 2007).
- May not produce desired close relationships due to time constraints of school.
- May be difficult to get participant buy-in; may not be valued by staff or administration.

There are some critical questions to answer when planning a school-based mentoring program. These questions should be shared with all stakeholders so that interested parties can discuss potential areas of concern before launching. Figure 6.2 lays out some elements to explore as you build a mentoring program at your rural school.

A third option for mentoring that might have an even greater benefit for the community at large is to establish a mentorship program with individuals from outside the school. As a classroom teacher, I started an informal mentoring program pairing my most at-risk students with members of the community who had volunteered to provide support to the middle school. All four volunteers were military retirees who lived in the community. With the support of my administration, I worked with the school counselor to train them and set up bimonthly mentoring meetings with my 6th grade students. All of the students, and their parents, were supportive of and participated in the arrangement. Meetings were informal and held during the school day, typically at lunch in my classroom or the library. What a difference those four

FIGURE 6.2

Elements of Planning a Mentorship Program

Planning Element	Critical Questions
Structure of the program	• What are the needs of the students who have been targeted for mentoring? • Who will the mentors be? • What will the student referral process look like? • What will the size and makeup of the initial student group be? • How will mentor matches be made? • How often will mentors meet with their mentees? Where? What will they do while they are together? • What facilities or resources are needed? • What, if any, funding is needed?
Roles and responsibilities	• Who will be responsible for managing the program? • What is the role of administration? Teachers? Other adults/staff? • What legal issues need to be considered? • What will the evaluation process look like? • What role will parents/caregivers play in the program? Who will serve as liaison? • What written program parameters will be completed (e.g., memorandum of understanding, action plan)?
Student referrals	• What are the selection criteria for student referrals? • Who will make referrals? • How will students be onboarded? • What happens when students choose not to participate?
Mentor recruitment	• What basics do potential mentors need to know about the program? What are the expectations for their involvement? • Who is likely to want to participate? How will you interest others? • How will you screen potential mentors to ensure a safe program? What happens if a potential mentor is screened out? • What are the basic criteria for a suitable mentor (e.g., availability, dependable, positive attitude, likes students)?
Training	• How and when will training be conducted? Who will conduct training? • What resources will be used in the training process? • What are basic training requirements for initial training (e.g., McKinney-Vento Act, duty to report)? What ongoing training will be provided?
Mentor-mentee matches	• What match criteria will be used? • Who will be responsible for deciding mentor-mentee matches? • Who will supervise the mentors and how often? • How will mixed signals about the purpose of mentoring be handled (e.g., tutoring vs. relationship building)? • How will mismatched pairs/absent mentors/absent students be handled? • How will off-program activities or meetings be addressed?
Closure	• What will the process for closing out the match (typically at the end of the year) look like? • How will you decide if a match needs to be closed sooner? What happens to the participants of a prematurely closed match?
Evaluation	• What data will be collected during the program? How will these data inform program goals? • How will outcomes be used to improve the program?

Source: Jucovy & Garringer, 2008.

individuals made in the lives of those young people! Attendance, attitude, engagement, and academics all improved.

As principal, I expanded on the idea and instituted an advisory period for all students. Much like the AVID model, students were matched with the same teacher for the course of their middle school years. Advisory was the first class period of the day and featured topics for discussion, team-building activities, and loosely structured relationship building among staff, students, and the community. Our high-risk students engaged in one-to-one mentoring with community volunteers and classified staff two or three times a week during advisory. Even on this larger scale, we saw the difference. These types of relationships help forge connections to the community that students can build on and grow as they get older—connections that can be foundational and life-altering, especially for students who are at risk.

All mentoring should focus on assets and growing strengths, which means that the rural leader must engage in some intentional planning and training. Many of the considerations for a community-connected mentoring program are the same as for a school-based program, although there are a few other elements that need to be addressed as well. Mentors who come from outside the school setting may require a significant amount of training to ensure that they know how to interact with students and feel equipped to deal with their needs. Additionally, background checks of volunteers will be needed to protect both students and the school.

Form Faith-Based and Other Nontraditional Partnerships

In most rural communities, faith-based organizations such as churches or ministries have already established a presence. Groups that are focused on service can be a key partner for schools dealing with issues of student poverty. Have conversations with leaders to establish what their core mission is and how it can align with the school's goals. These conversations can help establish a common purpose and lay the groundwork for what types of resources, people, and expertise are available. One group that does this type of collaboration is Pastors for Children, a national 501(c)3 that operates in several states. There are several advantages to partnerships with faith-based organizations:

- **Referrals.** Faith-based organizations can help the school to identify students and families who are at risk and in need of support and services, and can assist with referrals either to the school and its programs or to other aid in the community or region.

- **Events and fundraising.** While they may not be able to provide direct funds to the school, faith-based organizations may be able to sponsor events to fundraise for various school programs.
- **Microgrants.** Most faith-based organizations are not able to provide large amounts of funding to schools, but many can offer quick funding directly to a family in need in the form of security deposits, rent, utilities, or gas. Open communication between school and organization leadership can ensure that families that need an extra level of support are able to get it when necessary.
- **Ongoing conversations.** Faith-based communities are an important asset to tap into for support with any stakeholder discussions regarding changes, improvements, or other topics. Members of their circle often have pertinent expertise and valuable perspectives.

Faith-based communities are not the only benevolent organizations able to support collaboration with the school. Although differences in faith between the student populations and the organization have not been an issue in my community, be aware that your community may be more sensitive to this type of partnership. Expand your search for community partners to fire departments, police or sheriff departments, local businesses, civic employees, charitable associations, convenience stores, and local and regional medical facilities.

Seek Promise Neighborhoods Grants

One of the annual funding opportunities available through the U.S. Department of Education under the Every Student Succeeds Act is the Promise Neighborhoods grant program. This place-based program is modeled on Harlem's Children's Zone work, which connected organizations to the local school district to create and launch a variety of services aimed at improving academic and social outcomes for children who live in distressed urban neighborhoods. The focus of these initiatives is to break the cycle of generational poverty by providing support to children and their families from birth to college or career. The Promise Neighborhood model can also be successful in a rural setting; in fact, two of the three identified priorities for the program include both rural and Tribal neighborhoods that need assistance. Grants are awarded for up to five years, underscoring the need for project sustainability. Additionally, data collection requirements might be difficult to meet given the mobile nature of families dealing with poverty and restrictions on capacity for administrative work in a rural setting. However, investigating these programs might suggest some different ways to break down silos and work with the community at large on initiatives to support at-risk youth and their families in your rural community. The following ideas, inspired by the Promise Neighborhoods program, might spark conversation:

- **Share data.** Develop a system to share data between the school and partners in the community to identify gaps in services, needed supports, and other at-risk data points. Privacy laws can make this difficult, but several Promise Neighborhoods have found a way to make it work.
- **Set up liaisons between school and home.** Train individuals to serve as neighborhood "connectors" to ensure that students and families have access to needed supports and services. These connectors or liaisons can link the school to different community assets on an ongoing basis and act as a conduit for communication in real time. Setting up a liaison program using active community members is another way to build a sense of community ownership in the rural school.
- **Conduct a door-to-door needs and asset survey.** Use community volunteers to help collect information from families in the community. Not only will this practice help establish local context for future conversations about needed school initiatives, it can also quickly identify at-risk households (e.g., families struggling with illiteracy, job loss, homelessness).

Practice Trauma-Informed Care

One of the ways that rural schools are assisting students who have experienced one or more ACEs is through trauma-informed classroom practices. Any kind of standards-based instruction requires students to focus on the learning at hand, create connections and store them for later retrieval, and regulate their own behavior; the trauma from ACEs events can negatively affect all of these functions. TI practices aim to mitigate a child's ability to learn and function in the classroom setting, but TI instruction may be challenging in rural areas due to a lack of resources and support.

As previously stated, rural is not a monolith, and the type of care required will vary by region. Geography, cultural, and racial demographics, along with the local economy, all play a part in what the local community will tolerate and accept. One of the primary issues that rural leaders should be aware of is stigma surrounding mental health and trauma in many rural communities. These issues are often seen as weakness or personal failure, leading to the belief that people should "tough it out" rather than seek help, and TI practices may be viewed as unnecessary and overreaching.

Another issue to be aware of is the cultural viewpoint of a community that might value and prioritize traditional healing methods over Western approaches (e.g., members of the Tohono O'odham Tribal community in my school district). Additionally, other factors such as chronic poverty can magnify the effects of ACEs (Howley & Redding, 2021). Any TI strategy needs to be tailored to the needs of the individual student but should also take into consideration various community stakeholders' wants and needs. This can be accomplished by incorporating cultural competence into TI practices as well as involving community members, parents, local healers, and other community leaders into the development and implementation of TI instruction. Ensuring that local cultural practices, beliefs, stories, traditions, and history are integrated into TI practices make them more accessible and relevant to the community at large and ultimately ensure that students get needed support.

There are many frameworks that can be used to implement the components of a TI program, but all share three key areas of focus:

- A safe school environment
- Relationships and engagement within the school community
- Teaching emotion regulation and coping skills

There are a number of resources that can help you learn more about both ACEs research and TI practices. The following programs, which are adaptable to most rural settings, are a good place to start:

- **Trauma Responsive Equitable Education (TREE).** The TREE program involves a variety of stakeholders outside the school, including caregivers and community organizations, working together to ensure that all rural students have access to the same resources. The framework addresses systemic educational challenges often faced by rural, high-poverty communities, such as chronic adversity, stress, and trauma. Find out more at https://cobscookinstitute.org/tree.
- **Positive Behavioral Interventions and Supports (PBIS).** The Ohio Department of Education has a comprehensive website describing PBIS

and identifying resources aligned with the PBIS framework that are targeted toward building positive relationships and creating a positive climate for learning. There are also links to follow related to trauma and its impact on students and learning. Find out more at https://education.ohio.gov/Topics/Student-Supports/Ohio-PBIS.
- **National Center on Safe Supportive Learning Environments.** This organization offers a broad array of tools and resources as well as free training for leaders and teachers on TI practices, building positive relationships and environments, strategic planning guides for implementing TI frameworks, and current news and information on grants related to these types of programs. Type "rural" into the search bar to get examples of successful programs from across the country that can serve as templates for replication in other areas. A state-by-state menu of federal grants received for safe and supportive school programming is available. Find out more at https://safesupportivelearning.ed.gov.
- **HEARTS.** This program out of the University of California San Francisco focuses on TI in a safe, engaging, and equitable whole school teaching and learning environment. Structured using a Multi-Tiered System of Supports, the framework includes training for all stakeholders to improve school culture and build personnel capacity. A resource bank of HEARTS work is provided. Find out more at https://hearts.ucsf.edu/program-overview.
- **Collaborative Learning for Educational Achievement and Resilience (CLEAR).** Washington State University's program operates in 37 schools, a third of which are rural. The CLEAR framework focuses on providing professional development and school culture improvements over a three- to four-year period. Teacher pedagogy is the main focus, but leadership is also included. Ongoing support and feedback from the CLEAR team allow for adjustments along the way. Find out more at https://extension.wsu.edu/clear.

No matter what TI framework you choose to implement, keep in mind that changes may take years to fully play out. Additionally, local assets may influence what practices you are able to put in place, so during the planning phase, you will need to establish what might look different about TI programs in your context. There are strengths in every rural community that can be brought in to support staff and students dealing with trauma and its effects. Leaning into these strengths can create stronger school-community bonds and higher levels of engagement and support.

Focus on Building Student Assets

The last decade has seen a shift in terms of how adolescence is viewed (Frankland, 2021). The Positive Youth Development (PYD) model focuses on building assets through skill development and community engagement rather than focusing on deficits—a viewpoint that can further negatively affect students living in poverty or other at-risk circumstances. Eccles and Gootman (2002) use five different attributes to characterize the PYD framework (see Figure 6.3). Learning environments centered around building qualities in students have a greater likelihood of positive social and educational outcomes.

Lerner and colleagues (2005) define the five Cs of the PYD model as follows:

- **Competence**—A sense of capability in the areas of social, academic, cognitive, and vocational skills.
- **Confidence**—A global sense of self-efficacy and self-worth.
- **Connection**—Positive and two-way relationships with peers, family, school, and community.
- **Character**—Morality, integrity, and adherence to societal and cultural norms.
- **Caring**—Sympathy and empathy for others.

Students with these qualities engage with society, enhancing both the community they live in and their own development, leading to what is often

FIGURE 6.3

The Five Cs of Positive Youth Development

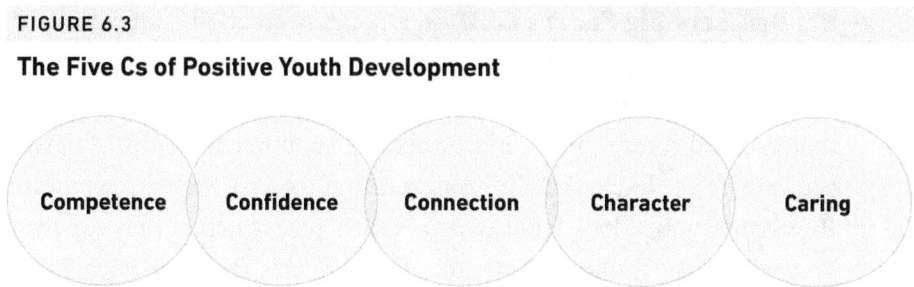

Source: Adapted from Eccles & Gootman, 2002.

referred to as the sixth C, Contribution (Lerner et al., 2005). When the community harnesses the strengths of engaged and connected youth, everyone can benefit. Youth involved with a PYD-based program are more likely to do better in school, less likely to adopt risky behaviors, and much more likely to be connected to their community.

Below is a list (not inclusive) of several national organizations that rural leaders can collaborate with to benefit their students. Largely funded with donations and grant dollars, they operate in most rural places across the United States. Take the time to research if any are local to you (or want to be) and how they can be partners in supporting students at risk. Many are looking to establish programming in rural communities.

- **4-H.** Nearly 6 million youth ages 5–18 have participated in the 4-H program, and almost half of those are from rural communities (4-H, n.d.). The program is delivered by public universities through Cooperative Extension programming in a variety of venues, both in and outside of school. Topics of focus are varied and largely driven by the interests and expertise of the local community. Broad program areas include STEM, agriculture, healthy living, and civic engagement. Find out more at https://4-h.org.
- **YouthBuild.** Operating in urban, rural, and Tribal communities, YouthBuild focuses on individuals ages 16–24 who do not have a high school diploma and lack financial resources. Programs are context-dependent and focus on the needs of the local community. Available assets include collaborative partners and resources to ensure that youth get the training, skill building, and supports needed to find long-term success and become contributing members of the local community. Find out more at https://youthbuild.org.
- **Big Brothers Big Sisters (BBBS).** Operating in all 50 states through 240 agencies, 70 percent of which are in rural places, BBBS launched a Rural Initiative in 2018 aimed at ensuring that children in small and underserved communities could access a supportive mentor. There is typically a waiting list of children wishing to be paired with a mentor. BBBS continues to look for partners in rural places so that they can grow and expand the number of mentors they are able to match with youth. Find out more at www.bbbs.org.

- **Native Youth Initiative for Leadership, Empowerment, and Development (I-LEAD).** Although this federally funded initiative is no longer in practice, it could serve as a template for programming that would benefit your community. Created through state-specific joint collaborations, I-LEAD operated in 21 areas to support leadership development for Native American youth ages 14–24. Programming focused on services and activities that supported social and economic development, promoted self-sufficiency, and built community connections. A video featuring several I-LEAD grantees is available at www.youtube.com/watch?v=Vitosze2HAc.
- **AmeriCorps.** In operation for decades, AmeriCorps is one of the few youth service programs that can be found in almost every rural community in the nation. Programming focuses on education, economic opportunity, disaster services, environmental stewardship, healthy futures, and veteran and military families. Community organizations can work with AmeriCorps to establish a partnership to address specific needs within a community, including those of the local school. There is an application process for both people to help run the programming and funding for launch. AmeriCorps is open to volunteers age 17 and older, and many current opportunities are targeted at engaging school-aged children in PYD-based opportunities. Find out more at https://americorps.gov.

It is possible that the best fit for your rural community and its young people is to develop your own PYD program, which can benefit all stakeholders in the rural community. When planning, ask the following questions to focus your time and effort on the right work:

- How will local youth be involved in the planning and implementation of the program?
- What assets in the local community need to be reinforced?
- What activities and resources are needed by the different stakeholder groups?
- What skills do involved adults have that can be leveraged by the program? What other stakeholder groups within the community are able to participate and how?

- What specific group of youth are being targeted initially? How will they be invited to participate? How will programming expand to other age groups and when?
- What are the short-term and long-term goals of the program? What action steps need to be taken to achieve those goals?
- What resources are needed for the program (e.g., people, funding, materials, facilities, marketing)?
- What role will youth play in creating program goals and objectives?
- Who will be responsible for tracking progress? Making adjustments as needed?
- How will youth be involved in evaluating the program? What are the identified success indicators? (National Clearinghouse on Families & Youth, 2007)

Every rural place has resources that can help young people in their community reach their full potential. Even impoverished areas have assets and strengths that can be drawn upon. Involving the youth themselves from concept to implementation will make any PYD program a richer and more meaningful experience for them—and once they are empowered at the local community level, they will be more likely to work within the community at large to ensure that it is a thriving place with potential and opportunity.

Find the Right Fit

As with all initiatives or new programming, one of the keys to success is the right fit for the local context. Many programs can be adapted to fit the needs of rural students and the availability of adults to work with them. However, some ideas or solutions will never be quite right and are therefore a waste of time and resources. In a rural area, where these commodities are as scarce as they are valuable, it is vital to assess the feasibility of a potential program or practice in the planning stages, during initial implementation, and as the program proceeds to adjust as necessary. Because most research on best practices for education has been done in the urban setting, it can be challenging to find exemplars that are the right fit for rural environments.

One of the ways to assess the fit of a potential program is to conduct an analysis using the Rural Fit Factor Assessment in Figure 6.4. Using this tool to guide stakeholder planning discussions about any change initiative can help to determine if the needs of the school and community are best served

FIGURE 6.4

Rural Fit Factor Assessment

1. Identify the program to be analyzed, the target population, and the stakeholders who will take part in planning discussions.
2. Discuss the following questions and record the group's answers.

Research and Evidence	
• What research is available regarding the effectiveness of the program/initiative, and what type of locale was the research conducted in? • What is the level of evidence in support of the program (use What Works Clearinghouse at https://ies.ed.gov/ncee/wwc as needed)? • What theory of change applies to the program? • What are the short-term and long-term outcome expectations for the program? • What data on outcomes for diverse populations are provided?	Notes:

Functionality	
• What are the components of the program, and are they clearly outlined for implementation? • What student populations is the program intended to serve, and how can it be used for different subgroups? • What current users or facilitators are operating the program who can serve as a reference? • How can fidelity of implementation be determined?	Notes:

Resources	
• What technical assistance or consultancy is available for both initial launch and ongoing support? How would these be provided in a rural setting? • What are the costs and deliverables for implementation and launch? Professional development? Ad hoc training? How does rurality impact these? • What consumables are included, and how often do they need to be replaced? • Are materials available in multiple languages and formats? • How responsive are materials/components to the needs of diverse populations?	Notes:

Need	
• Who will this program be used with? How will it fulfill the needs of those populations? • What has already been done for the target population, and to what degree of success? What are the population's skill gaps and strengths? • What do stakeholders identify as the target population's needs, and how will the program assist with those needs? • What are the desired outcomes, both short- and long-term, for the program?	Notes:

(continued)

FIGURE 6.4

Rural Fit Factor Assessment (*continued*)

Fit	
• Does the program align with the school's overall goals (i.e., mission, vision, core values)? • Does it align with other programming currently operating at the school? How will it intersect with other programming? Will other programming impede implementation and practice of the proposed program? • How does the proposed program fit with the local rural community? How might it be disruptive? • How might the program be adapted to the rural context?	Notes:

Capacity	
• What are the ongoing budgetary requirements for the program? What if there is no budget capacity? • What personnel are required, and what do they need to implement and maintain the program? Do they have capacity for these requirements? • What will the administrative burden for the rural leader be with this program? What skills does the leader need to manage launch and ongoing programming? • How will data be collected, and by whom, to monitor fidelity and areas for correction or improvement? • What current practices or procedures need to be adjusted to support implementation of the program? • What facilities will be required? Technology? Monitoring systems? Communication systems? Are any of these able to be adapted to the rural setting?	Notes:

3. Once the group has discussed all six areas for consideration, along with any issues or concerns not highlighted in the questions, they should make a recommendation about whether or not to move forward with the proposed programming or initiative.

by moving forward with implementation. The six different areas to consider can be divided into two categories. Research and evidence, resources, and functionality center around the program's effectiveness and what components are needed to operate in a school setting. Fit, need, and assets relate to how the program will align to the rural school community and how adaptable it is to the setting. For the clearest picture of a program's feasibility, the stakeholder group should be sure to address all parts of the Rural Fit Factor Assessment. If multiple programs are being considered, each should be individually examined.

The biggest concern for rural leaders is the ability to adapt a change initiative to the rural setting. It's important to note that while the program might not be the perfect one to move forward with, parts of it may be useable or paired with other programs currently being implemented at the site. Making sure any program you choose to implement will provide flexibility to meet the needs of students, staff, and the rural area is key.

◻ ◻ ◻

Supporting students living in poverty in rural communities requires a multi-faceted approach, incorporating establishing a safe and supportive learning environment, involving staff and community members, and addressing cultural differences that might influence how supports and interventions are perceived. By implementing programming and providing resources that address the unique needs of students living in poverty, including dealing with potential trauma, rural leaders can provide all students with the opportunity to succeed regardless of socioeconomic status.

7

Diversity in Rural Communities

A lot of people hold the misconception that rural America is racially and ethnically homogenous—in other words, predominantly white—but that has certainly not been my experience in southern Arizona. Many of the state's rural communities are reflective of their location. The Borderlands region is heavily Hispanic, but there are also ranching families that go back several generations. Tribal lands host some of the most remote communities. There are vast differences between the rural places along the North Rim of the Grand Canyon and Yuma, an agricultural powerhouse on the U.S.–Mexico border. The diversity in the land and its characteristics is reflected in the people who populate rural towns and unincorporated areas. Rural America is increasingly diverse, and not just in my home state. Talking to rural school leaders from across the country reveals astounding differences. The architecture, food, politics, and traditions are all unique and are extensions of people's values, cultures, and beliefs. Rural economies are also diverse—and changing—as some industries such as mining and agriculture slowly fade away and others such as tourism surge. The impacts of the recession and the global pandemic have forced many local mom-and-pop stores out of business while big box stores, potentially located many miles away, take over.

Challenge: Demographic Changes

Rural America is becoming increasingly diverse. According to the Housing Assistance Council's (HAC's) interpretation of 2020 U.S. Census data, three out of four rural residents are white and non-Hispanic, compared with 58 percent for the United States as a whole; this figure represents a decrease of 4.7 percent in the rural white non-Hispanic population over a 10-year period (HAC, 2021). Hispanic and Black rural residents make up 10.4 percent and 7.4 percent of this population, respectively, while Native Americans account for 2 percent in the same dataset. While the overall rural population increased slightly (0.3 percent) from 2010 to 2020, a decline of 4.7 percent in white, non-Hispanic rural residents corresponds with an increase in the racial diversity of rural places (HAC, 2021). Almost one in five of those new rural residents is Hispanic, and those who identify themselves as multiracial increased by 148 percent, accounting for 4 percent of the total rural population. Needless to say, these statistics point to a need for a true understanding of the emerging demographic trends in rural America. The more than 7 percent rise in rural minority students and equivalent decline in the percentage of white, non-Hispanic students is a trend to note.

These diversity trends in rural places across the country are not equally distributed, however. Both geography and culture play a role in creating growth clusters in specific regions or communities. This can lead to racial isolation and even segregation exacerbated by poverty and lack of access to resources. As the hub of the community, the rural school is often a place for those who have been marginalized in some way to turn for assistance and connections. Schools can help with issues of access to college and career opportunities, programs for multilingual learners and gifted students, or benefits for Native American and Indigenous communities. It is incumbent on rural school administrators to enact equitable practices and procedures that can benefit all students.

Solutions for the Resilient Rural Leader

Rural school leaders face unprecedented growth and change in the diversity of their schools, and with these comes the need to monitor and adjust their practices. Leaders are, to borrow an old timber logging term, the "key log" that can free up the way forward to a vibrant and thriving rural school. Addressing the unique needs of all learners in the building not only helps individual students, it also expands to the community as a whole. Let's take a look at some of the areas where you can shift the key log and free up the equity logjam.

Provide Resources for Native American Students

Native American students and their families have rich traditions and deep relationships within their communities. Many also come to school with unique challenges and needs specific to their Tribe or region. Just as rural is not a monolith, neither are Native populations. In fact, in Arizona, there are 22 federally recognized Tribes, each with their own concerns. As a whole, however, Native American students lag behind their peers in a variety of key indicators, including academic proficiency in both math and reading, graduation rates, chronic absenteeism, and postsecondary attainment. The strengths and challenges that face each Tribal community vary across the country, but overall, the cultures' focus on collaboration and intentionality can be leveraged to help Native American students. Following are some practices that can bolster your school's work with Native populations:

- **Tribal language instruction.** Establish a second language program with Tribal certification to instruct both Native and non-Native students in the local language and culture. This type of partnership between the school and the Native community benefits both groups and reflects a commitment to sustaining and preserving threatened cultures. Specific aspects of Native culture and religion may not be fully expressible in the majority language, especially given that oral tradition and storytelling carry a great deal of importance. Offering this type of collaboration also opens the door to other ways to work jointly to support students.
- **Culturally responsive teaching.** Implement culturally responsive pedagogy to ensure that curricular material is relevant to the background your students bring to the classroom. Integrate a culture-based framework into every subject taught.
- **Culturally appropriate programming.** Work with your local Tribal council to host cultural awareness events through the school, both during the school day and as evening activities. Including Native American students in planning and leading these events can be a means of helping them develop pride in their heritage. Many Tribal communities supply cultural awareness professional development for teachers and staff who work with their children so that faculty are prepared to connect with and support their unique needs.
- **Flexible scheduling and instruction.** Identify Native students who are migrant, following a seasonal traditional hunting, fishing, or harvesting calendar during the school year. To reduce the risk of learning loss, create personalized learning plans that incorporate a project-based approach. Connecting the curriculum and standards to the traditional

practices they are participating in gives students the opportunity to expand their learning in a relevant way while engaging in their culture.

- **Assistance with college preparation.** Many colleges and universities have programs that directly target Native American students for pre-graduation support with the college application process, financial assistance, and a variety of other requirements once they are enrolled in a program of study. Reach out to local community colleges to inquire about similar programs. Many Tribal communities desire that their youth get a college degree of some sort and then return to assist their community.
- **Federal funding.** Federal grants are available to help support and address the needs of Native American students in your district. In addition to a variety of local competitive and nonprofit grants, the three formula-based grants described below support rural schools with Native American programs:
  - *The Johnson-O'Malley Act.* Passed in 1934, this federal program is governed by the Bureau of Indian Education and distributed through SEAs to districts to support the academic and medical needs of eligible Native American students from preschool to 12th grade. The district must form an Indian Education Committee to work with the district on a wide variety of issues, including curriculum, programming, personnel employed by the grant, and goal setting. Learn more at www.njoma.com.
  - *Title VI Indian Education Formula Grants program.* These federal dollars from the U.S. Department of Education are used for two types of support: programming for American Indian and Alaska Native students that is culturally and linguistically responsive, and assistance with meeting academic standards. A Parent Advisory Council must be formed to help with grant administration. Typically, schools receive funding on a per-pupil basis in a noncompetitive formula grant. At the end of each grant cycle, grantees must submit an annual assessment of progress to the U.S. Department of Education. Learn more at https://oese.ed.gov/offices/office-of-indian-education/indian-education-formula-grants.
  - *Impact Aid.* While not targeted specifically to Native American students, the Impact Aid grant provides assistance to districts that include federally owned lands or those that have been removed from the tax

rolls (such as Native reservations) to counteract the loss in property tax revenue. The funds can be used for a wide variety of educational expenses, including staff salary and benefits, technology, curricular resources, and tutoring. All monies are distributed directly to the district's bank account. Learn more at https://impactaid.ed.gov/faqs.

Support English Learners (ELs)

One of the biggest concerns of rural leaders across the United States is figuring out how to accommodate the increasing number of students who do not speak English as their primary language. In many rural school communities, the number and diversity of students who do not speak English has increased. Many come from families who are considered migrant workers in agriculture, dairy, and meat packing. The increasing demand for EL proficiency and the Title III requirement to demonstrate that all students are making academic progress can be challenges for rural schools that may not have access to qualified EL teachers. Generalized classroom teachers often lack the experience and training necessary to teach EL classes effectively. Ineffective EL programs can lead to increased student dropout rates, limited workforce opportunities, and difficulty finding a place in the community as a fully participating citizen. In a 2016 survey, data showed that just 62 percent of ELs living in a rural area received some kind of instructional support designed to address their learning needs (Lewis et al., 2016). It is vital that rural schools implement systems and garner resources to assist both teachers and students in addressing the needs of English learners. The following suggestions are good places to start:

- **Build relationships.** Just as you do with other stakeholders, start by building trusting relationships between school staff and the families of EL students. This can be done through open houses, home visits, and school-to-home communication in the families' language. Invest in signage that either uses icons or includes multiple languages. Appoint a parent liaison, either formal or informal, who can reach out to families to provide information and serve as a conduit to the school when there are issues. Because distance to the school and transportation availability can be barriers to this relationship building, consider how to mobilize community assets to help or hold meetings at sites that are easily accessible to the families.

- **Train staff in EL programming.** Professional development for teachers and paraprofessionals who work with ELs is essential for success. Training in sheltered English instruction (SEI)—an approach that integrates English instruction with content instruction—can be arranged through many SEAs and colleges, as well as online. Most trainings include a cultural component that is helpful for incorporating lessons and interventions in the classroom. School administration should also attend training so that they can support the teachers' work. Knowing the qualities of a solid SEI program can help you tailor the programming offered to fit your school's context. For example, EL instruction might take place in students' general education classrooms, or ELs might come together at a designated time for targeted teaching.
- **Establish a mentoring program for staff.** If EL programming is new to your school, consider implementing a collaborative mentoring model in which staff who work with ELs have time to plan, share resources, and reflect with each other to enhance the programs likelihood of success.
- **Partner with other groups.** Typically, there is little funding available to assist with EL programming, and what funding is available can quickly be expended on training and resources. Create consortiums with nearby districts to cut training costs, especially for training that is available online. Also consider what community assets are available to assist with donations of resources and time. Partnering with other community-based organizations that support the families of EL students in other ways can help to ensure a continuum of support.

One specific group of students who will most likely need EL supports are designated as recently arrived immigrant English learners (RAIELs). Some of their families are fleeing conflict or unrest somewhere else in the world. Some students may be traveling unaccompanied or may be considered refugees. Some students may have attended school systems like those in the United States, but many may not have had that type of schooling—or may have had very little schooling altogether. Some may have arrived in the country last month, while others have been here for some time.

Students classified as RAIELs are likely to comprise a diversity of ethnicities that many rural leaders will be unfamiliar with. Cultural differences need to be taken into account, such as dietary needs or approaches to classes like physical education. Pop culture references may not always make sense, and curriculum may need to be adapted to accommodate an unfamiliarity with U.S. historical background. The bottom line is that RAIELs often need not only English language acquisition instruction but also more targeted social-emotional support for an extended period of time (Umansky et al., 2018). Some things to consider when working with RAIELs are highlighted in Figure 7.1. Remember that your school is serving as an ambassador to both the community and the country during these interactions. Providing a welcome that is open and supportive will help ease the newcomers' transition into the community.

As you begin to work with ELs as a rural leader, you should ask two essential questions: *Is the school's commitment to language diversity readily apparent?* and *How are we welcoming EL students and their families?* Do a walkthrough of your facility as if you were a non-English speaker and note what is and is not present. How can families navigate the building? What types of interactions

FIGURE 7.1

Considerations for Accommodating RAIEL Students

Requirement	Considerations
Enrollment paperwork	• Students may have limited or no documentation of previous schooling. • Enrollment forms may need to be modified or translated to get needed information. • Schedule enough time for the enrollment meeting to allow for a potentially time-intensive process.
Grade level/ subject placement	• Students may not be able to be placed in age-assigned grade. • Some pull-out or sheltered settings may be necessary. • Separate programming may be required based on the needs of the individual child (e.g., special education). • There may be competing core needs (e.g., language instruction, social-emotional learning).
Age-out extensions and flexible graduation requirements	• Students may need to attend school longer than their same-aged peers to get the instruction and services they require. • Transcript translation may be required to help with credit allocation. • Testing requirements may need to be adapted. • Supports for undocumented youth may be necessary.
Local policies	• Policies may need to be modified or created to eliminate barriers to accommodation.

might they have with school personnel? Once you know which items need attention, create an action plan to make the campus more supportive of the languages and cultures of your students.

Support Gifted Rural Students

Students who qualify for gifted and talented education (GATE) support in rural schools are often faced with a lack of programs, appropriate coursework, and mentoring opportunities. Some may criticize such services as elitist and claim that they divert resources away from other students, but it's important to recognize that gifted education is not a luxury for these students but a necessity. Providing them appropriate support and opportunities is essential for their academic and personal development. As I often tell my staff, everybody gets what they need, even if what they need looks different, depending on the student.

A smaller school setting is likely to field a smaller number of students who qualify for gifted education, meaning that the students are less able to connect with peers who have similar affinities. Difficulty in engaging a teacher with the pertinent skills and background to teach accelerated materials and curriculum means that rural GATE programs are often anemic. Distance to resources such as museums or cultural event centers further inhibit the ability to extend curriculum for a gifted program. Enrichment activities that typically take place after school or on the weekends, such as LEGO robotics or academic competitions, may be hindered by distance and lack of parent transportation. As with ELs, finding a different approach to providing programming for rural gifted students can mitigate the challenges born from the rural context. Consider the following suggestions:

- **Investigate prepackaged accelerated curriculum.** Most rural teachers have no training or background in gifted education, and those who do may not have enough time to devote to planning in addition to their other responsibilities. Implementing purchased curriculum and assessments will ensure that students get the content they need in a robust and enriching manner. Keep in mind that materials will probably need to be modified to fit your school's context and the needs of the community and the students.
- **Provide targeted professional development.** Offer training to teachers who have little or no background in gifted programs. Many are

available virtually and at low cost. Most states have an organization or association that supports teachers of gifted students that can be a resource. Connect with your SEA to access state-level resources and supports for teachers. To entice teachers into taking on the extra duty of gifted education, offer stipends or other incentives.
- **Use community members as resources.** Reach out to the community to create partnerships with local professionals, asking them to serve as guest speakers, volunteers working with students on specific projects, or mentors.
- **Leverage community assets.** Look to community assets when planning field trips or other fieldwork. A place-based focus on GATE curriculum is as effective as it is for general education. Partner with libraries, medical facilities, health clinics, and other governmental agencies for field experience lessons.
- **Broaden the population**. Because the number of students who qualify for GATE programs may be very small, especially in smaller and remote rural schools, you may need to consider ways to expand the targeted population. One approach is to include students who scored within a range of the cut score, up to the capacity for your program. Another is to collaborate with nearby districts on joint programming. If there are no schools close enough, virtual collaboration might fill the gap.
- **Differentiate instruction.** Train all staff in providing differentiated instruction so that gifted students have regular opportunities to expand their thinking. When gifted programs are incorporated into an advanced or even general curriculum, such teaching methods can benefit all students.

Practice Antiracism

Addressing racism in rural schools and communities requires comprehensive and sustained effort from school leaders, educators, families, and community members. It requires being active in the fight against racism by making "a conscious decision to make frequent, consistent, equitable choices daily" (National Museum of African American History & Culture, n.d., para. 9) and being open to talking about antiracism. These conversations are not easy and should be treated with sensitivity. If appropriate (or necessary), work with a trained facilitator to guide discussions as a neutral party. Following are some fundamental approaches that rural school leaders can take to address racism in their schools and communities:

- **Promote diversity and inclusivity.** Rural leaders can promote diversity and inclusivity by fostering an environment where all students feel welcome and valued. Some ways to achieve this include incorporating diverse perspectives and experiences into the curriculum, celebrating cultural diversity, and organizing schoolwide events that highlight different cultures.
- **Provide cultural competency training.** Schools and teacher preparation programs can provide cultural competency training to teachers, staff, and students to help them understand and appreciate diverse cultures. This training can include professional development on topics such as implicit bias, microaggressions, multicultural education, and culturally responsive teaching.
- **Create a safe and inclusive learning environment.** Ensure a safe and inclusive learning environment by establishing clear policies and procedures that prohibit discrimination, harassment, and bullying. Work with students and families to develop a culture of respect and kindness.
- **Engage in community outreach.** Racism is a community issue, and rural school leaders should engage in community outreach by partnering with local organizations and community members to promote racial equity and social justice. This outreach can include organizing community events, hosting parent-teacher conferences, and collaborating with community leaders to address systemic racial issues.
- **Recruit and retain diverse staff.** While the applicant pool for staffing a rural district may be limited, leaders can recruit and retain a diverse teaching staff by actively seeking out qualified candidates from diverse backgrounds and providing ongoing support and professional development. Diverse staff bring a range of perspectives and experiences to the classroom and can serve as role models and mentors for students from underrepresented backgrounds.
- **Foster student leadership and activism.** Rural school leaders can foster student leadership and activism by providing opportunities for students to engage in social justice issues and advocacy. These can include student-led clubs, service learning projects, and opportunities for students to participate in community-based organizations.

- **Introduce restorative justice practices.** Using restorative justice practices to address issues of racism and discrimination within schools has been shown to be effective at creating a culture of inclusiveness. Restorative justice focuses on repairing harm and building relationships through dialogue and mutual understanding, rather than punishing disciplinary transgressions.
- **Develop and implement an equity plan.** A comprehensive equity plan can help guide a district's efforts to address racism and promote inclusivity. The plan should include specific goals and objectives, along with strategies for achieving those goals. It's important to involve stakeholders, including parents, students, and community members, in the development of the plan to ensure that it reflects the needs and priorities of the community.
- **Address discipline disparities.** Discipline disparities can be a significant barrier to inclusive practices in the school setting. Be intentional about examining and addressing your school's discipline policies, practices, and data. Once you've identified any issues, you can begin the process of removing those barriers.

Here are some examples of successful programming and practices that rural leaders have put in place in their schools:

- The Camas School District in Washington State has implemented a comprehensive diversity plan that includes a focus on recruiting and retaining diverse staff, incorporating diverse curricula and literature, and hosting cultural events and celebrations. These practices have helped to create a more inclusive and welcoming learning environment for all students. Learn more at www.camas.wednet.edu/about-csd/csd-at-a-glance/equity-anti-racism.
- Together We Can Be Bully Free is a comprehensive program started in Union Parish, Louisiana, after a cluster of youth suicides due to bullying. The program is a collaboration among the local hospital, the sheriff's office, and Union Parish School District. Learn more at www.ruralhealthinfo.org/project-examples/950.
- Lame Deer School District in Montana collaborated with the Northern Cheyenne Tribe to develop a culturally responsive curriculum that incorporated Native American history, language, and traditions. The

partnership helped to promote cultural understanding and respect within the school and the larger community. Learn more at https://opi.mt.gov/Educators/Teaching-Learning/Indian-Education-for-All/Indian-Education-Curriculum/bringing-the-story-of-the-cheyenne-people-to-the-children-of-today-grades-1-12.
- Westside Community Schools in Nebraska have implemented a comprehensive equity plan that includes a focus on recruiting and retaining a diverse staff, incorporating diverse literature and curricula, and providing cultural competency trainings for all staff and students. The district has also implemented restorative justice practices to address discipline disparities and promote a culture of respect and empathy. Learn more at www.westside66.org/domain/445.
- An excellent resource for rural leaders to share with their staff is the Human Rights Campaign Foundation's Welcoming Schools website. The site provides lesson plans and activities for both the classroom and the school on a variety of diversity and inclusion topics. Learn more at https://welcomingschools.org.

Implementing the strategies and practices detailed in this chapter can help rural school leaders work toward creating a more inclusive and equitable learning environment that promotes cultural understanding and respect for all students. It is crucial for leaders to regularly assess and evaluate their strategies and practices to ensure that they are effectively addressing racism and promoting equity and inclusion in their schools and communities. There is no one-size-fits-all solution to addressing diversity in rural schools and communities. Each school and community will have unique challenges and opportunities, and it's important to work collaboratively with stakeholders to identify and implement effective strategies.

8

The Death of the Rural Community Center

Closing a school is an extremely emotional undertaking. Community relations were strengthened with those that supported the closure. But with those that did not, those relationships were irrevocably damaged. Even years later, this is still true.

—Arizona superintendent who led a rural school closure in 2008

Odden and Picus (2004) point out that educating the nation's children is an enormous undertaking. In most states, the majority of the governmental budget is dedicated to education expenses. In an era of shrinking public funding, ways to deliver services with maximum cost efficiency are at the forefront of educational discussions. Rural districts have always had to consider options for how best to use their limited resources to accomplish their mission. Unfortunately, one of those options—and one that has had varying degrees of success—is school closure.

School district reorganization, including both closures and consolidations, is not new to American education. In 1931, there were 127,531 school districts across the country; by 1982, the number had dwindled to 15,912—an astounding drop of close to 90 percent (Kliewer, 2001). The number of school sites has also plummeted. The National Center for Education Statistics reports that the longtime trend to close and consolidate schools resulted in a drop from

248,117 public schools in 1930 to 99,239 as of 2022 (NCES, 2022b). This drop occurred during the same time period that the number of students in public schools nearly doubled, which means that the number of students in each school increased dramatically. In the 1930s, the average size of a school was 81 students; in the mid-1990s, that number increased to 473 (Killeen & Sipple, 2000). Although school and district closures had slowed down after the 1970s, the practice seems to be on the upswing due to financial stress and declining student enrollment across the country.

Defining both types of restructuring here will help paint a clearer picture. *School closure* occurs when a school site is shuttered and the students who previously attended the school are reassigned to one or more designated receiving school sites within the same LEA. *School consolidation* takes place when two or more schools are combined into a single school site. Students from the closed school(s) are reassigned to a consolidated school facility.

School closure engenders strong emotions in any community. Schools are seen as a gathering place, a part of the community's identity, and are often the recipients of a great deal of personal investment. Nowhere is this more true than in rural areas. Rural schools are often the hub of the community, the glue that binds people together, and the center of the town's activities, and so losing a school places the community at a disadvantage (Kay, 1982; Lawrence et al., 2002). It's not surprising, therefore, that talk of school closures, reconfigurations, and consolidations is met with heated debate. Nelson (1985) and Gladson (2016) note the following arguments against school closures:

- More bureaucratic red tape
- Less participation in decision making by administrators and staff
- More tension between teachers and students
- Fewer opportunities to bring about change
- More time, effort, and money devoted to discipline
- Less parent-teacher involvement
- Less human contact, producing frustration and alienation and weakening morale of both students and school staff
- Timelines for closure that do not allow for organized efforts to challenge the decision to close

Additionally, research shows that schools with smaller enrollment numbers, which includes most rural schools, are better learning environments for students and staff. Some of the benefits to a smaller school include the following:

- Higher percentage of graduates and more students attaining postsecondary education
- Lower dropout rates
- Less violence, less vandalism, and a greater sense of belonging
- Better attendance rates, higher grade point averages, and more extracurricular participation
- Greater teacher satisfaction and more family involvement (Cotton, 2001)

Challenge: The Impact of Closure or Consolidation on the Local Community

Consolidation of districts and closure of schools is a perennial topic of legislative conversation at the state level, especially in relation to rural and remote school systems. In Arizona, consolidation bills have been proposed in each legislative session for decades. Multiple legislative ad hoc committees, the last in 2011, have been formed to study the potential effects of mandated rural school consolidation. The belief underpinning these consolidations is that larger school systems can be run more efficiently and will therefore be less costly to the state; the ability to create economies of scale would reduce the state's fiscal burden. While this may be true in some limited circumstances, the research shows that this narrow lens fails to capture the myriad other rural concerns and issues at play (Griffith, 2017).

One well-documented rural school consolidation battle in Illinois lasted for 30 years and is the focus of Alan Peshkin's (1982) book *The Imperfect Union*. Peshkin details the outcomes of an ethnographic study he conducted years after the state had mandated consolidation through legislation with House Bill 406 in 1945, forcing rural schools to reorganize. The book concentrates on a district in Page County called Unit 110 in the town of Killmer. At the time of the consolidation push, the district had 682 students and 47 attendance zones. The arguments both for and against the restructuring were the same as those that were being made in other states and ones that are still made today. When the vote on joining Unit 110 took place in 1948, consolidation passed by just one vote. The next hurdle was to determine how to restructure the area's high schools and which campuses the reorganized high schools would be located on. Killmer's school was slated to close. The town reacted by petitioning the state to allow them to open their own district, and the request was denied.

The school eventually reopened, but throughout the 30 years chronicled in his study, the constant upheaval instigated by the consolidation never went away.

Closing a school is socially disruptive. Student relationships with both peers and teachers are significantly affected, which can lead to lower participation rates in extracurricular activities and higher rates of absenteeism. The potential impact on academic performance has been well documented and can affect graduation rates. Adults in the building also see an impact, not only in relation to job loss but also to loss of community ties. Parents are less likely to volunteer and participate in school activities and governance (Flannery, 2023).

Geography of rural school districts should also be a consideration. Relocating students to more remote schools might result in transportation costs that eat into savings produced by consolidation and may outpace it. Additionally, long periods of time spent riding a bus are counterproductive for students' academic outcomes and their families' quality of life (Sadorf, 2013).

Economically, school closures can impact the community in terms of jobs, housing prices, tax rates, and property values. Communities with a school have a more stable population, keep businesses in the area, and have better housing markets (Lyson, 2002). A school is a sign of a healthy community, and especially in rural areas, it serves as a symbol of community control, tradition, autonomy, and identity (Peshkin, 1982). The research on the financial benefits of school closures is conflicting. Some studies have found that there is a cost savings when a school is closed and the district reorganizes. However, the extra funds are often spent on the cost of administration, transportation, or specialized staffing, which can negate the savings. There are also conflicting studies on when economies of scale come into play for a district (Sadorf, 2013).

Solutions for the Resilient Rural Leader

Closing a school is not the only option available to a rural district dealing with budget issues. Creating economies of scale, assigning multiple uses to buildings, and creating shared programming can all lead to cost savings and/or revenue generation. To head off potential restructuring, many rural leaders are being creative about filling gaps to ensure their students have the resources and support they need. However, sometimes it is just not possible to avoid restructuring. In either scenario, there are solutions that can ease the difficult process for students, staff, and the community.

Head Off Closure or Consolidation Through Partnerships and Shared Services

Although they may not be applicable to every district, some of the creative ideas described below have enabled rural leaders to better use their assets and those of their neighbors to shore up efficiencies. While pooling resources is not a new phenomenon, it can lead to some win-win situations and partnerships that support sustainability. By sharing space and assets, the school and the community can create more programming and services for all.

There are several models for these types of partnerships, all focused on fiscal savings (Deloitte, 2011). These partnerships can be either centralized (the decision making is done by a few individuals) or decentralized (the decision making is done by all participating districts). Colocation between the school and another organization is also a concept that has been successfully launched in some areas. This shared use of space makes it possible to maintain facilities that otherwise would not be affordable. Let's take a look at some examples of how partnerships can be advantageous to schools at risk of closure.

Shared administrative personnel. A hallmark of rural school communities is the "many hats" personnel model, where staff responsible for conducting the daily business of running a district combine responsibilities in myriad ways. In Colorado, where almost 85 percent of the districts in the state are classified as rural, approximately 40 districts are led by a dual-role superintendent/principal (DeNisco, 2019). However, shared administration service models to create economies of scale might be a more palatable option.

One model for smaller rural districts to consider is sharing a superintendent or entering into a cooperative leadership model. Not only can this arrangement be a cost-saving measure, but a leader overseeing multiple sites can more easily identify opportunities for collaborating and sharing other resources, such as curriculum or specialized teaching staff. This type of model is best served by an experienced superintendent who knows one of the districts well and has at least an understanding of the other. One such arrangement is in Washington in the GAR-PAL Cooperative Schools. Superintendent/Principal Brett Agenbroad is the superintendent of Garfield SD #302 and currently works with the Palouse SD #301 superintendent to share costs for such items as transportation, middle and high school services, business management, and noncore specialty faculty. He works with both districts and their boards and communities. It's important to note that this arrangement demands strong governing boards of education that understand the co-op model and its requirements of the leader and commit to a team approach for the operation of both districts.

Another administrator who can be shared is the director of special education. Because this position is a highly specialized area, and subsequently hard to fill in rural communities, it can be costly. A shared director who oversees and directs special education personnel at multiple sites can also identify opportunities to share related services such as therapists.

Shared service providers. A food service director is also a good candidate for a shared service agreement. Not only does this help with salary costs for the cooperating districts, it allows for additional cost savings due to the increased purchasing power of multiple districts. It also makes training nutrition workers less costly and can create a substitute pool from which staff can be assigned to multiple locations. Coordinating menu planning across multiple sites is another fiscal advantage to this arrangement.

IT support may cover multiple districts to provide tech support, maintain and upgrade infrastructure, and manage digital platforms. Having a shared central help desk managing these tasks would allow districts to maximize efficiency in terms of both costs and time. San Luis BOCES in Colorado arranged to bring a blended learning model to students in 14 rural districts who did not have access to broadband internet in their homes (Kafer, 2014). This is an excellent model of shared use working effectively. IT is ripe for the exploration of multiple types of partnerships.

Sharing payroll, accounting, and HR services across multiple districts allows for streamlined processes and can eliminate redundancies and create a more efficient business office. Additionally, sharing a procurement specialist not only reduces salary costs, it allows for more opportunities for saving through bulk purchasing.

Especially in the current climate, where employment candidates for transportation are few and far between, sharing transportation services is another cost-saving measure. A single transportation director can oversee the driver pool, provide training, attend to mechanical needs, and create busing routes for multiple districts. Establishing a larger pool of drivers who are already trained and familiar with all possible routes makes it easier to employ substitutes when necessary. Given the number of miles that rural buses typically travel each day, an efficient transportation department is key to a well-run school site.

It is important to note that nearby rural districts are not the only potential partners for shared services. Rural leaders should look to municipalities, local businesses, nonprofits, faith-based organizations, higher education, and community services for possible collaboration. Larger suburban or even urban districts that are close by are also worthy of consideration. At the start of my school year, I had an hourlong bus route with no driver. The high school district that serves my elementary district had a bus that traveled the same route to transport their students. We established a shared transportation agreement to have their driver pick up all students, K–12, in the mornings and drop my students off before heading to the high school. The short-term solution prevented those students from having to endure a much longer double route each day.

The Rural School and Community Trust (2003) recommends a variety of regional approaches to school administration (see Figure 8.1). These shared services can often make more sense to a rural community than a consolidation to meet the needs of the districts involved.

Sharing administrative personnel in a variety of positions and combinations can both save money and assist in the recruitment of necessary staff. The decision tree in Figure 8.2 can help you determine what solution will fill your district's needs. Keep in mind the possibility of burnout when looking at how to structure shared positions. Choosing the right individual and providing them support as needed is key.

No matter what model or agreement rural districts choose to share services, it is important to set schools up for success from the beginning. Articulate a common set of goals and expectations founded on input from the partner districts, identify early on who the lead will be, and determine what policies and regulations need to be taken into account as you get started. Starting small and scaling up can help avoid growing pains!

Professional development. Professional development is a common shared service in rural communities. These days, the availability of online training means there are more opportunities than ever to take advantage of more tailored and individualized professional development to meet the needs of rural educators. Shared services do not even have to be limited to schools in one state but can be a collaboration across multiple states. This is also true of peer networks of support. Here are some examples of professional development providers that meet the needs of rural communities.

- The Tucson Regional Educator Collaborative is a partnership between districts in three counties, the University of Arizona, several community

FIGURE 8.1

Regional Approaches to School Administration

Type of Unit	Governance	Membership Basis	Services Provided	Taxing Authority
Cooperative superintendency	Cooperative agreement entered into by two or more local districts	Voluntary	Joint hiring of superintendent serving all local districts; other administrative services as determined by agreement	None
Regional educational service agency	Nonprofit organization, interlocal government agency, or quasi-public corporation	Voluntary, but may be restricted to local districts within a defined service area	Any as mutually agreed, including advertising for staff vacancies, maintaining personnel files, coordinating professional development, fiscal management services, special education administration, grant writing, technology support, group purchasing of supplies (especially technology), employment services, maintaining substitute lists, letting unified bids for transportation, food services, and heating fuel, curriculum development, teacher contract negotiation	Usually none
Educational service districts	Public agency, usually subdivision of the state	Usually mandated by statute	Any authorized by law, including advertising for vacancies, maintaining personnel files, coordinating professional development, fiscal management, special education administration, grant writing, technology support, group purchasing (especially technology), employment services, maintaining substitute lists, letting unified bids for transportation, food services, and heating fuel, curriculum development, teacher contract negotiation	May have authority as provided by law
Regional supervisory district	Public officials either elected by voters or boards of member districts	Voluntary or mandatory, as provided by law	Joint superintendency, fiscal agency, including LEA status under federal law; may provide any of the services a local district provides	

Source: The Rural School and Community Trust, 2003. Used with permission.

FIGURE 8.2
Shared Services Decision Tree

```
                    Can the function
                      be shared?
             ┌────────────┴────────────┐
            Yes                        No
             │                          │
      What is the best          If not, what
      sharing structure?        vendors exist?
        ┌────┴────┐                     │
Cooperative:    Integrated:         Examine outsourcing
shared          education           efficiencies
superintendent, service agencies
cluster         (local, regional,
districts       state)
```

Source: Adapted from Deloitte, 2011.

colleges, and local business partners. The center focuses on providing professional development that fills the gap for smaller and rural schools that don't have the resources to hire high-quality consultants. Learn more at https://trecarizona.org.

- The Eastern Shore of Maryland Educational Consortium provides nine districts with shared services in operational effectiveness, professional development, and collective advocacy. Economies of scale have allowed the group to provide low-cost medical insurance to some members, occupational and speech services, and better rates for electricity. They also host an annual conference for leadership and teachers. Most recently, the consortium created an online library of curriculum resources to help teachers share lesson plans and ideas with each other across districts. Learn more at www.esmec.org.
- Since 2010, the Ohio Appalachian Collaborative has served 27 school districts in a cooperative model. Member districts share instructional and curricular resources and participate in online professional learning communities. Their group puts a strong emphasis on preparing students for college as an economic development strategy, a goal stemming from the low number of college graduates in the area. Learn more at https://battelleforkids.org/docs/default-source/publications/rec-case-studyoacfinal.pdf.

Voices from the Field:
Innovative Schools Cohort Shared Resource Model

In the state of Oklahoma, we have over 500 independent school districts. The state does not have any regional educational centers. The state department of education, located in Oklahoma City, is responsible for all corners of the state. Statewide nonprofits focused on one sector of the education system help schools with their day-to-day operations. One such organization is the Oklahoma Public School Resource Center (OPSRC). OPSRC is a membership organization that joins at the district level. OPSRC has services and programs to help employees and school board members within the districts. The five main domains for help and consultation are finance, technology, communications, legal, and teaching and learning.

In the teaching and learning area, schools can get several forms of professional development, such as state-mandated training, school board member training, principal evaluation training, or in-person training requested by the district. All of this training is included in the district's membership price for joining or renewing each year, so no matter how much training a district gets either at individual schools or as a district, there is no additional cost.

On top of this professional development training, OPSRC has a program they call the Innovative Schools Cohort. In this program, school districts create design teams of two to six people. The cohort meets for four in-person days, coming together to learn about future trends in education, network, learn about change management, and name a local innovation or change they would like to implement. The OPSRC staff leads these meetings. It allows for local district teams to collaborate around an idea and also network with other school districts from all corners of the state. Occasionally, the staff will bring in outside experts and innovators for the Innovative Schools Cohort districts to learn from.

In addition to the four days during the school year that districts come together, the OPSRC Innovative Schools Cohort team travels to the individual districts in the cohort to talk specifically about what innovation or change a district would like to implement that they feel would drive student achievement. During the meeting, the staff coaches the districts through implementation strategies, available resources, and organizational culture needs to make a successful change.

A membership with an organization like the OPSRC is a great example of using a shared resource. Members of the OPSRC are stretching their local dollars to get consultation and professional services at a cheaper rate than a district going out on their own for an individual service a district needs. By networking with other districts during OPSRC events like the Innovative Schools Cohort, district leaders are able to collaborate with other leaders who can help them better manage their own local districts.

—Jason Midkiff, director of learning and product development, Oklahoma Public School Resource Center

Special education services. Because of the itinerant nature of many related service providers working with students with individualized education plans, services for special education are an easy place to start a shared use model. Not only are the costs of related services hard for a rural district to absorb, the difficulty in finding a provider for these services can also be a challenge. Additionally, there are changing needs in the student population from year to year as caseloads and student goals change. A specialist may work with several schools over the course of the year, both in-person and virtually.

One example of shared special education services is the Navajo County Special Services Consortium, which serves students across the counties of Apache and Navajo in Arizona. The consortium employs a variety of specialists including occupational therapists, physical therapists, speech-language pathologists, and school psychologists. Learn more at https://navajocountyaz.gov/434/Special-Services-Consortium.

Another example of a shared services model is the Southeast Regional Resource Center in Alaska, established in 1981 by the Alaska state legislature, which serves the state's 53 largely rural school districts. The center provides a variety of services for districts, including operational support and facilities. The contracted services provided for special education focus on being culturally responsive to the unique needs of the students across the state. Additionally, the center offers professional development and administrative support. Learn more at https://serrc.org/special-education-services.

In Ohio, the special education department in Jefferson County Educational Service Center provides services to all of the school districts in a three-county area. Both direct and indirect services are offered through a variety of specialists. Also provided are services for early childhood and gifted education and professional development for district staff. Learn more at www.jcesc.k12.oh.us/SpecialEducation.aspx.

Infrastructure. Rural leaders often struggle to find cost-effective ways to manage budgets around the infrastructure of the schools they serve. Day-to-day operations to consider for partnerships include transportation, food service, technology, and purchasing. Administrative management of these areas has been previously discussed, but beyond personnel factors, sharing services offers other ways to create economies of scale, reduce redundancy, and standardize procedures and practices.

Voices from the Field: Shared Services Benefit All of Us

The definition of a rural school district has become as vast as the miles between our attendance boundaries. Whether by county or district or state, the lines determine the attendance of our students but not the cooperation and collaboration needed to address their every need.

I joined Laramie County School District 1 in Cheyenne, Wyoming, in 2021. Although it is the largest school district in the state, it is considered rural by general standards. When you live rural, you must plan ahead about something even as simple as borrowing a cup of sugar. Knowing your neighbors, their skills, and their availability is key to the success of a great community.

With this in mind, we have built capacity to leverage our assets and liabilities to better impact the system for students across the state. Some examples of this include sharing partnerships in a variety of areas. Our district's transportation department has the largest towing equipment in the region, so we are often asked to help tow buses, extract vehicles, and clear roads with the state department of transportation and neighboring districts. In return, many partner districts will transport our students within a region outside of ours when students are at regional or statewide competitions, including sports, clubs, and other activities. We provide our students with a safety net that includes transportation assistance so they can get to after-school care. Our food service team helps store bulk food and supports deliveries throughout the region. Collectively, our communities share facilities. Often, the schools are the only community recreation locations, and our districts work hard to provide shared spaces. Additionally, we share information regarding risk pool, insurance, and other contracts.

Often in rural communities, because of low population density, most people know each other personally. Due to the relationships, there are often conflicts of interest in the area of investigations with human resources and Title IX processes. We have developed a network of support for investigations, training, and decisions. This leads to other collaborations, including mentoring, coaching, sharing staff, and crisis support.

Sharing staff has been an incredible asset. When a specialized content area becomes difficult to staff, districts work together to share contracts and resources to best serve students. This is often seen in the areas of special education and career and technical education. Another area where staff sharing has been incredibly beneficial is the additional support when a crisis arises. In small, rural communities, when staff and students are so closely connected, the impact of a tragedy ripples through the entire community. By sending counselors and other support personnel, we can ease the pain and allow for healthier grieving and healing for all involved. As a collaboration, we are working on shared grant opportunities to help leverage funding across organizations. We have launched a major community-wide initiative engaging partners to provide a common language and support system for students and adults dealing with difficult situations.

Professional learning opportunities are an important facet for any business or organization. In education, since we are preparing our students for the future and for jobs that may not exist yet, that professional development allows our teachers and staff to keep up with the latest trends and developments so that we can provide our students with a 21st century learning experience. Because of our state's rural nature, we often work closely with other districts to provide shared training and conference opportunities. Not only are the teachers better able to collaborate with others in similar content or grade-level areas, we also are able to provide more cost savings and efficient large-scale learning for our region and state.

Our technology and finance departments have become a resource for districts both within and outside our state, as both of our directors are experts in their respective fields. We are always willing to share these resources for the benefit of students throughout our state. Our leaders also attend and host a variety of conferences throughout the state.

As a rural community, we have worked together to leverage our assets and build our systems to best benefit our students. We are so fortunate to come together in these ways to impact our future.

—Margaret Crespo, superintendent,
Laramie County School District 1, Wyoming

School-based health centers. A report from the American Hospital Association (2022) notes that 136 rural hospitals were closed between 2010 and 2021 across the country. These closures have a big impact on rural families. Creating a school-based health clinic can help high-risk children and their families who face barriers to care. Especially in remote and frontier communities, where medical services may be hours away and difficult to get to, locating a health clinic on a rural school campus is one of the best ways to meet the unique needs of the community. It allows providers to offer a broader range of medical care, improves care coordination services, and offers more convenient care options.

The center can provide a wide variety of basic health services, such as immunizations, health screenings, health education, and even primary care. Dental care, vision and hearing screenings, behavioral health services and even reproductive health services are also possible. With creative planning, a school-based health clinic can even provide spaces to host medical specialists from out of town on a regular basis.

In 2022, the U.S. Department of Health and Human Services (HHS) awarded $25 million to fund the creation of school-based health centers. The majority of funding recipients are located in rural communities (HHS, 2022). To access information about applying for funding to build a center, visit the Health Resources & Services Administration website at https://bphc.hrsa.gov/funding/funding-opportunities/school-based-service-expansion.

The Whole School, Whole Community, Whole Child model is an initiative by the Centers for Disease Control and Prevention (CDC) comprising eight key components, including health services. School leaders can access the CDC's School Health Index tool to perform a needs assessment for their district as well as an evaluation of the school's capacity to offer center services at www.cdc.gov/healthyschools/shi/index.htm.

Key questions to answer before implementing a school-based health center include the following:

- What are the vision and goals for programming?
- What financial resources are available, both short- and long-term?
- Which community partners can collaborate with the school team?
- What policies prescribed by the governing board or other entities need to be considered?

- How will privacy and confidentiality issues (e.g., FERPA, HIPAA compliance) be handled?
- What services will be provided and by whom?
- How will the center be evaluated for effectiveness?

Following are descriptions of just a few of the many rural communities that have launched successful school-based health service programs:

- The Kentucky Family Resource and Youth Services Centers are a network of centers that are adapted to meet the needs of local students and their families. The centers provide a wide range of services to address social and health-related barriers to learning. Learn more at https://chfs.ky.gov/agencies/dfrcvs/dfrysc.
- In Arizona, the Santa Cruz Adolescent Wellness Network focuses on students in K–12 as well as professional development for school leaders and teachers in their rural U.S.–Mexico border area. Learn more at www.adolescentwellness.net.
- In western North Carolina, where both staffing and transportation are persistent challenges, the Health-E-Schools program brings telehealth service to schools. Learn more at www.health-e-schools.com.
- In Louisiana, three rural parishes benefit from Arbor Family Health clinics, which provide a wide range of health services, including medical, dental, and behavioral. Learn more at www.arborfamilyhealth.org/school-clinics.

Open Rural School Facilities to Joint Use

The library. Many rural communities may not have a public library. In those that do, joining forces to provide services might make sense for the school and the community, as it creates a resource-sharing opportunity to help with staff, space, and equipment—as well as grant dollars—and encourages wider use by the community at large. Sharing facilities with the community library may also allow for enhanced services, less redundancy, greater security, more hours of operation, and increased opportunity to partner with other organizations. Some organizations that might be considered to inhabit a joint use library on a school campus include the following:

- Community centers
- Higher education space
- Rural fire or police station
- Community health center
- State emergency services center
- Early childhood center
- Post office
- Local history organization or museum
- Veterans Affairs office
- Tourism office
- Senior center

Social service agencies. Because the rural school is more often than not the hub of the community, it's a fitting location for providing wraparound services for students and their families. Co-located and joint use space on the school campus can host a variety of social service agencies. When putting any such an arrangement in place, be sure to establish a clearly defined set of expectations. These should address areas like facility maintenance, staffing, parking, access limits and security, custodial service, and emergency protocols and procedures.

Moving Forward in a Closure or Consolidation

If a closure or consolidation is unavoidable, steps can be taken to ensure the process is intentional, well planned, and communicated to the public in a way that maintains the community relationships that are so important. The Rural School and Community Trust (2006) created a set of 10 standards that can serve as guideposts for states or regions considering a consolidation or closure. To confirm that any consolidation plan is necessary and advisable, rural leaders should ensure that the plan meets the following standards:

- Maintains and improves small schools, making them more cost-effective.
- Provides sufficient funding for each school to meet program and outcome standards as defined by the state and to provide each child with an equal opportunity to achieve.
- Retains or places schools within communities and avoids placing them in isolated open country.

- Provides maximum participation in school governance by communities served by the school and the school district and requires community approval of school closings.
- Honors and reinforces a policy of racial desegregation.
- Makes best use of appropriate distance learning technologies to share students and faculty, enriching curriculum and instruction without enlarging schools or transporting students.
- Reduces disparity between districts in local tax capacity and effort.
- Protects children from bus rides exceeding 30 minutes each way for elementary students and one hour each way for high school students.
- Maximizes regional cooperation between districts, such as regional education service centers, to provide high-cost, low-demand services efficiently to schools and/or students who require them.
- Strengthens local economic and community development and supports and is supported by community patterns of work and commerce. (Rural School and Community Trust, 2006)

Real Life Lessons from a School Closure

I was a principal of a grades 6–8 middle school in Sierra Vista, Arizona, when my superintendent advised the governing board that the economically responsible way to address the fiscal cliff that was looming due to declining enrollment and increased business cost was to make changes to the structure of the district's schools. I was told in December 2009 that my current site would be closed. All 7th and 8th grade students would move to the district's other middle school site, and all elementary schools would change from serving grades K–5 to K–6. Timeline for completion? July 2010! The other middle school principal would move to an elementary site, and I would take over the newly formulated middle school as principal. To say the next six months were hectic is an understatement.

Based on my experience, and that of others in the same circumstance, here are some of the things I encourage you to consider if you are ever in this position. This list is not inclusive! Depending on your rural school communities, you may find that you have unique variables that need to be addressed. No matter the plan, though, transparency and ongoing communication are key.

A communication plan. Be sure to communicate with all stakeholders as early as possible and in a way that builds trust with the affected communities. Use forthright language with consistent messaging, no matter who is speaking. Keep communications limited to the topic of the closure for maximum clarity, and deliver the message with empathy.

A single spokesperson (most of the time). As with all good communication plans, having a single spokesperson deliver big or controversial messages is best practice. Ideally, the superintendent should serve as the face of the district. However, it is also important that leadership from all affected sites communicate as a consistent, united front. When announcing our closure and restructuring, my principal colleague and I addressed our staffs jointly so that everyone heard the same message.

FAQs and talking points. The finer details, along with the reasons behind the decision to move forward with a closure or consolidation, should be readily available to the public. As new action steps are taken, incorporate both anticipated and realized outcomes into the document. Closing a school is very disruptive to the plans, routines, and expectations of the families involved. Be sure they have the facts, time to weigh in, and support to plan for the new way of doing things.

Regular meetings with all community stakeholder groups, both collectively and individually. Meetings, which include public hearings by the governing board and superintendent, are vital to a successful process. As soon as the decision is being considered, involve the public and allow for their input to present a more transparent process throughout. Public meetings may even expose potential solutions that could prevent the consolidation process from moving forward. Providing the space for anger, sadness, grief, and fear—and dealing with each concern as it is shared—will go a long way to preserving the social fabric of the community. Consider facilitating listening sessions as a way to gain insights into stakeholder concerns and ideas for handling the transition skillfully. Don't rush this process! A period of three to six months is a minimum for collecting input from the community and establishing trust. It also gives the district an opportunity to share the fine points of why the closure is necessary.

The most current information located in multiple venues. Social media, school websites, the district website, blogs, email blasts, and newsletters are all ways to widely disseminate information. Ensure that all messaging and information is consistent.

Parent input opportunities. Parents will respond to news of the restructuring of the school community in a variety of ways, some for and some against. There may be no way to avoid all the negative responses from parents, but to the extent possible, the parents should be given a voice in the process. These are their children! Events that bring parents from affected schools together, such as open houses or volunteer campus beautification projects, will help establish goodwill and may alleviate concerns. They may also lay the groundwork for future involvement and volunteering efforts after the transition has been completed. Creating an outlet for hard feelings may help channel those concerns into forming a new combined parent group. This is just part of the reason parent input opportunities are important.

Student involvement opportunities. Involving students in the closure and consolidation process is essential to preparing families for the transition. Consider establishing student teams at each site that can collaborate with both sites' staff and student bodies. This also ensures that students are getting the same information on both campuses. Social interaction activities will help students form new friendships. Consider having teachers create and teach lessons that span multiple campuses. Start an intramural sport and put on academic events made of mixed-school student teams. Provide tours of future classrooms to alleviate student fears about the unknown. Take photos of the activities and share them through social media as a way to build excitement about the transition. Be sure to also let students know about the activities that the adults are doing to keep them engaged in the overall process.

Tapping into staff strengths. The formation of "transition teams" for staff members from affected sites is a way to ensure not only input opportunities but also the space to leverage staff in a different way. One of the members of the transition team members that I formed during my school closure had previously served in the military as a logistical specialist. I was able to put her in charge of moving all teacher classroom belongings and tracking them for relocation to their new rooms on the various campuses. Her recordkeeping and supervision of what needed to go where was invaluable. Without that transition team in place, the task would have fallen to me—and it would not have been nearly as successful. In fact, the need for coordination wouldn't have been on my radar at all if she had not brought it up to the group! As with students, having a venue to deliver consistent messaging and information to affected staff is vital to keeping trust and ensuring one group does not feel like they are not "in the know" about decisions being made.

Establish an archive. Restructuring, closure, and consolidation are the death of the old and the birth of something new. Old traditions may be laid aside for new ones, or things may be joined together to form something that combines the best of both schools. When my school closed and began the process of transitioning to new locations, we invited student input on things like school colors (students voted on two new colors, different from either previous school), the mascot (we brought the vacated school's mascot over and retired the receiving school's mascot), and the motto (newly combined staff created a new one together). But the history of both schools needs to be preserved. Be sure to archive photos, yearbooks, newspaper clippings, and other objects from both schools, as well as keep a collection of artifacts generated during the transition itself. Telling the story of the restructuring process helps to put the "new" combined school in context. As a part of the transition process, be sure to have a closing ceremony for the staff, students, and community. We held a ceremony for the community that was planned by teachers and students and even buried a time capsule in the courtyard. We'll see if anyone remembers where it is located in 50 years!

Dos and Don'ts of Rural School Closure or Consolidation

The area of focus for my dissertation, written in 2012–2013, was the impact that school closures in Arizona over a 12-year period had on both the fiscal health of the district and the relationship between the district and the surrounding community. Most of these closures were in rural areas. As part of my research, I talked to the superintendents who led 21 of those 34 closures from beginning to end and beyond. I wanted to gain some insights from them on whether they perceived those closures to be effective. How were relationships with stakeholders and staff affected? Was the fiscal impact what was anticipated? What effects did closure have on the governing boards of those communities? Was there any way to do a closure "right"? Figure 8.3 summarizes the key takeaways from that research.

Developing a Plan

As you begin the difficult process of closing a school or consolidating with another district, you will need to find and study available research, and lean into what other leaders have done that was effective. Keep in mind the dos and don'ts of school closures, and be sure to involve as many stakeholders as possible in the process from the outset. Remember that your role will often be one of coordinator and student advocate throughout community discussions and actions.

FIGURE 8.3

Dos and Don'ts of School Closures

Do	Don't
• Know that it will be, and should be, a long process.	• Expect quick results.
• Ensure full transparency with all stakeholders throughout the process.	• Underestimate the power of providing details and opportunities for communication.
• Be strategic in how the school being closed is selected.	• Ignore the potential controversy surrounding the selection of the building that will close.
• Allow for the voice of all stakeholders through multiple venues and opportunities.	• Fail to anticipate the impact on housing and businesses located near what may become an empty building.
• Take time to develop trust with the community.	• Forget that citizens expect local government agencies to operate efficiently.
• Be clear on anticipated and realized fiscal budget impacts of closure, both before and after.	• Fail to allow that closure in and of itself is only a portion of most fiscal savings plans, and that closures cost money, too.
• Ensure governing board members have all the necessary information to make effective decisions.	• Forget to allow that some board members may view this as cause to be unsupportive of district leadership.
• Keep students at the center of all discussions and decisions.	• Overpromise and underdeliver.
• Involve a professional demographer to collect necessary data and guide closure discussions.	• Let others tell the story without your input.
• Have a plan of action for the vacated building, whether mothballed or repurposed.	• Overlook the financial impact of a closure on surrounding property values.
• Have a clearly defined plan for where staff members, including the site principal, will be placed.	• Fail to gather input from staff on preferred placement and assigned roles.
• Consider what other cost-saving measures can be put in place to shore up savings.	• Ignore the importance of clearly defining what was implemented to stave off closure before it occurred.

Following is a collection of resources available to rural leaders that can serve as a guide or framework for your own work:

- *Closing a School Best Practices Guide.* This tool from the California Department of Education (2023) breaks the process into five large chunks: (1) gathering the facts, (2) deciding which school(s) to close, (3) making the decision, (4) making the transition, and (5) disposing of school property. While many aspects are California-specific, the guide discusses many useful topics, such as who to involve and what data to use in the decision-making process, and methods of communication that can be leveraged depending on the message going out. It also includes a timeline tool for major action items to consider. Learn more at www.cde.ca.gov/ls/fa/sf/schoolclose.asp.
- *School Closure Guide: Closing Schools as a Means for Addressing Budgetary Challenges.* This guide for school districts considering school closures to address budget shortfalls is produced by The Broad Foundation (2009). While the frameworks, timelines, and recommendations are based on closures in 10 urban school districts, many of the ideas and tools can be used or repurposed for a rural school context. The main points of the guide focus on whether to close and which school or schools to select, stakeholder communication, and how to carry out the closure. Of special interest are the appendices, which include a sample closure plan template, some pitfalls to be aware of, parent letter templates, guides for reassigning students, and suggestions for working with teacher unions during a closure event. Learn more at https://failingschools.files.wordpress.com/2011/01/school-closure-guide1.pdf.
- *Closing a School Building: A Systematic Approach.* This National Clearinghouse for Educational Facilities guide (McMilin, 2010) features a timeline and responsibility template document that includes the closure process as well as options for what to do with the building after closure. Repurposing ideas and a preventative maintenance plan for a mothballed building are provided. Learn more at https://files.eric.ed.gov/fulltext/ED512699.pdf.
- *School Redesign Models: A Guide to School Closure and Consolidation.* This document from the Texas Education Agency (n.d.) provides a case study to consider, guiding questions to walk through the process of a closure or consolidation event, and some general resources that might

be helpful. Much of the information is appropriate to rural contexts without adaptations. Learn more at https://tea.texas.gov/sites/default/files/School%20Redesign%20Model_Close%20Consolidate.pdf.

Given that many policymakers and influencers believe larger school systems can be run more efficiently and would therefore be less costly, school closures and consolidations are unavoidable topics of conversation in many rural communities. However, myriad other rural concerns and issues come into play. The loss of local control, the impact of geography, and the actual fiscal impact are all things to evaluate when discussing the possibility of shuttering a rural school. Rural communities lean heavily on their schools to provide a variety of services, resources, and even entertainment. A closure has a profound effect on the people and places involved, and care must be taken to help them through the process for a successful outcome for all.

9

Leaning into Rural Strengths

When talking about rural communities and their challenges, inevitably the notion of "brain drain" arises. The out-migration of young adults in their 20s and early 30s leaving to attend college, relocating for a job, or trying out urban living occurs from many rural places. Whether young adults stay because they feel trapped by circumstances or leave because they feel pushed out, brain drain in a rural community is a reality. The bottom line is that when this population leaves, they take both economic and intellectual potential with them. This out-migration is more likely to occur in rural places than in urban locales (Boethel, 2000). While some young people who left for education, employment, or social opportunities end up returning, most do not (Johnson & O'Hare, 2004).

However, one interesting trend noted in the last decade by rural sociologist Ben Winchester of the University of Minnesota Extension is that adults in their 30s and 40s are moving *to* rural communities (Peters, 2012). In his keynote address at the Arizona Rural Schools Association annual conference in 2022, Winchester noted that newcomers to rural areas are drawn not for jobs but rather by the simpler pace of life, the feeling of safety and security, and the lower costs of housing. Many of these young families have moved for work, sometimes telecommuting, and many have lived in rural places before. And these new arrivals to the rural areas have high levels of education, earning power, and experience—leading to a "brain gain" for the area (Peters, 2012). Importantly for rural schools, these newcomers often have children, resulting in an increase in rural school enrollment (Winchester, 2018).

As mentioned throughout the book, while rural schools face a variety of challenges that have required some innovative solutions, there are also many assets that can be leaned into in rural settings. Those unique strengths can be the reason many choose to live in and stay in their rural communities. The resilient and resourceful rural leader can and should take advantage of all of the assets available to them—which first means knowing what they are.

Solutions for the Resilient Rural Leader

There are many ways to identify and then leverage the strengths of a rural community. With family histories that can go back generations and strong ties to the land and to each other, there is a sense of investment that typically isn't felt quite as strongly in urban and suburban communities. That connection to the local community is something that the rural leader can use to secure needed assets for helping students succeed both during their school years and after graduation. You can tap into these assets to create programs, design new ways for the school to function alongside the local community, or invite different stakeholder groups to interact with the school and the students.

Conduct a Comprehensive Needs Assessment

Any plan, budget, or initiative that depends on the local community and its resources must first be grounded in the district's needs. Rural leaders should start by conducting a needs assessment to understand how the community stands in relation to the desired goal. Do students need a fine arts program? Are there concerns over the ability of the district to attract new staff to the area? Do outdated curriculum and assessments need to be replaced? No matter the issue being considered, a thorough understanding of it will help determine root causes and set priorities for future action. Many rural leaders of districts that receive federal Title grant funding are familiar with the process, as it is required each year for continued allocations. You can use the same framework when looking at a larger-scale community plan and deciding how to apply local assets.

All needs assessments are composed of two components. The first is a data analysis to identify trends and patterns over the course of several years. The second is an analysis of the root cause(s) of the outcomes seen in the data, especially when they indicate negative trends.

Most needs assessment frameworks of use to rural leaders are based on student academic and other data. Figure 9.1 lays out the five phases of a successful process. Each phase consists of actions to carry out before moving on to the next. Figure 9.2 offers examples of actions to take and critical questions to ask.

FIGURE 9.1

The Five Phases of a Needs Assessment

Plan → Collect and organize data → Analyze and interpret data → Establish priorities → Create action plan

FIGURE 9.2

Actions for Needs Assessment Phases

Phase	Actions	Critical Questions
Plan	• Define the need and desired outcome • Establish relevant actions, timeline • Identify stakeholders	• What impact do we seek? • What is the focus of the needs assessment? • Who needs to be involved, when, and to what extent? • What data will be collected and in what way?
Collect and organize data	• Collect data from multiple sources • Establish tools for collection • Determine how data will be presented	• What data already exists that can be curated? • What is the best method for gathering needed data? • How will data be presented?
Analyze and interpret data	• Look for patterns and revelations in collected data; disaggregation may be required • Use facilitator to help analyze data • Train stakeholders in disaggregation of data	• What do the individual and collective data show? What themes emerge? • Where are there differing perspectives on what the data show? • How can the results be presented to the larger community?
Establish priorities	• Note themes or trends as possible priorities • Determine if needs align with the local context • Set the number of priorities that can realistically be addressed	• What priority will have the greatest impact on need if addressed? • Will or should there be more than one priority? • What other needed data are missing?
Create action plan	• Create action steps for each priority • Identify root causes • Select interventions for action	• What are the anticipated changes of the priority intervention? • Is further data collection required? • How often will data be collected and reviewed during implementation?

Perform Personal Asset Mapping

Examining why individuals choose to live in a rural place can be a good starting point for promoting a specific school district in the area. People who are considering moving to a rural area are looking at what the community can offer on multiple fronts, such as food, shopping, entertainment, social connections, proximity to urban resources, and available jobs. Winchester (2018) notes that what people do for work and how they spend their leisure time are no longer as tied together as they once were. In fact, rural residents are much more willing to drive or otherwise commute to shop and play while living in their rural area. The idea that a rural town doesn't have to provide everything to be attractive to potential and current residents is something to note for recruitment and retention efforts, as well as for workforce development efforts.

To conduct your own personal asset mapping survey, locate a map of the area where you live and follow the instructions in Figure 9.3. (This could also be a joint faculty activity.) Personal asset mapping highlights that it's the area at large that matters to rural residents, not just the town itself. A comparison done by age range may reveal that the definition of desirable asset isn't universal for all residents. The distances rural residents are willing to travel may also vary with age.

FIGURE 9.3

Personal Asset Mapping Activity

★	Place a star where your home is located.
✕	Place an X where you work and one where your significant other works, if applicable.
○	Draw a circle around how far from home you go to shop and eat.
▢	Draw a square to capture how far you go from home for entertainment or recreation.
	Note your age range (20s, 30s, 40s, 50s, etc.).
	List three favorite assets within the boundaries you created (places, events, gatherings, etc.).

Knowing what assets are available both in the immediate area and beyond can help you tap into the ones that can make a difference in student success. It can also be used when putting together a marketing campaign specific to an age group that the district is trying to attract. Understanding what can "sell" the local area is important information for rural leaders to have. In a statewide initiative called the Michigan Cool Cities Survey, new and potential residents were surveyed about what assets would draw them to a rural area (Andresen, 2008). The top 10 "ideal" factors were not surprising:

1. Scenic beauty
2. Safe streets
3. Affordable
4. Place to raise family
5. Good schools
6. Sense of community
7. Low traffic
8. Concern for environment
9. Close to friends/family
10. Walkable streets

Consider the "ideal" personal assets within your school community and apply them not only to promoting the district but also to developing unique curriculum.

Conduct Community Asset Mapping

Most of the solutions presented throughout this book start with knowing what people and resources are located within the community. Community asset mapping (CAM) is a systematic approach to identifying all possible assets in the area. These can be businesses, faith-based organizations, civic organizations, individuals, and even the school itself. Anything that can improve the quality of life within the rural community can and should be considered an asset. Here is a listing of typical rural assets:

- School/district facilities, vehicles, technical capabilities, personnel
- Abilities and capacity of individual community members
- Faith-based facilities, members
- Civic assets such as libraries, municipal buildings, law enforcement capacity, common use sites like community centers, employees of the local government
- Health centers (hospitals, clinics, mobile units), medical personnel who work within and with the community
- Citizen associations such as parent-teacher organizations
- Service organizations such as 4-H, Future Farmers of America, veterans groups
- Local businesses/employers

The process for conducting CAM is both standard and simple. While you may want to customize the process to fit your context, you should include the following basic steps:

1. **Determine geographic boundaries for the "community."** What towns, regions, or neighborhoods will be included? Does the community cover specific places such as land grants, leased or preserved lands, or federal properties? Involve stakeholders and those that live within and outside the proposed area in the determination.
2. **Identify stakeholders to be included in the mapping process.** Invite participation from a diverse grouping of community members to connect with the networks, historical context, and community knowledge needed. How many people to include depends on the size of your area and the interest and availability of potential stakeholders. While there is no ideal number, be certain your group is comprehensive enough to identify all possible assets.
3. **Set parameters for asset determination.** What assets will be investigated for inclusion on the map? Setting expectations at the start of the mapping process helps to focus time and effort on the right work. The need being considered should be the foundation for this focus. For example, if the identified need is creating and launching a mentoring program for teenagers in your rural area, then consider assets targeted toward making the program possible. Be certain to connect the need to the identified assets by asking, "How would this possible asset help meet the need for a mentoring program?" If it doesn't support that effort, it should not be included in the CAM process.
4. **Compile a list of all assets located within the identified geographical area.** This list can be compiled by the mapping group or through the use of other resources such as directories, published membership lists for organizations, local news media including newspapers, community social groups, or recreational facilities. The compilation should include the location of the organization, contact information (including a point of contact), websites or social media links, types of services available, and assets (people, expertise, facilities) that can contribute to meeting the identified need (see Figure 9.4 for an example). Alternatively, the group could choose to identify individuals rather than groups. While the information being created is the same, keep in mind that there are more individuals in a rural community than there

FIGURE 9.4

Example of a Community Asset List

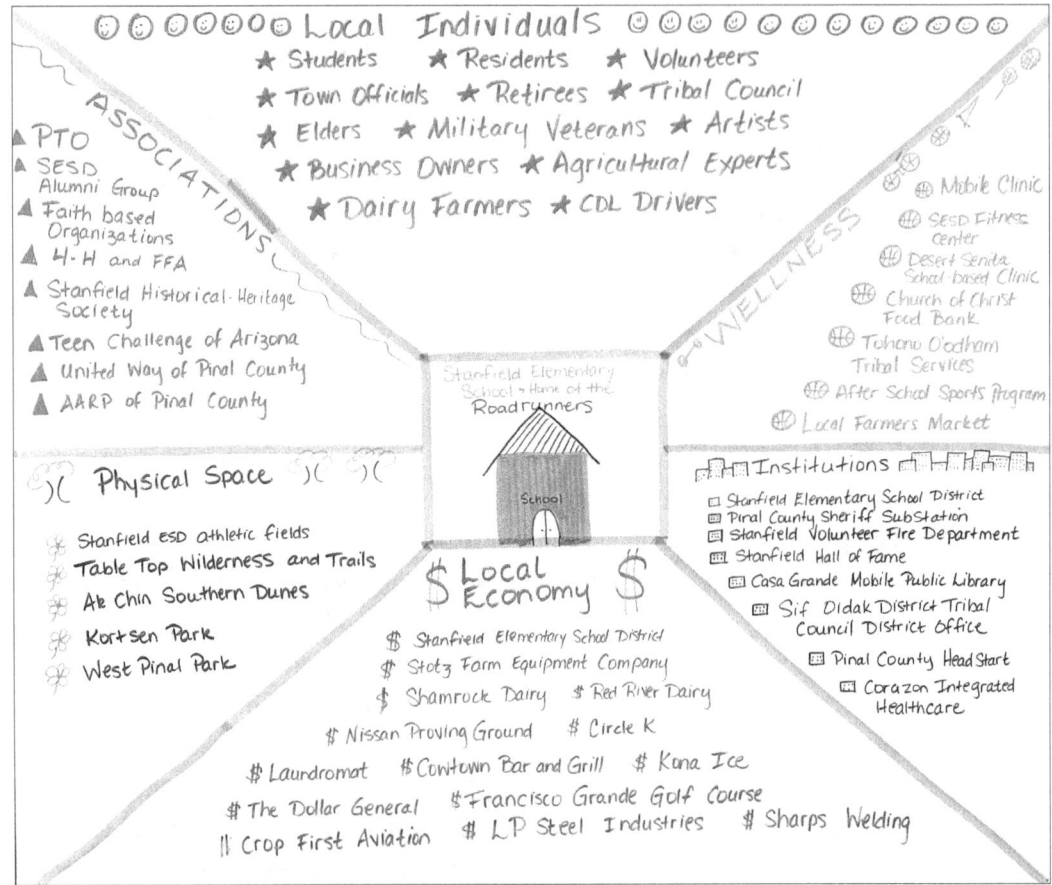

are specific groupings of community members. It may be time-efficient to start with groups and then identify any individuals who may also be able to assist in the solution. Here are some things to keep in mind while compiling this list:

a. *Determine what types of assets are needed.* Using the mentoring example, is academic support needed, and who can provide it? Does the program require a Spanish speaker? Be specific.

b. *Decide what methodology to use for asset screening.* Will there be a survey (online, door-to-door) or another way to collect asset data? Will there be group interviews or other face-to-face asset collection activities?

c. *Be sure to test any questions that are being sent out.* Before embarking on a large-scale canvass, test the questions on a smaller group to ensure that they result in the desired information from participants.

5. **Once identified, place all known assets on a physical map.** This process helps link assets together and identifies where gaps in goods and services might need to be addressed. Be sure to also indicate helpful landmarks or community resources such as parks or streets. One way to mark each identified asset is with color-coded dots. Assets like businesses or medical facilities can be assigned specific colors. Create a legend to keep the assets in order.

Asset mapping is not only a way to match school needs to community resources, it can also be the foundation for community or school district grants and provide a basis for anecdotal talking points when communicating with policymakers and influencers. Below are some resources that can help get the asset mapping process up and running in your rural community:

- Finding a map to plot identified assets can be difficult, depending on where the community is located. The state land office in each U.S. state can provide maps of specific areas within the state upon request. Contact your state office to see what is available. The U.S. Geological Survey's National Geospatial Program (www.usgs.gov/programs/national-geospatial-program/national-map) can create maps for specific areas and can also overlay resource filters as needed, including a 3D feature. Universities that are land grant institutions may also be a source of maps. If there is no specific office that offers cartography support, contact the university library system. Finally, you could use online Google Maps (www.google.com/maps) as a resource.
- The mapping process and the logistics of facilitating stakeholder discussions should be well structured. Some online resources and guides can be helpful in setting up the process. The website for MapGive, a humanitarian mapping initiative from the U.S. Department of State, offers resources for an OpenStreetMap mapping party, including printable table guides, question stems, and lists of activities, at https://mapgive.state.gov/box/#resources&event-guide. While not specific to rural community mapping, some of these items can be adapted for the context. The National Center for Farmworker Health has produced a

Community Asset Mapping Guide that outlines the process and has fillable templates that can be adapted to the individual rural area's needs at www.ncfh.org/uploads/3/8/6/8/38685499/ncfh_asset_mapping_tool.pdf. The Participatory Community Asset Mapping toolkit at https://communityscience.com/wp-content/uploads/2021/04/AssetMappingToolkit.pdf is a comprehensive toolkit by the Advancement Project and Healthy City that outlines the mapping process, offers guidelines for community meetings, and has a comprehensive library of templates and other helpful tools.

Another way to define rural strengths is to use a SWOT analysis, a tool that focuses on strengths, weaknesses, opportunities, and threats (see Figure 9.5). Start with the identified need and evaluate factors that can benefit the anticipated program or derail its success. Don't rush this process! Dedicating one meeting for each quadrant allows the team to thoroughly examine the context and helps all stakeholders be a part of the discussion. When all voices are able to contribute, the outcome or decision has more meaning to more of the community, creating greater connection and buy-in to the solutions selected.

Once all parts of the SWOT analysis have been gathered and discussed, create a plan of action rooted in the reality of what you need to consider in order to launch your plan successfully. Be sure to keep in mind underutilized assets or gaps in assets that need to be addressed. Identifying those gaps and then discussing how to either fill in with existing assets or create a new asset will help meet school needs in a substantial manner. Once the CAM process has been completed, sharing the results of the work will help in the next CAM process.

Promote Place-Based Education

There is a growing interest in place-based education (PBE), in which curriculum and instruction incorporate the unique assets of a particular place. PBE is the polar opposite of standards-based instruction. In a rural community, where the school is the hub, conscious efforts to link instruction to the local community create a relevant curriculum, highlight the effective skills and knowledge of local residents, and lend credibility to a rural way of living. PBE can dovetail with other education trends, such as project-based learning, service learning, and socioemotional learning. It is easily personalized

FIGURE 9.5
Sample SWOT Analysis

SWOT Analysis for Our Rural District	
Strengths	**Weaknesses**
• Close-knit community • Lower student-to-teacher ratios • Local traditions and culture • Community pride and support • Safer environment • Slower pace of life • Place-based learning opportunities	• Limited funding and lack of resources • Restricted access to technology and broadband internet • Fewer extracurricular, AP, dual enrollment opportunities • Geographic isolation • Recruitment challenges for staff • Transportation issues (long distances to travel) • Aging infrastructure • Limited career exposure
Opportunities	**Threats**
• Technology grants or other revenue streams • Community involvement • Distance learning • Entrepreneurship education programs to match local needs • Ecotourism and environmental education through natural surroundings • Teacher residencies with housing or stipends	• Urban-centric policy changes • Population decline • Cultural insularity may not prepare students for a globally connected world • Loss of local business • Lack of health services and other supports • Federal and state funding cuts can disproportionately hurt rural schools

and has many benefits. Start small and grow the idea of expanding learning beyond the classroom and into the community with these steps (Pieratt, 2016):

- **Investigate possible pathways for PBE and select just one.** PBE can take the form of community fieldwork, guest speakers, subject matter experts working with students, or a shadowing experience out in the community.
- **Connect goals to community assets.** Train staff to set up successful PBE opportunities by determining essential questions and goals for the learning and then crosswalking that to identify who or what could bring that learning to life.
- **Map assets that can be used in PBE and keep the map current.** Share access to the database and make it a living document that

everyone can use and modify or add to. Additionally, create a resource bank of email templates, call scripts, and other aids that can assist in making community connections and outreach. These tools can help ease the burden for staff designing PBE activities.
- **Keep information up-to-date.** Establish consistent data collection practices for teachers and students to use when they are out in the community. Is there a database of information on businesses and their contact information? Is there a call log with dates and requests to ensure a specific community asset is not overleveraged? Is there a living list of assets that is added to on a regular basis, as well as updated to remove assets that are no longer available? Assigning one person to the role of database administrator can streamline the process and ensure nothing gets lost.
- **Evaluate and share results.** Monitor how PBE is going throughout the school year and ask staff to share their challenges and successes with each other to encourage incorporating community assets into the curriculum.

At Stanfield School, place-based education came about to meet a need for more opportunities for students to learn computational thinking. As a result of developing a community asset map, the principal and staff were able to create a list of local businesses and professionals that could serve as guest speakers for classrooms doing activities like coding, mentors for teachers who didn't have expertise in working with devices like the Raspberry Pi, and support for other aspects, such as speaking to the real-world application of what they were learning in the local industries of agriculture and dairy farming. The curricula that teachers were able to launch was much more meaningful when we pulled in the local community and made the learning relevant to the students.

Lean on Community Schools and Partnerships

On its website, the Coalition for Community Schools defines the Community School Model as a "local engagement strategy that creates and coordinates opportunities with its public school to accelerate student success. It serves as a vehicle for hyper-local decision making that responds to the unique needs of each community." In discussing ways to meet both academic and non-academic needs of students in rural communities, educators often talk about wraparound services. As discussed previously, some of the issues that these students face include a lack of medical and dental care, a dearth of opportunities to connect with counseling assistance for social and emotional problems, and little to no access to social opportunities outside the school day. While the Community School Model is most often found in urban or suburban areas, it can be a good fit for rural communities in that it models supplying these services and more in a manner that is probably already being done. It is really not possible, especially in a rural community, for the school to operate as a silo.

Even if your district decides not to follow the formal Community School Model, solid partners are beneficial for everyone. Securing these partnerships takes advantage of the place of the school and invites the community to be involved in their students' education in a meaningful manner. It also gives students the information needed to make an informed choice about where they want to live and work. Being able to provide authentic work experiences within the local area is essential to not only workforce development but also the maintenance and growth of a vibrant rural community that is able to potentially mitigate some of the brain drain previously discussed. The Community School partnership is a way to set up a structured way for the rural community to support students with education and curriculum that can impact their future after high school.

There are some challenges to consider when building partnerships in rural places. First, transportation and distance that must be traveled to maintain a partnership can be a barrier. Another potential challenge is a lack of economic diversity. Are there only one or two industries in the area, such as mining or agriculture? In addition, limited funding can affect the format of a partnership and the number of students and staff that can participate. Knowing what assets the community has in place can help point to solutions to these barriers and allow for a robust school–community partnership.

Conducting a needs assessment and community mapping puts rural leaders in a position to consider specific partners within the community who might be willing and interested in creating a more formalized partnership with the school. At the start of any partnership, you should ask the following questions:

- Why is the community entity a good partner for the district, and how does the partnership align with the school's goals?
- How will a partnership with this entity benefit the school and the students? How will a partnership benefit the entity?

- In what capacity will this entity become a partner?
- How will interactions be structured with this entity? How will they be sustained?
- What compensation will be expected from the district to maintain the partnership? From the entity?
- What types of volunteerism can and should be expected from the entity? What will that look like in practice, and how will it be set up, monitored, and evaluated?
- Which students will interact with the community partner? Which staff will interact with the community partner? Who will determine the structure?

The answers to these questions can help guide the selection and onboarding of particular community partners. It is important to note that rural leaders serve as the bridge between the school and the community. There is a cyclical process that can assist in partnership development and growth. Adapted from the work of Kilpatrick & Johns (2004), the framework in Figure 9.6 can help guide the different stages in developing and growing school–community partnerships, including evaluating the programming in the Sustainability stage, which allows for starting the process over again.

Any school–community partnership, formal or informal, is going to have a positive impact on students. When everyone in the community rallies together, students profit in myriad ways: mentorship, tutoring, job skill development, value building, and community renewal and growth. Shared commitments and shared responsibilities to the young people in a rural area translate to student-centered actions that benefit all. Let's take a look at some successful partnerships:

- A specific example of a school–community partnership that grew from a successful program designed to meet needs in a rural district to a multistate, replicable program is Collegiate Edu-Nation, a collaboration between rural districts in Texas and Texas A&M University for career and technical education coursework. Founded in 2001 in rural Texas, the collaboration with the local business community was intended to combat the cycle of generational poverty that was forcing young people out of the area. The district and the community both committed to implementing the Rural P–20 System Model (i.e., covering students from preschool to future workforce participation) to prepare students for

FIGURE 9.6

School–Community Partner Building Cycle

Stage	Leadership Action	Community	Services Provided	Taxing Authority
Trigger	Identify need or problem that affects the community.	• Rural leader • Community leaders	• Hold listening sessions, focus groups.	• Boundary spanner with external partners. • Gain understanding of school and community. • Articulate educational vision.
Initiation	Collaborate with stakeholders.	• Rural leader • Identified partner	• Build support. • Identify resources. • Sell the plan.	• Establish procedures, process for partnership. • Leverage networks.
Development	Create formal action plan.	• Rural leader • Identified partner • School staff	• Develop shared vision and goals. • Identify barriers. • Ensure match between school and partner.	• Leverage credibility to sell partnership. • Create effective teams. • Identify funding, resources.
Maintenance	Carry out process, manage efforts.	• Rural leader • Identified partner • School staff • Identified staff contact • Students	• Monitor program. • Collect data/feedback. • Manage resources. • Communicate.	• Build capacity by involving more stakeholders. • Allocate resources. • Support efforts.
Sustainability	Review and renew vision and goals.	• Rural leader • Community stakeholders • Identified partner • School staff	• Evaluate. • Collect and act on feedback. • Refine, expand, or revise partnership. • Grow new partnerships.	• Communicate status. • Secure ongoing funding/resources.

Source: Kilpatrick & Johns, 2004.

both the workforce and for life by providing paid internships in the community for high school students. Learn more at https://edu-nation.org.
- In Leslie County, Kentucky, a Full-Service Community Schools Model was established in 2018 with the assistance and support of Partners for Rural Impact. Up to that point, very little had been done to evaluate the effectiveness of the model in a rural community. Results are very promising, and the Leslie County Schools framework serves as a model for other rural schools interested in the same work. Learn more at https://edredesign.org/sites/default/files/documents/2023-11/leslie_county_fscs_case_final.pdf.
- In Batesville, Arkansas, the school district worked with the Arkansas Coalition for Community Schools to create a preschool through high school program that partners with community organizations to increase student and family support. Located in a high-poverty area, the district set a goal of coordinating academic, health, cultural, developmental, and other resources. The success of the program, funded by the National Education Association, can serve as a model for other rural schools. Learn more at www.batesvilleschools.com/communityschools.
- ReVISION, in Nebraska, is another CTE-based program. Using Perkins grant funding, schools and districts participating in the program meet with local community partners and community colleges to learn about the workforce development needs of the community in an effort to target student learning. These rural career pathways have been so successful that the program has expanded over the course of a decade, leading to millions of dollars allocated for the program. Learn more at www.education.ne.gov/nce/revision/

To solidify your understanding of the Community Schools Model, look at how community schools have been structured not only in rural places but also in urban and suburban areas. The Coalition for Community Schools (www.communityschools.org) and the National Center for Community Schools (www.nccs.org) both feature an extensive resource library as well as regular publications for rural leaders looking to expand the scope and influence of their district in the community. To financially support your efforts, look at federal funding available through the Office of Elementary and Secondary Education within the U.S. Department of Education.

Voices from the Field:
Passion Engages Rural Communities

Holbrook Unified School District is a rural school system in Northern Arizona that spans 1,500 square miles and includes nine different communities, six of which are located on the Navajo Nation. The district serves 1,800 students in grades pre-K through 12, of which 59 percent are Navajo, 18 percent are Hispanic, 16 percent are white, 6 percent are multiracial, and 1 percent are Black and Asian.

The general rally around rural schools is always strong in rural settings. Inherently, most rural school systems are the largest employers in their communities, are central organizations for facility use, organize community gatherings and services, and generally are the core organization within a rural community. Rural schools are often central to the success of a community, which makes a strong school system extremely important.

While there is a general consensus that schools are pivotal to the livelihood of rural communities, one of the challenges for school boards, administration, and staff in rural schools may be transferring the generalized support of rural schools to garnering support for specific projects to help rural schools continue to thrive within the community. Gaining momentum to accomplish specific outcomes such as securing votes for bonds and overrides, rallying support around a new program, or generating public interest in special projects may not reflect the same general public support within rural school systems.

Something for rural school systems to consider for generating enthusiasm and support is tapping into specific passions to engage communities. Recently, one of the members of our governing board presented the idea of using district property to establish a bike path at an elementary school that could be used for biking programs for students as well as by communities the district serves. While the concept seemed novel but achievable, the key to the project was to garner support, both financial and practical, to make sure the project became a reality.

What happened when we explored how to make the bike path a reality was nothing short of amazing. Gathering people with similar passions around biking became a core concept to creating the SiiHasin Bike Path (*SiiHasin* is Navajo for "hope"). Project supporters included members of the local school community, community members within and outside the district boundaries, and bike path lovers from Oregon to Colorado. Operating out of the elementary school gym and building the path with picks, rakes, and shovels, volunteers gathered weekend after weekend until the first two phases of the bike path were achieved!

What has turned out to be a low-cost, volunteer-based project has simply been an amazing demonstration of how rural communities can come together through shared passions to grow and provide services and programs that may not otherwise be affordable or even possible. The SiiHasin Bike Path has caught the attention of local and national organizations, sparking donations of bikes, helmets, and funds and spawning possibilities for both sustainability and growth of the bike path and bike program.

When trying to build better school systems, rural leaders can search out passions and passionate people within their rural communities to explore possibilities. Connect with the passionate people in your community whom you can build momentum behind. It is the first step to engaging rural communities.

—Robbie Koerperich, superintendent,
Holbrook Unified School District #3, Arizona

Foster Rural Development Hubs

Similar to the Community Schools Model, Rural Development Hubs operating in regions across the United States harness the assets of a rural place for the good of the community as a whole. Partnerships go beyond the transactional giving and getting of services to transforming the area by capitalizing on and leveraging contributions from businesses, networks, and individuals. The Aspen Institute characterizes Rural Development Hubs as "place-rooted organization[s] working hand-in-glove with people and organizations within and across a region to build inclusive wealth, increase local capacity, and create opportunities for better livelihoods, health and well-being" (Community Strategies Group, The Aspen Institute, 2019, p. 16). Rather than operating at a narrow local level, these entities look at broader areas in a region to engage in more and greater opportunities to address workforce development, integrate local solutions, and remove barriers that might not otherwise be moveable. While rural leaders are not the ones to take the lead in such an organization, being aware of their work and acting as a voice for the education community can help inform their programming. Learn more about Rural Development Hubs at www.aspeninstitute.org/wp-content/uploads/2019/11/CSG-Rural-Devel-Hubs.pdf.

Engage Student Voice

Taking a look at your community's needs and assets from the perspective of an adult or a community stakeholder is important. However, it leaves out the voice of the most important stakeholder in the conversation: your students. Consider running a needs assessment or asset mapping activity with students to see what their priorities are. Scott Crisp, principal of Jackson Hole High School in Jackson Hole, Wyoming, took a deep dive into learning his students' perspectives on growing up rural. He then went a step further and created a podcast to share students' lived experiences. These efforts can be easily replicated in any rural school community, even in low- or no-tech ways, such as by holding focus groups or listening sessions. The student perspective is a powerful one.

Voices from the Field: Hearing from Us—A Collection of High School Student Interviews

Schools have an obligation to incorporate student feedback to assist in the development of a positive culture in the school and schoolwide systems. Educators and policymakers can collect student voices and incorporate them into the educational decision-making process. The Hearing from Us project, completed as part of my work as a U.S. Department of Education school ambassador principal fellow and principal of Jackson Hole High School in Teton County, Wyoming, elevates student voice. Developed and created in 2021, the primary goal of the project was to provide a space for students to articulate their thinking about key issues and to link high school student voices to educators, administrators, and policymakers at the local, state, and national levels.

Students who live in the western United States have unique stories. The West reflects a place of unique natural features and human stories. High school students interviewed for the project were from western Wyoming, with a long-term goal of capturing the voices of students in other rural western regions. Sometimes students' lives can be grounded in particular places. Student interviews provided a forum to get student feedback on potential causes of educational barriers and successes.

The Hearing from Us project is a collection of audio interviews of 20 high school students who live in rural and semirural western Wyoming. Season 1, episodes 1–13, are interviews with students who reflect a wide spectrum of student backgrounds (10 males, 10 females; 11 Hispanic, 9 Caucasian). Each student participant was asked the following key questions during the interview:

- Tell me about your family, background.
- Can you tell me about someone who has had a substantial influence on your life? What lessons did that person teach you?
- Do you enjoy school? Why or why not?
- What kind of student do you consider yourself?
- What advice would you give to younger students?
- Are there teachers, a teacher, or a coach who has had a particularly strong influence in your life? Why?
- What activities or other things are you involved in? What events in your life led you to start doing those?
- Have you had a job, volunteer experience, or participated in an event that you are most proud about? Why?
- How do you think growing up in the West has impacted your life?
- What has been a big failure or flop in your life?
- When have you experienced the greatest "aha" moments? Were you in a particular place, reading a particular book, listening to particular music, talking to a particular person?
- Is there something in school or in life that you are most proud about and why?

- If you could change one or two things in schools to make them better places for student learning, what would that be and why?

Needless to say, conducting recorded interviews with students presented a couple of challenges. For some students, it was their first experience being interviewed and recorded. Some interviews had to be conducted several times to assist with the student comfort level. Challenges also existed with translation with our English language learner (ELL) students. Also, given that my professional background encompasses being a classroom teacher and high school principal, I experienced technical challenges when it came to editing student audio interviews and merging student responses in order to produce a collection of student answers listed by each interview question.

What were some of the overarching feedback and comments from students? The majority of students clearly articulated the importance of the positive connection between the teacher and student, which was by far the strongest feedback provided by students. During the interviews, relationships were mentioned 23 times. What does this mean? School staff need to continually revisit the focus area of developing positive relationships with students.

In addition to the importance of strong teacher-student relationships, students also frequently mentioned the importance of school staff encouraging and supporting students to enroll in and complete challenging courses. Specifically, students requested direct teacher encouragement and individual support to take challenging courses. What does this mean? How students see themselves as learners has a significant impact on their learning opportunities and ability to take learning risks. Educators should play a large role in providing positive support to aid in student self-perception regarding their ability to take challenging courses.

As a principal, I found the project to be a constructive avenue to authentically connect with students and learn about their individual backgrounds, life experiences, challenges, successes, and ultimately, what our school (or any school) can do to improve the educational experience for students. Listen to *Hearing from Us: A Collection of High School Student Interviews* on Apple Podcasts and Spotify.

—Scott Crisp, principal of Jackson Hole High School, Wyoming

Concluding Thoughts

At the end of this year, I will complete my 13th year as a rural superintendent and 32 years as a rural educator. I can think of no greater gift than the one entrusted to me by the governing boards of education that hired me. I know that it is no accident that rural schools are the heart of their communities. Leading in a rural place is often difficult work, but the rewards far outweigh any of the challenges. As a newly seated rural leader, I had the gift of being mentored by the outgoing superintendent, something I know most new rural leaders don't receive. Without someone guiding me through those first few years, I would have struggled to wear the many hats rural leaders are expected to throw on. This book is meant to serve as a starting point for finding solutions for the many challenges and barriers that face today's rural administrator. But while it is broad-ranging, it is certainly not exhaustive! Local context, demographics, state and local policies, and the unique needs of each rural community all play a part in how a rural leader will approach a problem of practice and look to solve it. With *The Resilient Rural Leader* as your guide, it is my hope that you will find success in the unique, complex, and fulfilling opportunity in front of you!

References

America Counts Staff. (2017, August 9). One in five Americans live in rural areas. *United States Census Bureau.* https://www.census.gov/library/stories/2017/08/rural-america.html

American Academy of Family Physicians. (2014). *Rural practice, keeping physicians in* [Position paper]. https://www.aafp.org/about/policies/all/rural-practice-keeping-physicians.html

American Hospital Association. (2022). *Rural hospital closures threaten access: Solutions to preserve care in local communities.* https://www.aha.org/system/files/media/file/2022/09/rural-hospital-closures-threaten-access-report.pdf

Andresen, W. (2008). *Attracting and retaining the "next generation" on the Gogebic Range December 10, 2008 Will Andresen Iron County UW-Extension.* https://slideplayer.com/slide/7610973/

The Arbinger Institute. (2006). *The anatomy of peace: Resolving the heart of conflict.* Berrett-Koehler Publishers.

Azano, A. P., Brenner, D., Downey, J., Eppley, K., & Schulte, A. K. (2020). *Teaching in rural places: Thriving in classrooms, schools, and communities.* Routledge.

Barshay, J. (2022). What the research says about 4-day school weeks. *MindShift.* KQED. https://www.kqed.org/mindshift/59801/what-the-research-says-about-4-day-school-weeks

Benton, K., Permenter, P., Richel, M., Sheley, P., Hartman, N., & Layland, A. (2022). *Supporting students in poverty with high-impact instructional strategies toolkit.* National Comprehensive Center at Westat. https://compcenternetwork.org/ccn-products/multimedia/supporting-students-in-poverty/

Bierly, C., Doyle, B., & Smith, A. (2016). *Transforming schools: How distributed leadership can create more high-performing schools.* Bain & Company. https://media.bain.com/Images/BAIN_REPORT_Transforming_schools.pdf

Blase, J., & Blase, J. (2000). Effective instructional leadership: Teachers' perspectives on how principals promote teaching and learning in schools. *Journal of Educational Administration, 38*(2), 130–141.

Boethel, M. (2000). *Thriving together: Connecting rural school improvement and community development.* ED 451020. Southwest Educational Development Laboratory. https://files.eric.ed.gov/fulltext/ED451020.pdf

Bradley, B., Restuccia, D., Rudnicki, C., & Bittle, S. (2017). *The digital edge: Middle-skill workers and careers.* Burning Glass Technologies.

The Broad Foundation. (2009). *School closure guide: Closing schools as a means for addressing budgetary challenges.* https://failingschools.files.wordpress.com/2011/01/school-closure-guide1.pdf

California Department of Education. (2023). *Closing a school best practices guide.* https://www.cde.ca.gov/ls/fa/sf/schoolclose.asp

Center on Education Policy. (2020). *History and evolution of public education in the US.* Graduate School of Education & Human Development, The George Washington University. https://files.eric.ed.gov/fulltext/ED606970.pdf

Center on Rural Education and Communities. (2023). *Poverty, housing insecurity and student transiency in rural areas.* Penn State College of Education. https://ed.psu.edu/academics/departments/department-education-policy-studies/eps-centers-councils-and-journals/center-rural-education-communities/poverty-housing-insecurity-and-student-transiency-rural-areas

Centers for Disease Control and Prevention. (2019, November). *Vital signs.* https://www.cdc.gov/vitalsigns/aces/pdf/vs-1105-aces-H.pdf

Chanlongbutra, A., Singh, G. K., & Mueller, C. D. (2018). Adverse childhood experiences, health-related quality of life, and chronic disease risks in rural areas of the United States. *Journal of Environmental and Public Health, 2018,* 7151297. https://doi.org/10.1155/2018/7151297

Clarksville-Montgomery County School System. (n.d.). Teacher residency programs. https://www.cmcss.net/teacher-residency-programs/

Coleman-Jensen, A., Rabbitt, M. P., Gregory, C. A., & Singh, A. (2022). *Household food security in the United States in 2021.* (Economic Research Report No. ERR-309). U.S. Department of Agriculture. https://www.ers.usda.gov/publications/pub-details/?pubid=104655

Colorado Department of Education. (2023, December 13). DISH_Dashboards: Fowler High School (3134). https://public.tableau.com/app/profile/colorado.department.of.education/viz/shared/7SBWY66YN

Communities in Schools. (2020). *Community matters. Communities in Schools national report: Focus on rural schools.* https://www.communitiesinschools.org/media/filer_public/08/64/0864d045-f351-452e-98ff-7e79c79dc2e3/2020_community_matters_report_web_06122020.pdf

Community Strategies Group, The Aspen Institute. (2019). *Rural development hubs: Strengthening America's rural innovation structure.* https://www.aspeninstitute.org/wp-content/uploads/2019/11/CSG-Rural-Devel-Hubs.pdf

Cotton, K. (2001). *New small learning communities: Findings from recent literature.* (ERIC Document ED 459539). Northwest Regional Educational Laboratory. https://files.eric.ed.gov/fulltext/ED459539.pdf

Crouch, E., Jones, J., Strompolis, M., & Merrick, M. (2020, September). Examining the association between ACEs, childhood poverty and neglect, and physical and mental health: Data from two state samples. *Children and Youth Services Review, 116,* 105155. https://www.sciencedirect.com/science/article/pii/S0190740920305922

Cruzeiro, P. A., & Boone, M. (2009). Rural and small school principal candidates: Perspectives of hiring superintendents. *The Rural Educator, 31*(1), 1–9. https://doi.org/10.35608/ruraled.v31i1.437

de Bono, E. (n.d.). *Six thinking hats.* https://www.six-thinking-hats.com/

Deloitte. (2011). *Shared services handbook.* https://www2.deloitte.com/content/dam/Deloitte/dk/Documents/finance/SSC-Handbook-%20Hit-the-Road.pdf

DeNisco, A. (2019, January 16). Rural K12 districts tackle enrollment declines and teacher shortages. *District Administration.* https://districtadministration.com/rural-k12-districts-tackle-challenges/

Eccles, J., & Gootman, J. A. (Eds.). (2002). *Community programs to promote youth development.* Committee on Community-Level Programs for Youth. Board on Children, Youth, and Families,

Division of Behavioral and Social Sciences and Education, National Research Council and Institute of Medicine. National Academy Press.

Enomoto, E. K. (2012). Professional development for rural school assistant principals. *Planning and Changing, 43*(3/4), 260–279.

Farrigan, T. (2014, March 4). Poverty and deep poverty increasing in rural America. *USDA Economic Research Service.* https://www.ers.usda.gov/amber-waves/2014/march/poverty-and-deep-poverty-increasing-in-rural-america/

Feeding America. (n.d.). *Hunger in rural communities.* https://www.feedingamerica.org/hunger-in-america/rural-hunger-facts

Felitti, V. J., Anda, R. F., Nordenberg, D., Williamson, D. F., Spitz, A. M., Edwards, V., Koss, M. P., & Marks, J. S. (1998). Relationship of childhood abuse and household dysfunction to many of the leading causes of death in adults: The adverse childhood experiences (ACE) study. *American Journal of Preventive Medicine, 14*(4): 245–258. https://doi.org/10.1016/s0749-3797(98)00017-8

Fields, J., & Surma, K. (2020, August 27). *Homeless people in rural America struggle to find help.* Howard Center for Investigative Journalism. https://cronkitenews.azpbs.org/howardcenter/covid-homeless/stories/rural-homeless.html

The Final Mile Project. (2022). *The project—Bringing broadband to the final mile.* https://www.finalmileproject.com/The-Project

Flannery, M. E. (2023, January 27). How educators are stopping school closures. *NEA Today.* https://www.nea.org/nea-today/all-news-articles/how-educators-are-stopping-school-closures

Food Research & Action Center. (n.d.). *National School Lunch Program.* https://frac.org/programs/national-school-lunch-program

4-H. (n.d.). *What is 4-H?* https://4-h.org/about

Frankland, M. (2021). Meeting students where they are: Trauma-informed approaches in rural schools. *The Rural Educator, 42*(2), 51–71. https://doi.org/10.35608/ruraled.v42i2.1243

Fullan, M. (2002). Leadership and sustainability. *Principal Leadership, 3*(4). https://michaelfullan.ca/wp-content/uploads/2016/06/13396047460.pdf

Gagnon, D. J., & Mattingly, M. J. (2016). Advanced placement and rural schools: Access, success, and exploring alternatives. *Journal of Advanced Academics, 27*(4), 266–284.

Gladson, K. (2016, October 3). School closings: Challenges for students, communities, and litigators. *American Bar Association.* https://www.americanbar.org/groups/litigation/committees/childrens-rights/articles/2016/school-closings-challenges-for-students-communities-litigators/

Gonzales, J. (2022, May 17). Rural Colorado students go to college at low rates. Tiny Fowler goes against the trend. *Chalkbeat Colorado.* https://www.chalkbeat.org/colorado/2022/5/17/23075901/fowler-high-school-colorado-rural-college-higher-education-success/

Griffith, M. (2017, August 2). In education funding, size does matter [Blog post]. *EdNote.* https://ednote.ecs.org/in-education-funding-size-does-matter/

Grissom, J. A., Egalite, A. J., & Lindsay, C. A. (2021). *How principals affect students and schools: A systematic synthesis of two decades of research.* The Wallace Foundation. https://www.wallacefoundation.org/knowledge-center/Documents/How-Principals-Affect-Students-and-Schools.pdf

Grissom, J. A., Loeb, S., & Mitani, H. (2015). Principal time management skills: Explaining patterns in principals' time use, job stress, and perceived effectiveness. *Journal of Educational Administration, 53*(6), 773–793.

Haynes-Maslow, L., Hardison-Moody, A., & Byker Shanks, C. (2020). Leveraging informal community food systems to address food security during COVID-19. *Journal of Agriculture, Food Systems, and Community Development, 10*(1), 197–200. https://doi.org/10.5304/jafscd.2020.101.005

Healthy Schools Campaign. (2015, September 3). *Teledentistry: Reducing absenteeism by supporting student health.* https://healthyschoolscampaign.org/blog/teledentistry-reducing-absenteeism-by-supporting-student-health

Herrera, C., Grossman, J. B., Kauh, T. J., Feldman, A. F., McMaken, J., & Jucovy, L. Z. (2007). *Making a difference in schools: The Big Brothers Big Sisters school-based mentoring impact study*. Public/Private Ventures. https://ppv.issuelab.org/resource/making-a-difference-in-schools-the-big-brothers-big-sisters-school-based-mentoring-impact-study.html

Heynoski, K., Douglas-McNab, E., Khandaker, N., Tamang, T., & Howell, E. (2022). *5 shifts to address the national educator shortage: Findings from the National Educator Shortage Summit*. American Association of School Personnel Administrators. https://assets.noviams.com/novi-file-uploads/aaspa/AASPA-5_Shifts_NESS_FINAL.pdf

Hobson, A., Brown, E., Ashby, P., Keys, W., Sharp, C., & Benefield, P. (2003). *Issues for early headship—Problems and support strategies*. National College for School Leadership. https://www.researchgate.net/publication/237254566_Issues_for_Early_Headship_-_Problems_and_Support_Strategies

Hohlfeld, T. N., Ritzhaupt, A. D., Dawson, K., & Wilson, M. L. (2017, October). An examination of seven years of technology integration in Florida schools: Through the lens of the Levels of Digital Divide in Schools. *Computers & Education, 113,* 135–161. https://doi.org/10.1016/j.compedu.2017.05.017

Housing Assistance Council. (2021, September 28). *The United States is becoming more racially diverse—And so is rural America*. Rural Research Briefs. https://ruralhome.org/united-states-becoming-more-racially-diverse-so-is-rural-america/

Howley, C., & Redding, S. (Eds.) (2021). *Cultivating rural education: A people-focused approach for states*. Information Age Publishing.

Huang, G., & Howley, C. (1991). *Recent trends in rural poverty: A summary for educators*. ERIC Digest (ERIC Document 335180). http://files.eric.ed.gov/fulltext/ED335180.pdf

Idaho Public Charter School Commission. (2013). *Idaho College and Career Readiness Academy charter petition (1st hearing)*. https://chartercommission.idaho.gov/meetings/archive/2013/10-10-13/TAB%20B1%20-%20IDCCRA%20Charter%20Petition%20-%201st%20Hearing.pdf

Ingersoll, R. M., & Tran, H. (2023). Teacher shortages and turnover in rural schools in the US: An organizational analysis. *Educational Administration Quarterly, 59*(2), 396–431. https://doi.org/10.1177/0013161X231159922

Institute for Research on Poverty. (2018). *Rural poverty 50 years after "The People Left Behind" | Bruce Weber and Ann Tickamyer*. YouTube. https://youtu.be/dNWNKElbdXU

Institute for Research on Poverty. (2020, January). *Many rural Americans are still "left behind."* Fast Focus Research/Policy Brief No. 44-2020. https://www.irp.wisc.edu/resource/many-rural-americans-are-still-left-behind/#_edn1

Insurance Institute for Highway Safety & Highway Loss Data Institute. (2023). *Fatality facts 2021: Urban/rural comparison*. https://www.iihs.org/topics/fatality-statistics/detail/urban-rural-comparison

Johnson, K. M., & O'Hare, W. P. (2004). Child poverty in rural America. *Reports on America, 71*. https://scholars.unh.edu/soc_facpub/71

Jucovy, L., & Garringer, M. (2008). *The ABCs of school-based mentoring: Effective strategies for providing quality youth mentoring in schools and communities*. Hamilton Fish Institute on School and Community Violence & National Mentoring Center. https://educationnorthwest.org/sites/default/files/abcs-of-mentoring.pdf

Kafer, K. (2014). *School district partnerships help Colorado K–12 blended learning take flight*. Independence Institute. https://i2i.org/wp-content/uploads/2014/07/IP_2_2014_web_b.pdf

Kay, S. (1982). Considerations in evaluating school consolidation proposals. *Small School Forum, 4*(1), 8–10.

Killeen, K., & Sipple, J. (2000). *School consolidation and transportation policy: An empirical and institutional analysis*. Working paper for the Rural School and Community Trust Policy Program. https://files.eric.ed.gov/fulltext/ED447979.pdf

Kilpatrick, S., & Johns, S. (2004). *Leadership for rural school–community partnerships.* Paper presented at AARE Annual Conference, Melbourne, Australia. https://www.aare.edu.au/data/publications/2004/kil04172.pdf

Kliewer, L. (2001). Small, rural schools face uncertain future due to predictions of declining enrollment. *Firstline Midwest, 8*(3).

Klocko, B., & Justis, R. J. (2019). Leadership challenges of the rural school principal. *The Rural Educator, 40*(3), 23–34. https://doi.org/10.35608/ruraled.v40i3.571

Knutson, P., & Del Carlo, D. (2018). Impact of multiplex relationships on rural science education.pdf. *The Rural Educator, 39*(2), 21–35. https://doi.org/10.35608/ruraled.v39i2.203

Kupersmidt, J., Stelter, R., Karcher, M., & Garringer, M., Shane, J. (2020). *Peer mentoring: Supplement to the elements of effective practice for mentoring.* Mentor. https://www.mentoring.org/wp-content/uploads/2020/08/Peer-Mentoring-Supplement-to-the-EEP.pdf

Lawrence, B. K., Bingler, S., Diamond, B. M., Hill, B., Hoffman, J. L., Howley, C. B., Mitchell, S., Rudolph, D., & Washor, E. (2002). *Dollars & sense: The cost effectiveness of small schools.* KnowledgeWorks Foundation. https://files.eric.ed.gov/fulltext/ED473168.pdf

Learning Forward. (n.d.). The principal story learning guide [Toolkit]. https://learningforward.org/toolkits/the-principal-story-learning-guide

Leithwood, K., Louis, K. S., Anderson, S., & Wahlstrom, K. (2004). *Review of research: How leadership influences student learning.* The Wallace Foundation.

Lerner, R. M., Almerigi, J. B., Theokas, C., & Lerner, J. V. (2005). Positive youth development: A view of the issues. *The Journal of Early Adolescence, 25*(1), 10–16. https://doi.org/10.1177/0272431604273211

Lewis, L., Gray, L., & Ralph, J. (2016). *Programs and services for high school English learners in public school districts: 2015–16: First look.* National Center for Education Statistics.

Lichter, D. T., & Parisi, D. (2008, Fall). Concentrated rural poverty and the geography of exclusion (Policy brief). *Rural Realities.* https://scholars.unh.edu/cgi/viewcontent.cgi?article=1054&context=carsey

Love, H. E., Schlitt, J., Soleimanpour, S., Panchal, N., & Behr, C. (2019). Twenty years of school-based health care growth and expansion. *Health Affairs, 38*(5), 755–764. https://doi.org/10.1377/hlthaff.2018.05472

Lyson, T. A. (2002). What does a school mean to a community? Assessing the social and economic benefits of schools to rural villages in New York. *Journal of Research in Rural Education, 17*(3), 131–137.

Master, B., & Doss, C. (2022, March 7). Analysis: Study of 6 "grow your own" teacher prep programs shows how they can improve the diversity of the workforce. *The 74.* https://www.the74million.org/article/analysis-study-of-6-grow-your-own-teacher-prep-programs-shows-how-they-can-improve-the-diversity-of-the-workforce

Mattingly, M., Johnson, K., & Schaefer, A. (2011). *More poor kids in more poor places: Children increasingly live where poverty persists* (Issue Brief No. 38). Carsey Institute. https://files.eric.ed.gov/fulltext/ED536107.pdf

Maxwell, J. C. (2011). *The five levels of leadership: Proven steps to maximize your potential.* Center Street.

McArdle, E. (2019, May 23). The middle of somewhere. *Ed. Magazine.* Harvard Graduate School of Education. https://www.gse.harvard.edu/ideas/ed-magazine/19/05/middle-somewhere

McMilin, E. (2010). *Closing a school building: A systematic approach.* National Clearinghouse for Educational Facilities. https://files.eric.ed.gov/fulltext/ED512699.pdf

Mejia, B. (2019, July 20). Vail school district hopes that tiny homes help attract, keep teachers. *AZPM.* https://news.azpm.org/p/news-topical-edu/2018/7/20/133567-vail-school-district-hopes-tiny-homes-help-attract-keep-teachers/

Metz, A., & Louison, L. (2018). *The Hexagon tool: Exploring context.* National Implementation Research Network, Frank Porter Graham Child Development Institute, University of North Carolina at Chapel Hill.

Metz, A., & Louison, L. (2019). *The Hexagon: An exploration tool: Hexagon discussion & analysis tool instructions*. National Implementation Research Network, Frank Porter Graham Child Development Institute, University of North Carolina at Chapel Hill. http://files.eric.ed.gov/fulltext/ED606133.pdf

Mitgang, L. D. (2003). *Beyond the pipeline: Getting the principals we need, where they are needed most*. The Wallace Foundation. https://www.wallacefoundation.org/report/beyond-pipeline-getting-principals-we-need-where-they-are-needed-most-getting-principals-we

Montana State University–Northern. (n.d.). *Teachers of Promise Pathways (TOPP)*. https://www.msun.edu/academics/coeasn/TOPP.aspx

Montgomery, M. R. (2010). *Small rural school districts in Nebraska: A case study of challenges and solutions* (Doctoral dissertation, University of Nebraska—Lincoln). https://digitalcommons.unl.edu/dissertations/AAI3432054/

Moore, R., Vitale, D., & Stawinoga, N. (2018). *The digital divide and educational equity: A look at students with very limited access to electronic devices at home*. ACT Center for Equity in Learning. https://equityinlearning.act.org/wp-content/themes/voltron/img/tech-briefs/the-digital-divide.pdf

Morton, E. (2023). Effects of 4-day school weeks on older adolescents: Examining impacts of the schedule on academic achievement, attendance, and behavior in high school. *Educational Evaluation and Policy Analysis, 45*(1), 52–78. https://doi.org/10.3102/01623737221097420

Morton, M. H., Dworsky, A., Samuels, G. M., & Patel, S. (2018). *Missed opportunities: Youth homelessness in rural America*. Chapin Hall at the University of Chicago. https://www.chapinhall.org/wp-content/uploads/Youth-Homelessness-in-Rural-America.pdf

Myers, S. R., Branas, C. C., French, B. C., Nance, M. L., Kallan, M. J., Wiebe, D. J., & Carr, B. G. (2013). Safety in numbers: Are major cities the safest places in the United States? *Annals of Emergency Medicine, 62*(4), 408–418. https://www.ruralhealth.us/NRHA/media/Emerge_NRHA/PDFs/Myers-cities-safer.pdf

National Center for Education Statistics. (n.d.a). Children in rural areas and their family characteristics. *Condition of Education*. https://nces.ed.gov/programs/coe/indicator/lfa/family-characteristics-rural

National Center for Education Statistics. (n.d.b). *Educational institutions*. https://nces.ed.gov/fastfacts/display.asp?id=84

National Center for Education Statistics. (n.d.c). *Locale definitions*. https://nces.ed.gov/surveys/ruraled/definitions.asp

National Center for Education Statistics. (2017). *Selected statistics from the public elementary and secondary education universe: School year 2015–16*. https://nces.ed.gov/pubs2018/2018052/tables/table_04.asp

National Center for Education Statistics. (2021). Table 203.72. Public elementary and secondary school enrollment, by locale and state: Fall 2019. *Digest of Education Statistics*. https://nces.ed.gov/programs/digest/d21/tables/dt21_203.72.asp

National Center for Education Statistics. (2022a). Principal turnover: Stayers, movers, and leavers. *Condition of Education*. U.S. Department of Education, Institute of Education Sciences. https://nces.ed.gov/programs/coe/indicator/slb

National Center for Education Statistics. (2022b). Table 214.10. Number of public school districts and public and private elementary and secondary schools: Selected school years, 1869–70 through 2021–22. *Digest of Education Statistics*. https://nces.ed.gov/programs/digest/d22/tables/dt22_214.10.asp

National Clearinghouse on Families & Youth. (2007). *Putting positive youth development into practice: A resource guide*. https://rhyclearinghouse.acf.hhs.gov/sites/default/files/document/PosYthDevel_0_0.pdf

National Museum of African American History & Culture. (n.d.). *Being antiracist*. Smithsonian. https://nmaahc.si.edu/learn/talking-about-race/topics/being-antiracist

National Rural Education Association. (n.d.). *Welcome to NREA*. https://www.nrea.net

Nelson, E. (1985). School consolidation. *ERIC Digest, 13*. https://eric.ed.gov/?id=ED282346

North Carolina School Report Cards. (n.d.). *East Wilkes High School*. https://ncreports.ondemand.sas.com/src/school?school=970320&year=2019

Odden, A., & Picus, L. O. (2004). *School finance: A policy perspective* (3rd ed.). McGraw-Hill.

Office of Elementary & Secondary Education. (2019). *Effective communication strategies for building local stakeholder engagement and ownership*. U.S. Department of Education. https://oese.ed.gov/resources/oese-technical-assistance-centers/state-support-network/blog/effective-communication-strategies-for-building-local-stakeholder-engagement-and-ownership/

Office of Management and Budget. (2000). Standards for defining metropolitan and micropolitan statistical areas. *Federal Register, 65*(249), 82227–82238. https://www.federalregister.gov/documents/2000/12/27/00-32997/standards-for-defining-metropolitan-and-micropolitan-statistical-areas

Office of the Comptroller of the Currency. (2014). *Community Reinvestment Act* (Fact sheet). https://www.occ.gov/publications-and-resources/publications/community-affairs/community-developments-fact-sheets/pub-fact-sheet-cra-reinvestment-act-mar-2014.pdf

Office of the Maricopa County School Superintendent. (n.d.). *Stay interviews: The no-cost, high-impact retention strategy*. https://static1.squarespace.com/static/55314ad4e4b04c1bc645ad3e/t/6165b8a361716c18b949451b/1634056356078/Stay+Interview+Quick+Guide+2021.pdf

Peshkin, A. (1982). *The imperfect union: School consolidation & community conflict*. University of Chicago Press.

Peters, D. (2012, May 16). "Brain gain" study: People in 30s, 40s still moving to rural Minnesota. *Ground Level Blog*. https://www.mprnews.org/story/2012/05/16/brain-gain-study-people-in-30s-40s-still-moving-to-rural-minnesota

Petersen, V. (2019, September 10). A perennial challenge in rural Alaska: Getting and keeping teachers, home-grown versus out-of-state. *Education Week*. https://www.edweek.org/leadership/a-perennial-challenge-in-rural-alaska-getting-and-keeping-teachers/2019/09

Pieratt, J. (2016, August 23). Five tips for testing the place-based education waters. *Getting Smart*. https://www.gettingsmart.com/2016/08/23/five-tips-testing-place-based-education-waters/

Podolsky, A., Kini, T., Bishop, J., & Darling-Hammond, L. (2016). *Solving the teacher shortage: How to attract and retain excellent teachers* [Research brief]. Learning Policy Institute. https://learningpolicyinstitute.org/sites/default/files/product-files/Solving_Teacher_Shortage_Attract_Retain_Educators_BRIEF.pdf

Preston, J. P., Jakubiec, B. A., & Kooymans, R. (2013). Common challenges faced by rural principals: A review of the literature. *The Rural Educator, 35*(1). https://doi.org/10.35608/ruraled.v35i1.355

Rath, A. (2015, March 15). Why is the risk of youth suicide higher in rural areas? *All Things Considered*. https://www.npr.org/2015/03/15/393192543/why-is-the-risk-of-youth-suicide-higher-in-rural-areas

Reform Support Network. (2020). From "inform" to "inspire": A framework for communications and engagement. https://oese.ed.gov/files/2020/10/rsn_framework-communications-engagement_1.pdf

Ridlen Bowen, K. J. (2022). *IntraHousing: Housing for student teachers in rural school districts* (Unpublished master's thesis, Texas A&M University). https://hdl.handle.net/1969.1/196023

Rispens, S. (2022, July 24). How to build a teacher: Montana programs work to combat longstanding educator shortages issue. *Missoulian*. https://missoulian.com/news/local/how-to-build-a-teacher-montana-programs-work-to-combat-longstanding-educator-shortages-issue/article_45156e7c-9728-570e-a356-8748b6c98923.html

Rosenkoetter, S. E., Irwin, J. D., & Saceda, R. G. (2004). Addressing personnel needs for rural areas. *Teacher Education and Special Education, 27*(3), 276–291.

Rural Health Information Hub. (2022). *Healthcare access in rural communities.* https://www.ruralhealthinfo.org/topics/healthcare-access

The Rural School and Community Trust. (2003). *Alternative ways to achieve cost effective schools.* https://mrea-mt.org/wp-content/uploads/2017/08/RSCT-Anything-But-Research.pdf

The Rural School and Community Trust. (2006, March). Anything but research-based: State initiatives to consolidate schools and districts. *Rural Policy Matters.*

Rural Schools Collaborative & National Rural Education Association. (n.d.). Celebrating great teachers in rural places. *IAmARuralTeacher.* https://iamaruralteacher.org

Sadorf, M. A. (2013). *The effects of kindergarten through eighth grade school closures in Arizona from 2000–2012* (Doctoral dissertation, Northern Arizona University). Retrieved from ProQuest (3606835). https://www.proquest.com/openview/c62842673fd371891d5ad9239ff0b1d6/

Schmidt, C. (2019, August 28). MSU programs collaborate on solution for rural teacher housing shortage. *Montana State University.* https://www.montana.edu/news/18946/msu-programs-collaborate-on-solution-for-rural-teacher-housing-shortage

Schuman, A. L. (2010). *Rural high school principals: Leadership in rural education* (Unpublished doctoral dissertation, Temple University). https://digital.library.temple.edu/digital/collection/p245801coll10/id/71128/

Setchel, B. A. (2008). *How distributed school leadership practices are implemented in a rural Northeast Georgia elementary school* (Doctoral dissertation, Georgia Southern University). https://digitalcommons.georgiasouthern.edu/etd/267

Shapiro, S. M. (2023, June 15). Young and homeless in rural America. *The New York Times Magazine.* https://www.nytimes.com/2022/09/29/magazine/rural-homeless-students.html

Smith, A. A. (2007). Mentoring for experienced school principals: Professional learning in a safe place. *Mentoring & Tutoring, 15*(3), 277–291.

Steiner, E. D., Doan, S., Woo, A., Gittens, A. D., Lawrence, R. A., Berdie, L., Wolfe, R. L., Greer, L., & Schwartz, H. L. (2022). *Restoring teacher and principal well-being is an essential step for rebuilding schools: Findings from the State of the American Teacher and State of the American Principal Surveys.* RAND Corporation. https://www.rand.org/content/dam/rand/pubs/research_reports/RRA1100/RRA1108-4/RAND_RRA1108-4.pdf

Sturtevant, L. (2019, March 7). Local solutions in action: School district–owned land. *LSA.* https://lsaplanning.com/local-solutions-in-action-school-district-owned-land/

Texas Education Agency. (n.d.). *School redesign models: A guide to closure and consolidation.* https://tea.texas.gov/sites/default/files/School%20Redesign%20Model_Close%20Consolidate.pdf

Tieken, M. C. (2014). *Why rural schools matter.* University of North Carolina Press.

Umansky, I., Hopkins, M., Dabach, D. B., Porter, L., Thompson, K., & Pompa, D. (2018). *Understanding and supporting the educational needs of recently arrived immigrant English learner students: Lessons for state and local education agencies.* Council of Chief State School Officers. https://ccsso.org/sites/default/files/2018-04/Understanding%20and%20Supporing%20the%20Educational%20Needs%20of%20RAIELs.pdf

U.S. Census Bureau. (n.d.). *Zip code tabulation area ZCTA5 85172.* https://data.census.gov/profile/ZCTA5_85172?g=860XX00US85172

U.S. Department of Agriculture Economic Research Service. (2017). *Rural education at a glance, 2017 edition.* https://www.ers.usda.gov/webdocs/publications/83078/eib-171.pdf

U.S. Department of Agriculture Economic Research Service. (2021). *Rural education.* https://www.ers.usda.gov/topics/rural-economy-population/employment-education/rural-education/

U.S. Department of Agriculture Economic Research Service. (2022). *Rural poverty & well-being.* https://www.ers.usda.gov/topics/rural-economy-population/rural-poverty-well-being/

U.S. Department of Education. (2017). *2017 Title II reports: National teacher preparation data: Montana.* https://title2.ed.gov/Public/Report/StateHome.aspx?si=30

U.S. Department of Health and Human Services. (2022, May 3). *HHS awards nearly $25 million to expand access to school-based health services* (Press release). https://www.hhs.gov/about/news/2022/05/03/hhs-awards-nearly-25-million-expand-access-school-based-health-services.html

U.S. Government Printing Office. (2004). *Rural Teacher Housing Act: Hearing before the Committee on Indian Affairs, United States Senate.* (Senate Hearing 108-468). https://www.govinfo.gov/content/pkg/CHRG-108shrg92775/html/CHRG-108shrg92775.htm

Velazquez, T. (2022, August 29). School districts use funds for housing to help with teacher shortage. *KUNM.* https://www.kunm.org/local-news/2022-08-29/teacher-housing-could-solve-the-teacher-shortage-in-rural-areas

Verlinden, N. (2022). 21 best stay interview questions to ask. *Academy to Innovate HR.* https://www.aihr.com/blog/stay-interview-questions/

Vogels, E. A. (2021, August 19). *Some digital divides persist between rural, urban and suburban America.* Pew Research Center. https://www.pewresearch.org/short-reads/2021/08/19/some-digital-divides-persist-between-rural-urban-and-suburban-america/

Warschauer, M., & Matuchniak, T. (2010). New technology and digital worlds: Analyzing evidence of equity in access, use, and outcomes. *Review of Research in Education, 34*(1), 179–225. https://doi.org/10.3102/0091732X09349791

The Washington Post. (2013, June 8). The federal definition of "rural"—Times 15. https://www.washingtonpost.com/politics/the-federal-definition-of-rural--times-15/2013/06/08/a39e46a8-cd4a-11e2-ac03-178510c9cc0a_story.html

Whitaker, M. (2017, July 13). Ten tips for public education advocacy. *National Association of Secondary School Principals.* https://www.nassp.org/2017/07/13/ten-tips-for-public-education-advocacy

Winchester, B. (2018). *Rural migration: The brain gain of the newcomers.* University of Minnesota Extension Center for Community Vitality. https://umvrdc.org/wp-content/uploads/2018/05/BrainGain.pdf

Wood, J. N., Finch, K., & Mirecki, R. M. (2013). If we get you, how can we keep you? Problems with recruiting and retaining rural administrators. *The Rural Educator, 34*(2). https://doi.org/10.35608/ruraled.v34i2.399

The World Bank. (2022). *Rural Access Index (RAI).* https://datacatalog.worldbank.org/search/dataset/0038250

Youth Collaboratory. (2018). *Wide open spaces: Bridging the resource gap in rural mentoring.* https://www.youthcollaboratory.org/toolkit/rural-mentoring-toolkit

Index

accountability, school, 52
accounting services, 145
administration services, shared, 144–145, 147*f*
adverse childhood experiences (ACEs), 110–111, 118–121
advisory periods, 116
advocacy, 20–21
    change and, 22–23, 22*f*
    effectiveness, 23–24
    relationships and, 21–23
alumni speakers, 104
American Council on Rural Special Education, 29
American Rescue Plan, 49
Americans with Disabilities Act, 57
AmeriCorps, 123
antiracism, 136–139
Arbor Family Health clinics (Louisiana), 155
area amenities, 8
Arizona Student Opportunity Collaborative, 104
Arkansas Coalition for Community Schools, 178
Aspen Institute, 180–181
asset mapping
    community, 168–172, 170*f*
    personal, 167–168, 167*f*
    SWOT analysis, 172, 173*f*
Association of School Business Officials International, 18
associations and organizations, support
    federal, 29–30
    local level, 27–28
    regional level, 28–29
    state level, 28
attainment, 6, 103–106
AVID, 103, 113
Baldwin County School District (Georgia), 105
Batesville school district (Arkansas), 178
BBBS (Big Brothers, Big Sisters), 122
Big Brothers, Big Sisters (BBBS), 122

Board of Cooperative Educational Services (BOCES), 27
boards, school, 13–15, 15*f*
brain drain, 6, 164
BRIGHT Fellowship program, 59
broadband access, 84–85, 88–94, 92*f*
budgeting, 16–19, 89–94
burnout, 62

calendar management, 79–83
Camas School District (Washington State), 138
career readiness, 103–106
caring, 121
cartographic resources, for asset mapping, 170–171
change, 22–23, 22*f*, 52
character, 121
child care, 47
circadian rhythms, 79–80
classroom observations, 66
CLEAR (Collaborative Learning for Educational Achievement and Resilience), 120
Closing a School Best Practices Guide (California DOE), 162
Closing a School Building: A Systematic Approach (National Clearinghouse for Educational Facilities), 162
closures and consolidations, school, 140–142, 163
    archiving, 159–160
    avoiding, 144–155, 147*f*, 148*f*
    communication plan, 157–158
    dos and don'ts, 160, 161*f*
    FAQs and talking points, 158
    impact of, 142–143
    lessons from a real life closure/consolidation, 157–160
    library joint use, 155–156
    parent input, 158–159
    plan development, 160–163

closures and consolidations, school (*continued*)
    shared resource model, 149–150
    shared services case study, 151–153
    social service agencies joint use, 156
    spokespersons, 158
    staff transition teams, 159
    stakeholder involvement, 158
    standards for, 156–157
    student involvement opportunities, 159
coaching, leadership, 61–62, 61*f*
Coalition for Community Schools, 174, 178
cohort model, 59
collaboration, 66
Collaborative Learning for Educational Achievement and Resilience (CLEAR), 120
college access programs, 104–105
college readiness/preparation, 103–106, 131
Collegiate Edu-Nation (Texas), 176–178
communication
    open-door policies, 77–79, 78*f*
    stakeholder engagement, 56–57
community asset list, 169–171, 170*f*
community asset mapping, 168–172
Community Asset Mapping Guide, 172
community involvement
    antiracism efforts, 137
    gifted and talented education, 136
    instructional leadership and, 66, 67–68, 69
    mentoring, 114–116, 115*f*
    partnerships, 50–51, 54–57, 68, 174–178, 177*f*
    school closures and consolidations, 141–143
Community School Model, 174–178, 177*f*
competence, 121
confidence, 121
connection, 121
contract completion bonuses, 47
cost savings, 17
co-teaching, 44
coursework reimbursement, 47
COVID-19 pandemic, 2, 26, 84, 110
Crisp, Scott, 181–183
cultural competency training, 137
culturally appropriate programming, 130
culturally responsive teaching, 130, 133–134
curriculum development, 66, 68, 103
    gifted and talented education, 135–136
    Native American students, 130–131
curriculum implementation and assessment, 19

Dallas Independent School District, 59–60
data analysis, 66
decision-making, 72–73, 76–77
    alternatives, 73–74
    analyzing options, 74
    prioritizing, 74–76, 75*f*
    root causes, 73
depression, 62
differentiated instruction, 136
digital equity, 88–94, 92*f*, 104
discipline disparities, 138
distant locale code, 5
distributed leadership, 69–72, 71*f*
district reorganizations. *See* closures and consolidations, school

diversity, 128
    antiracism, 136–139
    demographic changes, 128–129
    English language learners, 132–135, 134*f*
    gifted students, 135–136
    Native American students, 129–132

Eastern Shore of Maryland Educational Consortium, 148
East Wilkes High School (North Carolina), 105
economies of scale, 17
Education Service Agencies (ESAs), 27
email, 83
emergency responder capacity, 87
employee referral programs, 42
employment contracts, 41
energy audits, 17
English language learners, 17, 132–135, 134*f*
enrollment, student, 16
equity plans, 138

facilities and maintenance issues, 87–88, 100–102
FAFSA (Free Application for Federal Student Aid), 104
faith-based partnerships, 116–117
federal resources, 29–30
    facilities maintenance, 102
    funding programs and grants, 17–18, 25
    for Native American students, 131–132
final mile connectivity, 89
finance studies, leadership preparation programs, 14, 16
financial aid, student, 104
firearms and suicide, 87
fiscal management
    digital equity funding, 89–94
    equitable funding and resources, 69
    governing boards and, 14
    principal's role, 19–20
    superintendent's role, 15–19
Fishbone Diagram strategy, 73
5 Whys strategy, 73
The Five Levels of Leadership (Maxwell), 27
food insecurity, 85–86, 95–97, 108
food services, 145
Foundation of the American Institute for Conservation, 102
4-H, 122
four-day workweeks, 45
Fowler High School (Colorado), 106
Free Application for Federal Student Aid (FAFSA), 104
fringe locale code, 4
funding, state system, 16–19, 69

Gaining Early Awareness and Readiness for Undergraduate Programs (GEAR UP), 105
GATE (gifted and talented education), 135–136
GEAR UP (Gaining Early Awareness and Readiness for Undergraduate Programs), 105
gender differences, attainment, 6
Getty Foundation, 102
gifted and talented education (GATE), 135–136
governing boards, 13–15, 15*f*

Government Finance Officers Association, 18
grant funding, 25, 117–118
Grow Your Own (GYO) leadership programs
    principal pipeline, 58–60
        teacher recruitment and retention, 38–42

health centers, school-based, 154–155
Health-E-Schools program (North Carolina), 155
HealthierUS School Challenge, 107
health-related gaps, 86–87, 97–98
Hearing from Us project (Wyoming), 181–183
HEARTS program, 120
higher education preparation programs, 17, 58, 60
hiring and firing, governing boards and, 14
Holbrook Unified School District (Arizona), 179–180
homelessness, 109–110
housing issues, 87, 99–100
human capital management planning, 35–36
human resources department, 47, 145
Human Rights Campaign Foundation's Welcoming Schools website, 139

I-LEAD (Native Youth Initiative for Leadership, Empowerment, and Development), 123
immigrant students, 17
Impact Aid grants, 131–132
The Imperfect Union (Peshkin), 142
industry certification programs, 104
Influence Pyramid, 22–23, 22*f*
inform, 56
information forums, 43
infrastructure shared services, 151
inquire, 56
inspire, 56
instruction, flexible and connected, 130–131
instructional leadership, 19, 65–66, 67–69
internet access, 84–85, 88–94, 92*f*
involve, 56
IT support services, 145

Jackson Hole High School (Wyoming), 181–183
Jefferson County Educational Service Center (Ohio), 151
Johnson-O'Malley Act (1934), 131

Kentucky Family Resource and Youth Services Centers, 155

Lame Deer School District (Montana), 138–139
Leader Excellence, Advancement and Development (LEAD) division (Dallas), 59–60
leadership, rural school
    advocacy, 20–24, 22*f*
    development opportunities, 43
    multiclassroom leadership, 44
    policy and regulatory assessment, 24–25
    principals, 19–20
    roles and responsibilities, 12–13
    superintendents, 13–19, 15*f*
    support networks, associations, and organizations, 25–30
leadership preparation programs, 12, 14, 16, 51, 59, 60
leadership teams, 69–72, 71*f*
Leslie County Schools (Kentucky), 178

library services, joint use, 155–156
living conditions, 8
loan forgiveness programs, 42
locale codes, rural, 4–5
local-level support services, 27–28

MapGive, 171
marketing videos, 37–38
McKinney-Vento Homeless Assistance Act of 1987, 110, 111
medical and health-related gaps, 86–87, 97–98
medical care benefits, 47
mentorships, 61–62, 61*f*, 103, 112–116, 113*f*, 115*f*, 133
middle mile connectivity, 88–89
migration to rural areas, 164
Mind Maps strategy, 73
minority attainment, 6
mobility, tracking student, 112
multiclassroom leadership, 44
multitasking, 82–83

National Agricultural Library (USDA), 29
National Center for Community Schools, 178
National Center on Safe Supportive Learning Environments, 120
National Park Service, 102
National Register of Historic Buildings, 102
National Rural Education Advocacy Coalition, 29
National Rural Education Association, 2, 3
Native American students, 129–132
Native Youth Initiative for Leadership, Empowerment, and Development (I-LEAD), 123
Navajo County Special Services Consortium, 150
needs assessments, 165, 166*f*
North Carolina State University, 59
Northeast Leadership Academy, 59

Ohio Appalachian Collaborative, 148
The Ohio State University, 59
Oklahoma Public School Resource Center (OPSRC), 149
onboarding and support, teacher, 42–43
online training, professional, 146
open-door policies, 77–79, 78*f*

parent involvement, 66
Pareto Principle, 74–75
Participatory Community Asset Mapping toolkit, 172
partnerships
    anti-poverty, 116–117
    community schooling and, 174–178, 177*f*
Pastors for Children, 116
payroll services, 145
PBE (place-based education), 172–174
PBIS (Positive Behavioral Interventions and Supports), 119–120
peer mentoring, 113–114, 113*f*
The People Left Behind (Institute for Research on Poverty), 108
personal asset mapping, 167–168, 167*f*
personalized instruction, 68
personnel management, 17
    governing boards and, 14
place-based education (PBE), 172–174

policies
    advocating for, 20–24
    assessment of impact of, 24–25
    governing boards and, 14
Pomodoro Technique, 81
Positive Behavioral Interventions and Supports (PBIS), 119–120
Positive Youth Development (PYD) model, 121–122, 121*f*
poverty, 85, 107–108
    adverse childhood experiences, 110–111, 118–121
    building student assets, 121–124
    faith-based partnerships, 116–117
    homelessness, 109–110
    impacts of, 108–111
    mentorships and, 112–116, 113*f*, 115*f*
    nontraditional partnerships, 116–117
    Promise Neighborhoods Grants, 117–118
    Rural and Low-Income School (RLIS) Programs, 112
    rural fit factor program assessments, 124–127, 125*f*–126*f*
    Small, Rural School Achievement (SRSA) Program, 112
    student mobility tracking, 112
    trauma-informed care, 110–111, 118–121
Principal Preparation for Excellence and Equity in Rural Schools (PPEERS) program, 60
principal preparation programs, 58, 60
principals, leadership. *See also* leadership, rural school
    areas of, 64–65, 65*f*
    decision-making tools, 72–77, 75*f*
    distributed leadership, 69–72, 71*f*
    instructional leadership, 65–66, 67–69
    management challenges, 66–67
    open-door policies, 77–79, 78*f*
    time management, 79–83
    volunteerism and, 79
principals, recruitment and retention
    Grow Your Own, 58–60
    mentorships and coaching, 61–62, 61*f*
    networking, 60–62, 61*f*
    professional development resources, 51–52
    role diversification, 51
    rural contexts in principal preparation programs, 60
    rurality and, 50–51
    school accountability, 52
    strategies for, 48, 53, 54*f*
    stress management and wellness, 62–63
    visibility and access, 54–57
principals, school
    attributes of successful, 52–53
    challenges and duties, 49
    influence and importance, 48, 64
    roles and responsibilities, 19–20
The Principal Story Learning Guide, 72
privacy, 3
Pro-Con T-Chart strategy, 74, 76
professional development
    English language learning instruction, 133
    gifted and talented education, 135–136
    for principals, 51–52
    as shared service, 146–148
    teacher preparation funding, 17

professional support issues, 8
Project HOPE-Virginia, 111
Promise Neighborhoods Grants, 117–118
purchasing cooperatives, 17
PYD (Positive Youth Development) model, 121–122, 121*f*

racism, 136–139
RAI (Rural Access Index), 84
REAP (Rural Education Achievement Program), 112
recently arrived immigrant English learners (RAIELs), 133–134, 134*f*
recruitment, teacher, 41–42
    antiracism and diversity, 137
    case study, 39–41
    Grow Your Own programs, 38–42
    human capital management planning, 35–36
    marketing videos, 37–38
    rurality transparency, 38
    social media engagement, 36–37, 36*f*
recruitment and retention strategies, principals, 48, 53, 54*f*
Regional Education Laboratory (REL) Program (USDOE), 28, 29–30
regionalization of school services, 144–155, 147*f*, 148*f*
regional-level support services, 28–29
relationships, advocacy and, 21–23, 132
remote locale code, 5
remote work, 44
resources
    broadband and digital equity, 84–85, 88–94, 92*f*
    facilities and maintenance issues, 87–88, 100–102
    food insecurity, 85–86, 95–97
    housing issues, 87, 99–100
    lack of, 7, 8, 84–88
    medical and health-related gaps, 86–87, 97–98
restorative justice practices, 138
retention, teacher, 47
    flexible staffing models, 43–45
    four-day workweeks, 45
    onboarding and support, teacher, 42–43
    stay interviews, 45, 46*f*
return on investment, 18
revenue, 18
ReVISION (Nebraska), 178
RLIS (Rural and Low-Income School) Programs, 112
Rural Access Index (RAI), 84
Rural and Low-Income School (RLIS) Programs, 112
Rural Development Hubs, 180–181
rural education
    area amenities and living conditions, 8
    attainment rates, 6
    community and, 5–6
    definitions, 3–5
    resources, 7, 8
    rewards and draw, 3
    versus urban education, 1–2, 7–8
    variations in, 7
Rural Education Achievement Program (REAP), 112
rural education associations, 28
Rural Education Leaders Network (RELN), 26–27

rurality, and recruitment, 38, 50–51
Rural School and Community Trust, 146, 156–157
Rural Schools Collaborative, 3, 28

Santa Cruz Adolescent Wellness Network (Arizona), 155
scheduling, flexible, 130–131
school-based health centers, 154–155
school boards, 13–15, 15*f*
school closure, 141
School Closure Guide: Closing Schools as a Means for Addressing Budgetary Challenges (Broad Foundation), 162
school closures and consolidations. *See* closures and consolidations, school
school consolidation, 141
School Redesign Models: A Guide to School Closure and Consolidation (Texas Education Agency), 162–163
service organizations, local, 28
shared school services, 144–155, 147*f*, 148*f*
signing bonuses, 47
Six Thinking Hats strategy, 74
social media engagement, 36–37, 36*f*, 78
social service agencies, joint use, 156
socialization, teacher, 42–43
Southeast Regional Resource Center (Alaska), 151
special education services, 150–151
spending, 17
Spillane, James, 72
staff–student mentoring, 113–114
staffing models, 43–45
stakeholders, engaging, 51, 54–57
    and anti-poverty programs, 124–127, 125*f*–126*f*
    community asset mapping, 169
    digital equity, 89
Stanfield School, 58, 108, 174
state-level support services, 28
stay interviews, 45, 46*f*
stress management, 62–63
student assets, building, 121–124
student leadership and activism, 137
student mobility tracking, 112
student teachers, 41
student voice, 181–183
suicide rates, 87
superintendents. *See also* leadership, rural school
    challenging roles, 13
    fiscal performance, 15–19
    governing boards and, 13–15, 15*f*
    roles and responsibilities of, 15*f*
support services, 69
support systems, 26
    ad hoc, 26–27
    federal resources, 29–30
    local level, 27–28
    regional level, 28–29
    state level, 28
SWOT Analysis strategy, 74, 172, 173*f*

teacher development, 68
teacher evaluation, 66
teacher preparation programs, 17, 31, 40–41
teacher recruitment and retention
    AASPA recommendations, 32–34
    attrition and turnover, 31–32
    flexible staffing models, 43–45
    four-day workweeks, 45
    Grow Your Own programs, 38–42
    human capital management planning, 35–36
    marketing videos, 37–38
    onboarding and support, 42–43
    PESTLE analysis, 32–34, 33*f*
    recruitment strategies, 35–42
    retention strategies, 42–47, 46*f*
    rurality transparency, 38
    social media engagement, 36–37, 36*f*
    stay interviews, 45
    upsides and challenges, 34
    workforce shortage, 31–34, 33*f*
teamwork, 66
technology, 68. *See also* digital equity
time management, 79–83
Title I funding, 25
Title II-A funding, 42
Title VI Indian Education Formula Grants program, 131
to-do lists, 83
Together We Can Be Bully Free (Louisiana), 138
Transforming Schools (Bierly et al.), 72
transparency, 19, 34, 38, 46, 57, 78, 157–158, 161*f*
transportation issues, 68, 85, 86, 143, 145, 151
trauma-informed care, 111, 118–121
Trauma Responsive Equitable Education (TREE), 119
TREE (Trauma Responsive Equitable Education), 119
Tribal language instruction, 130
TRIO Programs, 105
Tucson Regional Educator Collaborative, 146–147

University of Maine, 60
University of West Alabama, 60
Upward Bound, 105
Urgent–Important Matrix strategy, 75–76, 75*f*
U.S. Department of Agriculture (USDA), 4
    National Agricultural Library, 29
U.S. Department of Education (USDOE)
    Regional Education Laboratory (REL) Program, 28, 29–30
    Rural Education Resource Center (USDOE), 29

visibility, in community, 50–51, 54–57
vision, 66
volunteerism, 79

Wallace Foundation, 48, 64, 72
Welcome Teams, 43
wellness initiatives, 62–63
Westside Community Schools (Nebraska), 139
Whole School, Whole Community, Whole Child model, 107, 154
Winchester, Ben, 164

YouthBuild, 122

About the Author

 **Dr. Melissa A. Sadorf** is the superintendent of the Stanfield Elementary School District in Arizona. In her rural district, she also serves as the business manager, federal grant programs director, and HR director. Prior to her work with Stanfield, Melissa was a teacher, literacy coach, assistant principal, and principal. Melissa is the executive director of the Arizona affiliate of ASCD and for the Northern Arizona University Rural Schools Resource Center. She is also executive director of the Arizona Rural Schools Association and sits on the National Rural Education Association as president of the executive board. She facilitates monthly roundtables for rural superintendents, has created a Rural Leaders Network that spans 16 western states, and produces and hosts a podcast called *The Rural Scoop,* which highlights best practices in rural school systems. She is also an assistant teaching professor for Northern Arizona University, teaching educational leadership and principal preparation courses. Melissa can be reached on social media at @dr_sadorf or through her website at www.velaconsultants.com.

Related ASCD Resources: Educational Leadership and Equity

At the time of publication, the following resources were available (ASCD stock numbers in parentheses):

Design Thinking for School Leaders: Five Roles and Mindsets That Ignite Positive Change by Alyssa Gallagher and Kami Thordarson (#118022)

Five Levers to Improve Learning: How to Prioritize for Powerful Results in Your School by Tony Frontier and James Rickabaugh (#114002)

Fix Injustice, Not Kids and Other Principles for Transformative Equity Leadership by Paul Gorski and Katy Swalwell (#120012)

Is My School a Better School Because I Lead It? by Baruti K. Kafele (#120013)

School Culture Rewired: Toward a More Positive and Productive School for All (2nd Edition) by Steve Gruenert and Todd Whitaker (#123029)

School Leadership That Works: From Research to Results by Robert J. Marzano, Timothy Waters, and Brian A. McNulty (#105125)

The Six Priorities: How to Find the Resources Your School Community Needs by Luis Eladio Torres (#122022)

Small Shifts, Meaningful Improvement: Collective Leadership Strategies for Schools and Districts by P. Ann Byrd, Alesha Daughtrey, Jonathan Eckert, and Lori Nazareno (#123007)

Stop Leading, Start Building: Turn Your School into a Success Story with the People and Resources You Already Have by Robyn R. Jackson (#121025)

Teaching with Poverty and Equity in Mind by Eric Jensen (#120019)

For up-to-date information about ASCD resources, go to www.ascd.org. You can search the complete archives of *Educational Leadership* at www.ascd.org/el. To contact us, send an email to member@ascd.org or call 1-800-933-2723 or 703-578-9600.

WHOLE CHILD TENETS

1. HEALTHY
Each student enters school healthy and learns about and practices a healthy lifestyle.

2. SAFE
Each student learns in an environment that is physically and emotionally safe for students and adults.

3. ENGAGED
Each student is actively engaged in learning and is connected to the school and broader community.

4. SUPPORTED
Each student has access to personalized learning and is supported by qualified, caring adults.

5. CHALLENGED
Each student is challenged academically and prepared for success in college or further study and for employment and participation in a global environment.

ascd whole child

The ASCD Whole Child approach is an effort to transition from a focus on narrowly defined academic achievement to one that promotes the long-term development and success of all children. Through this approach, ASCD supports educators, families, community members, and policymakers as they move from a vision about educating the whole child to sustainable, collaborative actions.

The Resilient Rural Leader relates to the **engaged**, **supported**, and **challenged** tenets.

For more about the ASCD Whole Child approach, visit **www.ascd.org/wholechild.**

Become an ASCD member today!
Go to www.ascd.org/joinascd
or call toll-free: 800-933-ASCD (2723)

DON'T MISS A SINGLE ISSUE OF ASCD'S AWARD-WINNING MAGAZINE.

ascd educational leadership

If you belong to a Professional Learning Community, you may be looking for a way to get your fellow educators' minds around a complex topic. Why not delve into a relevant theme issue of *Educational Leadership*, the journal written by educators for educators?

Subscribe now, or purchase back issues of ASCD's flagship publication at **www.ascd.org/el**. Discounts on bulk purchases are available.

To see more details about these and other popular issues of *Educational Leadership*, visit **www.ascd.org/el/all**.

ascd

2800 Shirlington Road
Suite 1001
Arlington, VA 22206 USA